Mark Hopkins

Evidences of Christianity : lectures before the Lowell Institute,

January 1844

Mark Hopkins

Evidences of Christianity : lectures before the Lowell Institute, January 1844

ISBN/EAN: 9783337263133

Printed in Europe, USA, Canada, Australia, Japan

Cover: Foto ©Lupo / pixelio.de

More available books at **www.hansebooks.com**

EVIDENCES OF CHRISTIANITY.

LECTURES

BEFORE

THE LOWELL INSTITUTE,

JANUARY, 1844.

REVISED AS A TEXT BOOK.

BY

MARK HOPKINS, D.D.
PRESIDENT OF WILLIAMS COLLEGE.

BOSTON:
T. R. MARVIN & SON, 42 CONGRESS ST.
NEW YORK:
SHELDON AND COMPANY.
1867.

Entered, according to Act of Congress, in the year 1863, by
MARK HOPKINS,
In the Clerk's Office of the District Court of the District of Massachusetts.

ELECTROTYPED AT THE
BOSTON STEREOTYPE FOUNDRY.

The following Lectures, published seventeen years since, having been extensively used as a text book, are now revised, with the hope of adapting them more fully to that end. In doing this, the arguments have been separated from each other, and captions have been given to the paragraphs. Changes have also been made in arrangement, a few things have been omitted, and some additions have been made. Neither these, nor the reasons for them, need be specified. The general form and substance of the Lectures have been retained, but, as now presented, it is hoped that the arguments will be both more readily apprehended and more easily remembered.

The Lectures were originally written on the invitation of JOHN A. LOWELL, Esq., to deliver them before the Lowell Institute; and my sense of his kindness and courtesy were expressed in connection with their former publication. That expression I desire to renew, and to add that the same kindness and courtesy have been still further illustrated in connection with the present edition.

MARK HOPKINS.

WILLIAMS COLLEGE, September, 1863.

PREFACE

TO THE FIRST EDITION.

The following Lectures are published as they were delivered. Perhaps nothing would be gained, on the whole, by recasting them; but they must be expected to have the defects incident to compositions prepared under the pressure of other duties, and required to be completed within a limited time.

When I entered upon the subject, I supposed it had been exhausted; but on looking at it more nearly, I was led to see that Christianity has such relations to nature and to man, that the evidence resulting from a comparison of it with them may be almost said to be exhaustless. To the evidence from this source I have given greater prominence than is common, both because it has been comparatively neglected, and because I judged it better adapted than the historical proof to interest a promiscuous audience. It was with reference to both these points, that, in the arrangement and grouping of these Lectures, I have departed from the ordinary course; and if they shall be found in any degree peculiarly adapted to the present state of the public mind, I think it will be from the prominence given to the Internal Evidence, while, at the same time, the chief topics of argument are presented within a moderate space.

The method of proof of which I have just spoken has one disadvantage which I found embarrassing. If Christianity is compared with nature or with man, it must be assumed that it is some specific thing; and hence there will be danger, either of being so general and indefinite as to be without interest, or of getting upon controversial ground. Each of these extremes it was my wish to avoid. That I succeeded in doing this perfectly, I cannot suppose. Probably it would be impossible for any one to do so in the judgment of all. My wish was to present the argument. This I could not do without indicating my sentiments on some of the leading doctrines of Christianity up to a certain point; and if any think that I went too far, I can only say that it was difficult to know where to stop, and that, if I had given the argument precisely as it lay in my own mind, I should have gone much farther. It is from the adaptation of Christianity as providing an atonement, and consequently a divine Redeemer, to the condition and wants of man, that the chief force of such works as that of Erskine, and "The Philosophy of the Plan of Salvation," is derived; and I should be unwilling to have it supposed that I presented any thing which I regarded as a complete system of the Evidences of Christianity, from which that argument was excluded.

But if, in some of its aspects, the evidence for Christianity may be said to be exhaustless, it may also be said that several of the leading topics of argument have probably been presented as ably as they ever will be. Those topics I thought it my duty to present, and in doing so I had no wish to sacrifice force to originality, and did not hesitate to avail myself freely of such labors of others as were within my reach. If I had had time to do this more fully, no doubt the Lectures would have been improved.

For much recurrence to original authorities in the historical part, I had not time. The quotations in that part are generally taken from Paley or Horne, or from some source equally common. Those quotations, however, are of unquestioned authority; they are to the point, and perhaps nothing could have more usefully occupied the same space.

The importance of the object intended to be accomplished by the founder of the Lowell Institute, in this course of Lectures, cannot be over-estimated. Let there be in the minds of the people generally a settled and rational conviction of the truth of Christianity, such as a fair presentation of the evidence could not fail to produce, and there will be the best and the only true foundation laid for a rational piety, and for the practice of every social and civil virtue. That these Lectures were useful, to some extent, when they were delivered, in producing such a conviction, I had the great satisfaction of knowing; and I now commit them to the blessing of God, with the hope, though there are so many and so able treatises on this subject already before the public, that they will have a degree of usefulness that will justify their publication.

Williams College, April, 1846.

CONTENTS.

LECTURE I.

Object of the Course. — Responsibility of Men for their Opinions. — Revelation provable. — This shown from a Comparison of Mathematical and Moral Evidence, and from an Analysis of the Argument of Hume. 13

LECTURE II.

Preliminary Observations. — Revelation probable: First, from the Nature of the Case; secondly, from Facts. — Probability of Miracles, aside from their Effect in sustaining any particular Revelation. — Connection between the Miracle and the Doctrine. — The Christian Religion, or none. 39

LECTURE III.

Internal and External Evidence. — Vagueness of the Division between them. — Reasons for considering the Internal Evidences first. — Argument first: From Analogy. 68

LECTURE IV.

Argument second: Coincidence of Christianity with Natural Religion. — Argument third: Its Adaptation to the Conscience as a perceiving Power. — Peculiar Difficulties in the Way of establishing and maintaining a perfect Standard. — Argument fourth: If the Morality is perfect, the Religion must be true. 97

LECTURE V.

Argument fifth: Christianity adapted to Man. — Division first: Its Quickening and Guiding Power. — Its Adaptation to the Intellect, the Affections, the Imagination, the Conscience, and the Will. 125

LECTURE VI.

Argument fifth, continued: Division second: Christianity as a Restraining Power. — Argument sixth: The Experimental Evidence of Christianity. — Argument seventh: Its Fitness and Tendency to become universal. — Argument eighth: It has always been in the World. 155

LECTURE VII.

Argument ninth: Christianity could not have been originated by Man. 183

LECTURE VIII.

Argument tenth: The Condition, Character, and Claims of Christ. 210

LECTURE IX.

The External Evidence. — General Grounds on which this is to be put. — Argument eleventh: Authenticity and Integrity of the Writings of the New Testament. 238

LECTURE X.

Argument twelfth: Credibility of the Books of the New Testament. 269

LECTURE XI.

Argument thirteenth: Prophecy. — Nature of this Evidence. — The General Object of Prophecy. — The Fulfillment of Prophecy. 299

LECTURE XII.

Objections. — Argument fourteenth: The Propagation of Christianity. — Argument fifteenth: Its Effects and Tendencies. — Summary and Conclusion. 328

EVIDENCES OF CHRISTIANITY.

LECTURE I.

OBJECT OF THE COURSE.—RESPONSIBILITY OF MEN FOR THEIR OPINIONS.—REVELATION PROVABLE.—THIS SHOWN FROM A COMPARISON OF MATHEMATICAL AND MORAL EVIDENCE, AND FROM AN ANALYSIS OF THE ARGUMENT OF HUME.

In entering upon this course of lectures, there is one impression against which I wish to guard at the outset. It is, that I come here to defend Christianity, as if its truth were a matter of doubt. Not so. I come, not to dispute, but to exhibit truth; to do my part in a great work, which must be done for every generation, by showing them, so that they shall see for themselves, the grounds on which their belief in the Christian religion rests. I come to stand at the door of the temple of Truth, and ask you to go in with me, and see for yourselves the foundation and the shafts of those pillars upon which its dome is reared. I ask you, in the words of one of old, to walk with me about our Zion, and go round about her, to tell the towers thereof, to mark well her bulwarks, to consider her palaces, that ye may tell it to the generation following.*

Persons to be benefited. — In doing this, I shall hope to be useful to three classes of persons.

First Class. — To the first belong those who have received Christianity by acquiescence; who have, per-

---

* Psalm xlviii. 12, 13.

haps, never questioned its truth, but who have never examined its evidence. This class is large, — it is to be feared increasingly so, — and it does not seem to me that the position of mind in which they are placed, and its consequences, are sufficiently regarded.

The claims of the Christian religion present themselves to those who enter upon life in a Christian country, in an attitude entirely different from that in which they were presented at their first announcement, when they made such rapid progress, and when their dominion over the mind of man was so efficient.* Then, no man was born a Christian. If he became one, it was in opposition to the prejudices of education, to ties of kindred, to motives of interest, and often at the sacrifice of reputation and of life. This no man would do except on the ground of the strongest reasons, perceived and assented to by his own mind. Christianity was an aggressive and an uncompromising religion. It attacked every other form of religion, whether Jewish or pagan, and sought to destroy it. It "turned the world upside down" wherever it came; and the first question which any man would naturally ask was, "What are its claims? What are the reasons why I should receive it?" And these claims and reasons would be examined with all the attention that could be produced by the stimulus of novelty, and by the deepest personal interest.

Now, however, all this is changed. Men are born nominally Christians. The truth of the religion is taken for granted; nothing leads them to question it, nothing to examine it. In this position the mind *may* open itself to the reception of the religion from a perception of its intrinsic excellence, and its adaptation to the deep wants of man; but the probability is that doubts will arise. The occasions of these are abundant on every

---

* See Whately's Logic, Appendix, p. 325.

hand — the strange state in which the world is; the number of sects; the conduct of Christians; a companion that ridicules religion; an infidel book. One objection or doubt makes way for another. The objections come first, and, ere the individual is aware, his respect for religion, and his confidence in it, are undermined. Especially will this be so if a young man travels much, and sees different forms of religion. He will see the Hindoo bowing before his idol, the Turk praying toward Mecca, the Papist kneeling before his saint, and the Protestant attending his church; and, as each seems equally sincere, and equally certain he is right, he will acquire, insensibly perhaps, a general impression that all religions are equally true, or — which is much the same thing — that they are equally false, and any exclusive attachment to the Christian religion will be regarded as bigotry. The religion itself will come to be disliked as a restraint, and despised as a form. It is chiefly from this class that the ranks of fanaticism, on the one hand, and of infidelity, on the other, are filled; and it will often depend on constitutional temperament, or accidental temptation, whether such a one shall become a fanatic or an infidel.

At this point, there is doubtless a fault both in Christian parents and in Christian ministers. Where there is a proper course of training, this class can never become numerous; but it is numerous in all our congregations now. Needless doubts are not to be awakened, but it is no honor to the Christian religion to receive it by prescription. It is no fault to have those questionings, that desire for insight, — call them doubts if you will, — which always spring up in strong minds, and which will not be quieted till the ground and evidence of those things which they receive are distinctly seen. Are there such among my hearers? Them I hope to benefit. I hope to do for them what Luke did for the most excellent Theophilus — to show them the "*certainty*" of those things in which they have been instructed; to refer them, as he does again the same person in the Acts, to those "infallible proofs" on which the religion rests.

Second Class. — To the second class whom I hope to benefit belong those who have gradually passed from the preceding class into doubt and infidelity. For such, I think, there is hope. They are not unwilling to see evidence. Their position has led them to look at objections first, and they have, perhaps, never had time or opportunity to look at the embodied evidence for Christianity. They have fallen into infidelity from association, from vanity, from fashion; they have not found in it the satisfaction they expected, and they are willing to review the ground, or rather to look candidly, for the first time, at the evidences for this religion.

Exceptions. — Besides this class of infidels, there are, however, two others, whom I have very little hope of benefiting. One is of those who are made so by their passions, and are under the control of appetite, or ambition, or avarice, or revenge. As these were not made infidels by argument, argument will not be likely to reclaim them. "They never think of religion but with a feeling of enmity, and never speak of it but in the language of sneer or abuse." Another class is of those who have been well characterized as "a cold, speculative, subtle set of skeptics, who attack first principles and confound their readers or hearers with paradoxes." Apparently influenced by vanity, they adopt principles which would render all argument impossible or nugatory, and which would lead to fundamental and universal skepticism. This class seems not to be as numerous or as dangerous at present as at some former times.*

* Alexander's Evidences, p. 9.

Third Class.—The third class whom I hope to benefit consists of Christians themselves.

Certainty and Efficiency.—It is one of the conditions of Christian character and efficiency, that, on some ground, there should be such a conviction of the truth of Christianity as to form a basis of action and of self-sacrifice, which, if it should be required, would be carried even to martyrdom. The grounds of such a conviction cannot be too well examined. There is no man, who finds himself called to act upon any conviction, who does not feel his self-respect increased, and his peace of mind enhanced, and his strength for action augmented, when he has a clear perception of the ground of the conviction upon which he acts. And even though he may once have seen the Christian evidences in all their force, and been astonished at the mass of proof, and have been perfectly convinced, yet, after a time, these impressions fade away, and it is good for him to have them renewed. It is as when one has looked at the Falls of Niagara, and stood upon the tower, and gone round upon Table rock, and been rowed in the little boat up toward the great fall, and had his mind filled with the scene, but has again been occupied in the business of life till the impression has become indistinct on his mind. He would then gladly return, and have it renewed and deepened.

This feeling of certainty seems to have been one of the elements of the vigorous piety of ancient times. They believed; therefore they spoke. They knew whom they believed; therefore they were ready to be offered. They spoke of "certainty," of "infallible proofs," of being "eye-witnesses," of the "more sure word of prophecy." Their tread was not that of men who were feeling their way in the twilight of doubtful evidence, but that of men who saw every thing in the light of clear and perfect vision.

I would not, indeed, limit the amount of knowledge and conviction with which piety may exist. If it can spring up in the twilight, and grow where doubts overshadow it, and where it never feels the direct rays of truth, we ought to rejoice; but, at the same time, we ought to know that the growth will be feeble, and that the plant must be despoiled of the beauty and fragrance which it will have when it grows as in the light of the open day. To produce this feeling of certainty in one already a Christian, was the avowed object for which the Gospel of Luke was written; and it is this feeling, containing the elements both of peace and of strength, that I hope to produce and to deepen in the minds of Christians.

Coöperation needed. — But if I am to be useful to either of these classes, it must be with their own coöperation. The principle involved in this assertion, in reference to all moral truth, and, indeed, to all truth the acquisition of which requires attention, is as obvious to philosophy and common sense as it is plainly announced in the Bible. Nothing is more common, in reference to their present, as well as their future interests, than for men to "have eyes and see not."

Objection — Belief necessary. — Here, however, I am met by the objection that the belief of a man is not within his own power, but that he is compelled to believe according to certain laws of evidence. This objection I do not apprehend to be of very wide influence; but I have met with a few men of intelligence who have held to it, and it has been sustained by some names of high authority. I am therefore bound to notice it.

In this case, as in most others of a similar kind, the objection involves a partial truth, from which its plausibility is derived. It *is* true, within certain limitations, and under certain conditions, and with respect to certain kinds of truth, that we are not voluntary in our belief; but then these conditions and limitations are such as entirely to sever from this truth any consequence that we are not perfectly ready to admit.

We admit that belief is in no case directly dependent on the will; that in some cases it is entirely independent of it; but he must be exceedingly bigoted, or unobservant of what passes around him, who should affirm that the will has *no* influence. The influence of the will here is analogous to its influence in many other cases. It is as great as it is over the objects which we see. It does not depend upon the will of any man, if he turns his eyes in a particular direction, whether he shall see a tree there. If the tree be there, he must see it, and is compelled to believe in its existence: but it was entirely within his power not to turn his eyes in that direction, and thus to remain unconvinced, on the highest of all evidence, of the existence of the tree, and unimpressed by its beauty and proportion. It is not by his will directly that man has any control over his thoughts. It is not by willing a thought into the mind that he can call it there; and yet we all know that through attention and habits of association the subjects of our thoughts are, to a great extent, directed by the will.

It is precisely so in respect to belief; and he who denies this, denies the value of candor, and the influence of party spirit, and prejudice, and interest, on the mind. So great is this influence, however, that a keen observer of human nature, and one who will not be suspected of leaning unduly to the doctrine I now advocate, has supposed it to extend even to our belief of mathematical truth. "Men," says Hobbes, "appeal from custom to reason, and from reason to custom, as it serves their turn, receding from custom when their interest requires it, and setting themselves against reason as oft as reason is against them; which is the cause that the doctrine of right and wrong is perpetually disputed both by the pen and the sword; whereas the doctrine of lines and figures is not so, because men care not, in that subject, what is truth, as it is a thing that crosses no man's ambition, or profit, or lust. For, I doubt not, if it had been a thing contrary to any man's right of dominion, or to the interest of men that have dominion, that the three angles of a triangle should be equal to two angles of a square, that doctrine should have been, if not disputed, yet by the burning of all books of geometry suppressed, as far as he whom it concerned was able." "This," says Hallam, from whose work I make the quotation, "does not exaggerate the pertinacity of mankind in resisting the evidence of truth when it thwarts the interests or passions of any particular sect or community."* Let a man who hears the forty-seventh proposition of Euclid announced for the first time, trace the steps of the demonstration, and he *must* believe it to be true; but let him know that, as soon as he does perceive the evidence of that proposition so as to believe it on that ground, he shall lose his right eye, and he will never trace the evidence, or come to that belief which results from the force of the only proper evidence. You may tell him it is true, but he will reply that he does not know, he does not see it to be so.

So far, then, from finding in this law of belief — the law by which it is necessitated on condition of a certain amount of evidence perceived by the mind — an excuse for any who do not receive the evidence of the Christian religion, it is in this very law that I find the ground of their condemnation. Certainly, if God has provided evidence as convincing as that for the forty-seventh of Euclid, so that all men have to do is to

* Literature of Europe, vol. iii.

examine it with candor, then they must be without excuse if they do not believe. This, I suppose, God has done. He asks no one to believe except on the ground of evidence, and such evidence as ought to command assent. Let a man examine this evidence with entire candor, laying aside all regard for consequences or results, simply according to the laws of evidence, and then, if he is not convinced, I believe God will, so far forth, acquit him in the great day of account. But if God has given men such evidence that a fair, and full, and perfectly candid examination is all that is needed to necessitate belief, then, if men do not believe, it will be in this very law that we shall find the ground of their condemnation. The difficulty will not lie in their mental constitution as related to evidence, nor in the want of evidence, but in that moral condition, that state of the heart, or the will, which prevented a proper examination. "There seems," says Butler, " no possible reason to be given why we may not be in a state of moral probation with regard to the exercise of our understanding upon the subject of religion, as we are with regard to our behavior in common affairs. The former is a thing as much within our power and choice as the latter."

When truth has a fair chance. — And here, I remark incidentally, we see what it is for truth to have a fair chance. There are many who think it has this when it is left free to combat error without the intervention of external force; and they seem to suppose it will, of necessity, prevail. But the fact is, that the truth almost never has a fair chance with such a being as man, when the reception of it involves self-denial, or the recognition of duties to which he is indisposed. Let " the mists that steam up before the intellect from a corrupt heart be dispersed," and truths, before obscure, shine out as the noonday. Before the mind of one with the intellect of a man, but with the purity and unselfishness of an angel, the evidence of such a system as the gospel would have a fair chance.

Is it true, then, that, if a perfectly candid attention be given to its evidences, a certainty of the truth of Christianity will be produced in the mind at this late day, and in these ends of the earth? I say, Yes; and I say it in full view of the kind of evidence by which Christianity is supported, and which, by some, is supposed incapable of producing certainty. Let us look at this point.

The kind of evidence — probable and mathematical evidence compared. — What, then, is the *kind* of evidence by which Christianity is supported? And here I am ready to say, it is moral evidence, as opposed to mathematical, and what is called probable evidence, as opposed to demonstrative. Is, then, mathematical evidence a better ground of certainty than moral evidence? On this point, and also respecting the subjects to which mathematical evidence can properly be applied, there is a wrong impression extensively prevalent, not only in the community at large, but among educated men. Figures, it is said, can not lie; and there seems to be an impression that where they are used, the result must be certain. But when a surveyor measures the sides and angles of a field, and ascertains the contents by calculation, is he certain he has the exact contents of that field? He may be so if no mistake has been made in measuring the sides and angles. But of that he never can be certain; or, if he is, it can not be by mathematical evidence. His accuracy will depend upon the perfection of his instruments, of which he never can be certain. So it will be found in all cases of what are called mixed mathematics. There are elements entering into the result that do not depend on mathematical evidence, and therefore the evidence for that result is not demonstrative. Even in those results in which the greatest confidence is felt, and in which there seems to be, and perhaps is, an entire coincidence with fact, the certainty that is felt does not result from mathematical evidence. No man, who understands the nature of the evidence on which he proceeds, would say he had demonstrated that there would be an eclipse next year. His expectation of it would depend, not on mathematical evidence, but upon his belief in the stability of the laws of nature. And even in accordance with those laws, it is not impossible that some new comet may come in athwart the orbit of the earth or the moon, and disturb their relative position.

Facts can not be demonstrated. — But, says the objector, I speak of *pure* mathematics, and of the certainty of its evidence. I say, then, with regard to pure mathematics, that it has no application to facts. No fact can be demonstrated. Nothing whatever, no assertion about any thing that ever did exist, or ever can exist, can be demonstrated, that is, proved by evidence purely mathematical. This will be assented to by all who understand the nature of mathematical evidence, and it can be easily shown. It can be demonstrated that the two acute angles in every right-angled triangle are equal to the right angle; but can this be demonstrated of any actually existing triangle? Draw what you call a right-angled triangle, and can you demonstrate it about that? No. You can not demonstrate that your given triangle is right-angled. Whether it is or not will depend upon the perfection of your instruments and the perfection of the senses. Accordingly, demonstration never asserts, and never can assert, of any triangle, that it *is* right-angled; but its language is, Let it be a right-angled triangle, suppose it to be, and then the two acute angles will be equal to that right angle. It asserts nothing whatever about any thing that actually exists, but only the connection between a certain supposition and a certain conclusion.* Whatever certainty we have, therefore, about any thing that actually exists, or has existed, or can exist, is derived, not from mathematical, but from what is called moral or probable evidence.

What, then, shall we say of the reasonableness, or rather of the folly, of those who ask for mathematical evidence to prove the truth of the Christian religion, when that evidence can not be applied to prove any one fact whatever?

I would by no means disparage mathematics. I acknowledge its extensive utility and application. I am surprised at that skill in the construction of instruments by which truths demonstrated concerning supposed lines and figures can be so correctly and generally applied to the purposes of practical life. I look with wonder upon that structure of the universe, by which truths demonstrated concerning these same abstract propositions are found to apply with so much exactness to its forms, and forces, and movements; but still, I would have this science keep within its own sphere, and not arrogate to itself a certainty which does not belong to it in virtue of its own authority, and which operates practically to throw distrust upon our conclusions in other departments.

Either, then, there is certainty on other ground than mathematical evidence, or there is no certainty concerning any fact or existing thing whatever, and there will be no stopping short of that absolute skepticism which denies the authority of the human faculties, and doubts of every thing, and finally doubts whether it doubts.

Grounds of certainty. — If, then, such certainty may be attained, our next inquiry will be, What are

---

* Stewart's Elements, vol. ii. chap. ii. sec. 3.

the grounds of it? And of these there are no less than six.

First: Consciousness. — The first ground of certainty is consciousness. By this we are informed of what is passing within our own minds. We are certain that we think and feel.

Second: Reason. — The second is that which is now commonly called reason in man, or by some *the* reason, by which he perceives directly, intuitively, necessarily, and believes, with a conviction from which he can not free himself, certain fundamental truths, upon which all other truths, and all reasoning, properly so called, or deduction, are conditioned. It is by this that we believe in our own existence and personal identity, and in the maxim that every event must have an adequate cause. This belongs equally to all men, and, within its own province, its authority is perfect. No authority can be higher, no certainty more full and absolute, than that which it gives. No man *can* believe any thing with a certainty greater than that with which he believes in his own existence; and, if we may suppose such a case, he who should doubt of his own existence, would, in that single doubt, necessarily involve the doubt of every thing else.

Third: the Senses. — The third ground of certainty is the evidence of the senses. I do not deny that the senses may deceive us — that they sometimes do; but I affirm that generally the evidence of the senses is the ground of entire certainty to the mass of mankind. To them "seeing is believing," and they can conceive of no greater certainty than that which results from this evidence. Whatever doubt some may attempt to cast over this subject, it is obvious that no event whatever — not the flowing of water toward its source — can be a greater violation of the laws of nature, more in opposition to its ordinary sequences, than would be a deception upon the senses of men with respect to certain things and under certain circumstances. It would be as great a miracle to make three millions, or one million, of people believe that they went out and gathered manna — that they saw, and felt, and tasted it — when they really did not, as it would if water should flow back toward its source, or should divide and stand up in heaps.

Fourth: Memory. — The fourth ground of certainty is the evidence of memory. Without entire confidence in this, no testimony could be taken in a court of justice, no criminal could be convicted. When its testimony is perfectly clear and distinct, it leaves no doubt on the mind.

Fifth: Testimony. — The fifth ground of certainty is testimony. With respect to this, I would say substantially the same that I have said of the senses. No doubt, as has been said by Hume, and as every body knows, testimony sometimes deceives us; but it has not been enough insisted on, that testimony may be given by such men, and so many, and under such circumstances, as to form a ground of certainty as valid as any other can possibly be. I do not now say that the testimony for the Christian religion is of this character; but I say, if it is not, the difficulty lies, not in the kind of evidence, as distinguished from mathematical, but in the degree of it in this particular case.

Sixth: Reasoning. — The sixth ground of certainty is reasoning. That this is so in mathematics, all will admit. On other subjects, the certainty may be equally full and absolute. When Robinson Crusoe saw the track of a man's foot upon the shore of his island, he was as certain there had been a man there as if he had seen him. It was reasoning; it was inferring, from a fact which he knew by sensation, another fact which he did not thus know; but how perfectly conclusive! The skeptic never lived who would have doubted it. This kind of evidence is capable of every degree of probability, from the slightest shade of it upward. It often requires that a large number of circumstances should be taken into the account, and, in many cases, does not amount to positive proof. In many others, however, it does; and the circumstance on which I wish to fix attention is, that it may be the ground of a belief as fixed and certain as any other.

These, then, are the grounds of certainty, and each has its peculiar province. Of these, each of the first three — consciousness, reason, and the senses — is entirely competent within its own sphere, and, indeed, scarcely admits of collateral support. Not so the last three. The evidence of memory, of testimony, and of reasoning, may mutually assist and confirm each other. It is upon the last two, the evidence of testimony and of reasoning, that we rely for the support of what are called the external proofs of Christianity; and if one of these is capable of producing certainty, much more, if certainty admitted of degrees, would they both when conspiring together.

A habit of doubt — credulity and skepticism equally weak. — I have dwelt on this subject because it seems to me that many persons indulge themselves in a sickly and effeminate habit of doubt on all subjects without the pale of mathematics and physics, and more especially on the subject of religion. So much has been said, there are so many opinions and so much doubt respecting different points of the religion itself, that this feeling of doubt has been transferred to the evidence by which the religion is sustained. I wish, therefore, to have it distinctly felt that the kind of evidence by which Christianity is sustained is capable of producing certainty, and I claim that the evidences are such that, when fully and fairly examined, they will produce it. They amount to what is meant by a moral demonstration. There are many subjects on which, from want of evidence, or because they are beyond the reach of our faculties, it is wise, and the mark of a strong mind, to doubt; and there are also subjects on which it is equally the mark of a weak mind to doubt, and of a strong one to give a full assent. The day, I trust, has gone by when a habit of doubt and of skepticism is to be regarded as a mark of superior intellect.

Possible conflict of reasoning and testimony — the argument of Hume. — But, though testimony and reasoning may produce the certainty of mathematical demonstration in some circumstances, yet is it not possible that one of these sources of evidence may so come in conflict with the other as to leave the mind in entire suspense? Is it not possible that an amount of testimony which, when we look at it by itself, seems perfectly conclusive, may yet be opposed by an argument which, when taken by itself, seems perfectly conclusive, and thus the mind be left in a state of hopeless perplexity? This may be conceived; and, putting the testimony for Christianity in the most favorable light, it is precisely the condition in which it is claimed, by Hume and his followers, that the mind of a reasonable person must be thrown, by his argument on miracles. Shall I, then, go on to state and answer that argument? I am not unwilling to do so; because it will, I presume, be expected; and because it is still the custom of those who defend Christianity to do so, just as it was the custom of British ships to fire a gun on passing the port of Copenhagen, long after its power had been prostrated, and its influence had ceased to be felt.

According to Hume, "Experience is our only guide in reasoning concerning matters of fact." Our belief of any fact from the report of eye witnesses is derived from no other principle than experience; that is, our observation of the veracity of human testimony. Now, if the fact attested partakes of the marvelous, if it is such as has seldom fallen under our observation, here is a contest of two opposite experiences, of which the one destroys the other as far as its force goes, and the superior can only operate on the mind by the force which remains. "But," says Hume, "in order to increase the probability against the testimony of witnesses, let us suppose that the fact which they affirm, instead of being only marvelous, is really miraculous; and suppose, also, that the testimony, considered apart and in itself, amounts to an entire proof; in that case there is proof against proof, of which the strongest must prevail, but still with a diminution of its force in proportion to that of its antagonist. A miracle is a violation of the laws of nature; and as a firm and unalterable experience has established these laws, the proof against a miracle, from the very nature of the fact, is as entire as any argument from experience can possibly be imagined."

Again, Hume says, "It is experience only which gives authority to human testimony; and it is the same experience which assures us of the laws of nature. When, therefore, these two kinds of experience are contrary, we have nothing to do but to subtract the one from the other, and embrace an opinion either on one side or the other, with that assurance which arises from the remainder. But, according to the principle here explained, this subtraction, with regard to all popular religions, amounts to an entire annihilation; and therefore we may establish it as a maxim, that no human testimony can have such force as to prove a miracle, and make it a just foundation for any such system of religion."

The claim — no room for it on the ground of Theism. — The claim here is, not that we are to be cautious, as doubtless we are, in regard to all evidence for prodigies and miracles, but that the latter hold such a relation to the grounds of our belief that they can not be proved by human testimony. Let the question, however, be argued, as Hume claims to argue it, on the ground of theism, and let it be fairly stated, and it would seem impossible that there should be any difficulty respecting it. Do we believe in the existence of a personal God, intelligent and free?— not a God who is a part of nature, or a mere personification of the powers of nature, but one who is as distinct from nature as the builder of the house is from the house? Do we believe, with our best philosophers, either that the laws of nature are only the stated mode in which God operates; or that all nature, with all its laws, is perfectly under his control? Then we can find no difficulty in believing that such a God may, at any time when the good of his creatures requires it, change the mode of his operation, and suspend those laws. Would Hume accept this statement of the question? If so, the dispute is at an end; for this relation of God to nature involves the possibility both of a miracle and of its proof. It is incompatible with this relation, that experience should ever attain that character of absolute and necessary uniformity, in virtue of which alone its evidence can be set in opposition to that of testimony. If he would not accept this statement, he is an atheist or a pantheist; and we are not yet prepared to argue the question of miracles, for that can not be argued till it is fully conceded that a personal God exists.

Two spheres and movements — the mind adapted to both. — The above seems to me a sufficient answer to the argument of Hume. Our minds are constituted with reference to our position under both the natural and the moral government of God. But Hume does not take the moral government of God into his account at all. This is his great mistake. It is like the mistake of the astronomer who should carefully notice the recurring movements of the planets around their primary, but should fail to notice that mightier movement by which, as we are told, the planets and suns are all borne onward toward some unknown point in infinite space. Experience may enable him to determine and to calculate the movements of the first order; but if he would know that of the second, he must inquire of Him who carries it forward. The moral government of God is a movement in a line onward toward some grand consummation, in which the principles, indeed, are ever the same, but the developments are always new, — in which, therefore, no experience of the past can indicate with certainty what new openings of truth, what new manifestations of goodness, what new phases of the moral heavens may appear. To this movement, the circular and uniform one, in which alone experience is possible, is entirely subordinate; and it accords with our natural expectations and grounds of belief that the less important should be flexible to the demands of that which is more so. It is on this double movement, and the subordination of the lower, that the high harmonies of the universe depend. The constitution of our nature is adapted to both movements separately, and as related; and that nature is true to itself and to its position when men readily accept evidence for miraculous events. To render such events fully credible, we only need to show that they are demanded by great moral interests. The presumption of uniformity is then balanced by that of interposition, and the full weight of testimony comes in without a counterpoise. It is thus that there is provision for both the scientific and the supernatural element; and the system that would exclude either is narrow and inadequate.

The difficulty with the most of those who have opposed Hume has been, that they have permitted him, while arguing the question ostensibly on the ground of theism, to involve positions that are really atheistic. They have permitted him to give, surreptitiously, to the mere laws of nature a sacredness and a permanence which put them in the place of God. If we grant to Hume that the laws of nature are absolutely uniform, we preclude, of course, all proof for a miracle. This is really, though not avowedly, the essential premise by which he attempts to show that a miracle can not be proved by testimony; and whoever grants him this, grants the very point in dispute. The laws of nature, when once it is conceded that they are invariable, are of equal authority; and it is in vain to attempt to invalidate the authority of one by bringing against it that of another, by whatever amount of induction it may have been established.

Reply of Dr. Chalmers. — This does not seem to have been perceived by Dr. Chalmers in his very elaborate attempt to refute the argument of Hume. He grants that the laws of nature are uniform, and says that there are laws of testimony that are a part of the laws of nature, as uniform as any other, and that there are certain kinds of testimony in regard to which the uniform experience is, that they do not deceive us; and then he goes on to show, with great power, how the force of testimony may be accumulated so as to overbalance any improbability whatever. I admit fully all that he says on the force of testimony. But let its force be ever so great, if it were a fact that no testimony was ever known to deceive us, yet even then, if we admit the premise of Hume as he would have it understood, we only balance uniform experience against uniform experience, and thus produce the very case of perplexity spoken of by him. Chalmers saw with great clearness the overwhelming force of testimony as proof. He says, in opposition to Campbell and others, that our belief in testimony is founded solely in experience, and that there are certain kinds of testimony of which we have uniform experience that they do not deceive us. But he failed to see that no uniform experience of the truth of testimony could prove a fact that had been already admitted to be contrary to "a firm and unalterable experience." "A firm and unalterable experience" of the truth of testimony, can never prove a fact which can be fairly shown to be contrary to another "firm and unalterable experience."

The argument of Hume is not avowedly against the possibility of miracles, though, as he must, if he would not beg the question, he constantly insinuates, and implies in his definitions, that they are impossible. The avowed argument is against the possibility of the proof of miracles by testimony.

Testimony and experience not in conflict. — But if we allow the possibility of a miracle, the authority of testimony and of experience can not be fairly set against each other, because one is positive and the other negative. Experience can not prove a negative. It can not testify that a miracle has *not* taken place. That is the point in question, and to prove it, would require the positive testimony of every human being who has lived from the beginning of time. Had Hume been asked why he believed the course of nature to be absolutely uniform, he must have answered that he believed it on the ground of experience. And then, if asked how he knew what that experience had been, he must have replied, by testimony, for there is no other possible way. And thus it would appear that, while he seems to oppose the evidence of experience to that of testimony, he is only opposing the evidence of testimony to that of testimony. And what would the testimony on the side of Hume amount to in such a case? Why, absolutely nothing, because it is, as has been said, negative. Let a thousand men swear, in a court of justice, that they did not see a murder committed, and it will not diminish in the least the force of the testimony of one man who swears that he did see it, unless the thousand pretend to have been on the spot, and to have had opportunity to witness it. In this case, the experience of the thousand men would be properly said to be contrary to that of the one. But in no such sense can experience be said to be contrary to the testimony for miracles. If any number of men, if the whole race, — with the exception of those who had an opportunity to see, and who did see, a miracle, — should testify that they did not see it, that would not invalidate, in the least, the testimony of those who did see it. We should judge of that testimony on its own proper merits.

Thus stands the argument, if, with Hume, we place our belief in the uniformity of nature on the ground of experience. But is this really the ground of that belief? I think not. Nor can I agree with Stewart and other metaphysicians, who place " the expectation of the continued uniformity of the laws of nature " among what they call the fundamental laws of belief, which we believe in necessarily, and without reference to experience. This is not the place for the full discussion of this point. I merely observe that, so far is this from being to the mind a law of belief, to the exclusion of supernatural agency, that narrations of such agency have been received in all ages upon the slightest evidence; and that, if this were the law, then no man ought to believe, or could believe, in the resurrection of the dead, or a future judgment, or in the destruction or change of the present order of nature in any way whatever. The difficulty lies in an incautious and narrow statement of the true law. The true law of belief is, that the same causes will, in the same circumstances, produce the same effects. This is the law; and when applied to the permanence or uniformity of the course of nature, it will stand thus: The present course of nature will be uniform and permanent, unless other causes than those now in operation shall intervene to interrupt or destroy it. The probability of the intervention of such causes is a point on which every man must decide for himself. To me it seems probable — to you, perhaps, improbable; but there is nothing in the nature of the case to prevent it from being proved, like any other fact.

Having thus put this question upon its true basis, it will be necessary to say very little of the particular fallacies and consequences connected with the argument of Hume. I will simply add, that, —

Hume's argument is a practical absurdity. — 1. According to Hume, the very fact that renders a miracle possible, must render the proof of it impossible. Without a settled uniformity, a miracle could not be conceived; with it, according to him, it can not be proved. To suppose that the mind can be placed in such a relation as this to any possible truth, is a practical absurdity.

Would contradict the senses. — 2. The argument of Hume proceeds on a principle which would make it unreasonable to believe a miracle on the testimony of the senses. There is precisely the same reason for opposing the evidence of experience to that of the senses, as for opposing it to that of testimony. If the argument would overthrow a "full proof" from testimony, the senses, standing as they do in the same relation to experience, could give nothing more.

Begs the question. — 3. Hume begs the question. The only way in which a miracle can be a violation of the course of nature, or contrary to experience, is, that it never happened, and was never observed; for if it had happened, and had been observed, then it would constitute a part of universal experience. But to say that a "violation," or, more properly, a suspension of the laws of nature never happened, because those laws are uniform, and to define a miracle as something "that has never been observed in any age or country," is taking for granted the very point in dispute. It is as bald and barefaced a begging of the question as can well be imagined. "But," says Hume, "it is a miracle that a dead man should come to life, because that has never happened in any age or country. There must therefore be a uniform experience against every miraculous event; otherwise the event would not merit that appellation." Is this reasoning?

He uses "experience" in two senses. — 4. Hume uses the term *experience* in two senses. Personal experience is the knowledge we have acquired by our own senses. General experience is that knowledge of facts which has been acquired by the race. If, therefore, Hume says a miracle is contrary to his personal experience, that proves nothing; but if he says it is opposed to universal experience, that, as has already been said, is begging the question.

Simply opposes testimony to testimony. — 5. He opposes the evidence of experience to that of testimony, evidently with the intention of opposing to testimony the high authority that belongs to personal experience; whereas, in the sense in which he must use the term " experience," — since, as has been said, we can know what general experience is only by testimony, — he is only opposing testimony to testimony.

Renounced by Hume. — And, finally, Hume has himself renounced the principle of his own argument. He seems to have had a perception of some of the absurd consequences to which it must lead, and therefore adds, "I beg the limitations here may be remarked when I say, that a miracle can never be proved so as to be the foundation of a system of religion. For I own that otherwise there may possibly be miracles, or violations of the usual course of nature, of such a kind as to admit of proof from human testimony." This single admission destroys at once the whole force of his argument. As an example, he says, "Suppose all authors, in all languages, agree that from the 1st of January, 1600, there was a total darkness over the whole earth for eight days; suppose that the tradition of this extraordinary event is still strong and lively among the people; that all travelers who return from foreign countries bring us accounts of the same tradition, without the least variation or contradiction; it is evident that our present philosophers, instead of doubting the fact, ought to receive it as certain." "But," he adds, with reference, however, to another example, "should this miracle be ascribed to any new system of religion, men in all ages have been so imposed upon by ridiculous stories of that kind, that the very circumstance would be full proof of a cheat, and sufficient, with all men of sense, not only to make them reject the fact, but to reject it without further examination." On the consistency and candor of this passage I make no comment. As showing a tendency of our nature, the argument is just the reverse. Who, after reading this, can fail to feel that Hume was guilty of a heartless, if not a malignant trifling with the best interests of his fellow-men?

Summary. — Thus, after mentioning the classes of persons whom I shall hope to benefit, I have endeavored to show, first, that you, my hearers, are responsible for the manner in which you use your understandings, and for the opinions you form on this great subject.

4

And, secondly, that there is nothing in the nature or kind of evidence by which Christianity is sustained, nor in any conflict of the evidence of experience and of testimony, to prevent us from attaining that certainty upon which we may rest as upon the rock, and which shall constitute, if not "the assurance of faith," yet the assurance of understanding.

LECTURE II.

PRELIMINARY OBSERVATIONS. — REVELATION PROBABLE : FIRST, FROM THE NATURE OF THE CASE; SECONDLY, FROM FACTS. — PROBABILITY OF MIRACLES, ASIDE FROM THEIR EFFECT IN SUSTAINING ANY PARTICULAR REVELATION. — CONNECTION BETWEEN THE MIRACLE AND THE DOCTRINE. — THE CHRISTIAN RELIGION, OR NONE.

The Christian religion admits of certain proof; and to show this was one object of the last lecture. But, in searching for that proof, we may proceed in two different methods. We may either try the facts in question by the laws of evidence, precisely as we would any other facts; or we may judge beforehand of their probability or improbability. In the first case, we should allow nothing for what we might suppose previous probability or improbability, nothing for the nature of the facts as miraculous or common. We should hold ourselves in the position of an impartial jury, bound to decide solely according to the evidence. This course alone is in accordance with the spirit of the inductive philosophy, which decides nothing on the ground of previous hypothesis, but yields itself entirely to the guidance of facts properly authenticated, and refuses no conclusion which the existence of those facts necessarily involves. Let those who are to judge of Christianity approach it in this spirit, and we are content.

Need of the philosophic spirit. — And surely, if this spirit was demanded when the processes of nature only were in question, — and the whole history of human conjecture *there* is but the history of weakness and folly, so that science made no progress till facts established by proper evidence were received without reference to hypothesis, — much more must this same spirit be demanded when the procedure of God in his moral government is concerned. On such a subject, nothing can be more contrary to that wise caution which adheres to facts, and balances evidence, and keeps the mind open to conviction, than to come to a decision under the influence of a prejudication of the case on the ground of any antecedent improbability.

Spirit of the age — tendency to reaction. — But, unphilosophical as such a course plainly is, it springs directly from the spirit of the age. The human mind, in its constant oscillations between the extremes of credulity and skepticism, is now ranging somewhere on the side of skepticism. There was a time, both before and after the revival of letters, when a belief in frequent supernatural agency was common. But when many things, supposed to be owing to supernatural influence, were referred, by the light of science, to natural causes, and a large class of superstitions was thus expelled, then men passed to the other extreme, and it became weak and superstitious to believe even in the possibility of any other causes than those that were natural. It was the progress of this feeling toward the utmost limits of skepticism, that was called by many the progress of light in the world; and it was taken advantage of, and urged on, by skeptics, in every possible way. But a general tendency of the human mind is never altogether deceptive. It is the indication of some great truth. This is so with the tendency of man, admitted even by Hume, to believe in supernatural agency. And when the reaction is over, and men settle down in the light of a large experience, it will be readily conceded, I doubt not, that, while the general course of nature is uniform, so as to lay a foundation for experience, and give it value, there is also something in the system to meet our tendency to believe in that which is supernatural; that there are powers, higher than those of nature, connected with the natural and moral administration of the universe, that may interfere for the welfare of man.

Facts to rest on evidence. — But, however this may be hereafter, it is not so now. The legitimate force of the evidence for Christianity is constantly neutralized by assertions, purely hypothetical, of the improbability of the facts. Now, we admit of no such improbability. We hold that no man has a right to construct a metaphysical balance in which he shall place an hypothesis of his own as a counterpoise for one particle of valid evidence. To do it, is to go back into the dark ages. It is to apply, in religion, maxims long since discarded in physics. It is, therefore, out of a regard to the exigencies of the time, and not because I think it essential to the Christian argument, that I proceed to adduce some considerations to show the antecedent probability of a revelation from God.

Probability — how judged of. — To judge of the probability of any event, we must know something of its causes, or of the intentions of the agent who may produce it. If we know nothing of these, we have no right to say, of any event, that it is probable or improbable. If we know all the causes that are at work, or all the intentions of the agents employed, we can foretell with certainty what will take place. It is obvious, therefore, that an event which may seem highly probable to one man, or, perhaps, nearly certain, may seem to another altogether improbable. So sensible, however, are most persons of their ignorance of the causes, and agents, and purposes, that may exist in this complex and wonderful universe, that it requires but a

4 *

slight amount of evidence to substantiate events of which we should have said, beforehand, that the chances against them were as a million to one. Especially is this the case when the actions of a free agent are concerned, and when we are but slightly acquainted with his character and purposes.

But this is precisely the case before us. The question is, whether it was probable, beforehand, that God would give a revelation to man. Of this we can judge only as we are acquainted with the character of God, and the emergency requiring his special interposition. That he could give such a revelation, and confirm it by miracles, every theist must admit; and the simple question is, whether, as a free Agent and a moral Governor, (for I acknowledge no man as a theist who does not admit these two characters of God,) he would think it best to give a revelation.

Objection. — I know it is said, by some, that this is ground on which we ought not to tread. God, they say, is an infinite Being, and the complexity of his plans, and the range of his operations, must be so great that it would be presumption in creatures like us, creatures of a day, dwelling in this remote corner of the universe, to judge what would, or would not, be probable under his government. Far better might the little child, yet learning its alphabet, judge of the probabilities respecting the purposes and actions of the Government of these United States.

What follows? — That this is sometimes said sincerely I am not disposed to deny; but there is often connected with it a fallacy which is by no means harmless. Admit, then, the justice of it all; and what will follow? An argument against the probability of a revelation? Certainly not. It will simply follow that we can not tell whether a revelation would be probable or improbable; and then a candid man will judge of the evidence for a revelation just as he would of that for any other event. And this is all we desire. Let no antecedent improbability be assumed, and we are willing to go at once to the evidence and the facts.

Objectors do that to which they object. — But is this the state of mind of those who speak of man as thus ignorant? Is it their object to produce such a state of mind? I think not, but rather to bring doubt and uncertainty over the whole subject. It is assumed that we are ignorant of the purposes of God, and then, from that ignorance, the *improbability* of a revelation is argued. But it seems to be forgotten that we need previous knowledge, to judge of the improbability, no less than of the probability, of events; and while these persons shrink back with a pious horror from the presumption of judging what God might or might not do, they covertly assume a knowledge of his purposes, or at least of what he probably will not do in a given case. We say, that whoever affirms it is improbable that God would give a revelation, assumes, in proportion to his confidence, a knowledge of the previous plans and purposes of God; and then we ask him where he obtained that knowledge. God has not told him so, for that would be a revelation. He can not know it from experience, for the case stands by itself. We have no experience of what God does with his creatures, if such there are, similarly situated in other worlds. The uniform course of nature can be no objection, for the very question at issue is, whether that course shall be suspended. It is admitted that God can do it with perfect ease; and how can such a man know that the exigencies of his moral government may not require it?

Not wholly ignorant. — I am, however, far from assenting to what is thus said of our ignorance on this subject. If we use the term "beforehand" in the strictest and highest sense, perhaps it would be presumption in us to judge what God would do. But, in all our arguments respecting Christianity, we take for granted the great truths of natural religion. We have some knowledge of God, and of his providential dealings with the race; and it is not presumption in us to say whether it would be in accordance with that character, so far as known, and analogous with his dealings in other respects, if he should give to man a revelation. This is the true question. Is there any thing in what we know positively of the character of God, in connection with the condition of man, that would render it probable or improbable that he would give a revelation?

Probability of a revelation — God a father. — And why should he not? I know not why it should be considered so strange a thing that God should make a revelation to man. If I mistake not, it would have been much stranger if he had not. It may be strange that he should have created the world at all, or put such a being as man upon it; but if we believe that God made him with a rational and a religious nature — a child — capable of communion with him, and of finding in him only the highest source of happiness and means of moral perfection, — then it would be exceedingly strange if God should not reveal himself to him. Shall not a father speak to his own child?

Communion with God needed — not a strange thing. — It is demonstrable, on the principles of reason, that, if man had continued in a state of innocence, the highest progress, and expansion, and felicity of his nature could not have been attained except by communion with God. *Man becomes assimilated to that with which he voluntarily holds communion.* And since God is the fountain of all excellence, why should he not communicate himself to an innocent creature whom he had made with faculties to know, and love, and enjoy him? In the original and highest sense of the word, a state of nature is a state of direct intercourse with God. Accordingly, the Bible, instead of regarding it, as infidels, and, I must say, many divines, do, as a strange thing that God should hold communion with men, speaks of it as a matter of course; and the traditions of all nations have connected with an age of innocence the frequent intercourse of man with the gods. There is nothing, either in the nature of the case or in the instincts of humanity, to give rise to that strangeness with which infidels have invested a revelation from God; but the reverse. It is strange that man is at all. It is strange that God is. In one sense, every thing is strange, and equally so. But supposing God to be, and to make such a creature as man, it is *not* strange that he should make a revelation to him. Indeed, to suppose God to make man a being capable of religion, requiring it in order to the development of the highest part of his nature, and then not to communicate with him, as a father, in those revelations which alone could perfect that nature, would be a reproach upon God, and a contradiction.

Nor, even in a state of innocence, would the revelation of God in his works have been sufficient, since in them he reveals chiefly his natural attributes, and not that holiness and perfection of moral character from which the great obligations, and interests, and duties, and the high delights of his service, are derived. Even now we sometimes find a man groping about this rigid framework of general laws, and exclaiming, "O that I knew where I might find him! that I might come even to his seat!" and how much less would man in a state of innocence have been satisfied without direct communion with God! The highest and most natural conception of the universe is that which makes God the Father of his rational and spiritual creatures, which constitutes them a family, and which implies communication between him and them as personal beings, he making known his will and character, and they obeying and adoring him.

Effects of sin — ground of hope. — If, indeed, an innocent being should sin, we could not say beforehand what would be done. We should naturally expect that justice would have its course. But, looking at the race as it is, evidently favored by God to some extent, visited by his rain and sunshine and by fruitful seasons, we should have as much reason to think, from the nature and position of man, that there would be such a thing as true religion on the earth, as that there would be such a thing as true science upon the earth. For that man has a moral and a religious nature is as evident as that he has an intellectual nature. Wherever he is found he makes the distinction between right and wrong, and worships some superior being. If there have been a few who have professed themselves atheists, and we were to give them that credit for entire sincerity which many facts would lead us to withhold, this would no more prove that man has not a religious nature, than the fact that a few men have overcome the social instinct, and withdrawn from society, proves that he has not a social nature.

Religious nature central. — Nor are these principles, which thus lead man to anticipate future retribution, and to recognize superior powers, merely secondary, or subordinate to others. They are peculiarly those by which man is distinguished from the brute. They are those, as shown by all history, in connection with the cultivation and full development of which, all the other powers of man reach their highest perfection; in connection with the perversion and debasement of which, all the other powers are ill regulated and dwarfed. So effective, indeed, has the influence of these principles been felt to be, that all former governments have sought their aid, and have endeavored to associate the power of religion with that of the temporal arm. It has been from these principles, rather than from any others, that motives to high resolve, and long endurance, and voluntary poverty, and a martyr's sufferings, have been drawn. Remove from the history of the past all those actions which have either sprung directly from the religious nature of man, or been modified by it, and you have the history of another world and of another race.

Ineradicable.—I know the manifestations of this principle have been exceedingly various, and sometimes as whimsical and debasing as can well be conceived. There is no absurdity which men have not received, no austerity which they have not practiced, no earthly good, and no natural affection, which they have not sacrificed, in the name of religion; and the very variety and absurdity of religious rites, with the sincerity of men in them all, has been made, and still is, a capital argument of infidels to show that there is nothing in any religion. But it has been well replied, that "the more strange the contradictions, and the more ludicrous the ceremonies, to which the pride of human reason has been reconciled, the stronger is our evidence that religion has a foundation in the nature of man." * Indeed, no fact can be better established, both by philosophy and by history, than that mankind are so constituted that they must have some religion. Man has a religious nature, which is a fundamental and elementary constituent of his being. This nature will manifest itself. Let the true religion be removed, and a false one will come in its place. This is a truth, the clear perception of which by the public mind I deem of great importance; for if society is to make progress, it must be by cultivating the faculties that belong to human nature, and not by attempting to eradicate them; and hence all

* Stewart.

indiscriminate attacks upon religion, as such, must retard that progress.

Its right exercise possible. — Man, then, has a religious nature; and what purpose could a wise and good Being have, in sustaining the race, which would not involve the right exercise of this nature, in view of its appropriate objects? And to suppose that God has furnished man with no such object to draw that nature out, is like supposing that he would create the eye without light or the ear without sound, or that he would place man, as an intellectual being, in a world of such disorder that no arrangement or classification, and consequently no science, would be possible. The whole analogy of God's works, and of his dealings with men, shows that, if man has a religious nature, we might expect to find the right exercise of that nature possible, and that there would be such a thing as true religion in the world.

Only through a revelation. — But if a rational being, capable of religion, had lost the moral image, and consequently the true knowledge of God, and it should be the object of God to restore him, it could be done in no other way than by a direct revelation. This is obvious from two reasons. First, there would be some things which it would be indispensable for such a being to know, and which he could not know except by a direct communication. They are of such a kind that nature can have no voice, no utterance, no *whisper*, respecting them. Such would be an answer to the inquiry, whether God would pardon sin at all, and, if so, upon what conditions. And, secondly, it is not possible that a sinful being should be restored to God, to purity, and love, except by some manifestation to him of the purity and love of God such as nature does not give. So far as we can see, there must be brought into operation that great principle of moral assimilation mentioned by the apostle when he says, "We all, beholding, as in a glass, the glory of the Lord, are changed into the same image, from glory to glory." If, then, it was probable that God would do any thing to restore a race of transgressors to himself, it was in the same degree probable that he would give a revelation different from any that nature can possibly give. So far as we can see, it would be impossible for him to do it in any other way.

Shown by experience. — And what we might thus infer, from the nature of the case, is amply confirmed by an appeal to facts. An impartial survey of the condition of those portions of the earth that have been without the light of revelation, shows conclusively that the reformation of man was hopeless without it. A full and fair experiment has been made. It has extended through thousands of years, and ample time has been given to test every principle, to follow out every tendency to its results, to call forth every inherent energy of man. It has been made in every climate, under every form of government, in all circumstances of barbarism and refinement, by individuals who, for intellectual endowments, have been the pride of the race, and by nations who have made the greatest advancement in literature, in science, and in the arts. What unassisted man has done, therefore, to disperse the religious darkness, and to remedy the moral maladies of the world, may be regarded as a fair exemplification of what he would do.

To show that the race has been, and would continue to be, hopelessly benighted and degraded without a revelation, has been the chief object of those who have attempted to show its probability. This they have done with much erudition and research, and this ground is so familiar that I shall not go over it at large, but content myself with a brief statement of some of the more important points.

Knowledge of the divine unity lost. — And, first, the great doctrine of the divine unity has been practically lost without a revelation. Every where the mass of men have been worshipers of natural objects, or of the powers of nature personified, or of idols, or of deified men; and if a few philosophers have seen the folly of this, and really held to the divine unity, it was rather to ridicule and despise, than to benefit, the multitude. It does not appear, however, that they held to the doctrine except as a matter of speculation, or that they had any habit of worshiping the one infinite God, or taught that he ought to be worshiped. What must have been the practical blindness and uncertainty, on this cardinal point, of that philosopher, who, among his last requests, could ask a friend not to forget to sacrifice a cock for him to Esculapius? And yet this did Socrates. What must have been the state of the public mind among the most enlightened people on earth, and in the Augustan age, who could erect a statue to a woman infamous for her profligacy, with the following inscription, making her no less a deity than Providence itself? "The Senate of the Areopagus, and the Senate of the Five Hundred, to the goddess Julia Augusta Providence!"

Of the holiness of God. — I remark, secondly, that the heathen nations have been entirely destitute of the knowledge of God, as a holy God, as having a perfect moral character, and as exercising a moral government, the principles of which reach the thoughts of the heart. Whether there were data for the knowledge of this in nature, perhaps we need not decide; but, without this knowledge of God, it is evident there can be no pure and spiritual religion. Generally, the moral character of God has been conceived of by transferring to him the moral character, the affections, the passions, and even the lusts, of men. No religion based on such a conception of the object of worship can benefit man. He must become debased under its influence.

Separation of religion and morality. — But, thirdly, this ignorance of the moral character of God has led, as it naturally must, to the introduction of forms of worship that can not be acceptable to him, and to that separation of religion from morality which has been so universal, and, in most instances, so entire, among heathen nations. What Bishop Heber said of the Hindoos may, with some modifications, be said of all heathen nations: "The good qualities that are among them are in no instance, that I am aware of, connected with, or arising out of, their religion, since it is in no instance to good deeds, or virtuous habits of life, that the future rewards in which they believe are proposed. Accordingly," he says, "I really have never met with a race of men whose standard of morality is so low, — who feel so little apparent shame in being detected in a falsehood, or so little interest in the sufferings of a neighbor not being of their own caste or family, — whose ordinary and familiar conversation is so licentious, or, in the wilder and more lawless districts, who shed blood with so little repugnance." The tendency to this separation of religion and morals is strong every where, and nothing can be more destructive both of true religion and of morality, or more fatal to every interest of man. Let men think to please God by gifts, by forms, by bodily sufferings, without regard to justice, and benevolence, and purity, and all the foundations of individual happiness and social order must be out of course. And how much more must this be the case, when the character of the object worshiped is such as to excite and to encourage every form of iniquity, and when, as is often the case, unnatural cruelty, and drunkenness, and obscenity, instead of being forbidden, become a part of the religious rites! "When the light that is in men becomes darkness, how great is that darkness!" This is a point of the greatest moment, since no false religion ever did, or ever can, teach, and adequately sanction, any thing like a perfect system of morality; and since morality, unsustained by religion, can never furnish an adequate basis of either individual or general progress.

Immortality.—I remark, fourthly, that without revelation, men have had very obscure and doubtful notions respecting the immortality of the soul, and, so far as this fundamental doctrine has been received, it has been made use of rather to control men in their conduct here, than to fit them for another state. A great part of the philosophers regarded this belief as a vulgar prejudice, and those who received it held it as doubtful. Even Cicero, who had carefully studied the arguments of Socrates, and added others of his own, says, "Which of these is true, God alone knows; and which is most probable, a very great question." And very many, too, who held the doctrine, held it in such connection as to destroy its practical influence for good. Some held it in connection with the doctrine of fate or necessity; some, as Plato, in connection with the doctrine of the transmigration of souls; and some, like the present Hindoos just noticed, severed all connection between the moral character here and the state of the soul hereafter. As a practical doctrine, therefore, "life and immortality were brought to light by the gospel." This alone has revealed it, with such authority and certainty, and in such connections, as to give it all its efficiency as a motive of action. Nothing can be more beautiful or philosophical than the manner in which Christianity extends the same moral laws and essential conditions of happiness over the present and the future life, so that the life of heaven is made to be nothing but the brightening and expansion of the life that is commenced here. In this respect, the coming in of Christianity was like the coming in of the Newtonian system; for as that shows, contrary to the doctrine of the ancients, that the same laws apply to things earthly and to things heavenly, to the floating particle of dust and to the planet in its orbit, so Christianity introduces unity and simplicity into the moral system, and shows that the humblest child, that is a moral agent, and the highest archangel, are subject to the same moral law.

In these four points, — the unity of God, his moral character, the kind of worship that would be acceptable to him, and the immortality of the soul, — it may be thought that the materials of knowledge were within the reach of man. But if this is true for any, it is not for the mass of men. The elements of the highest mathematical truths are within the reach of all, and those truths may be said to be discoverable; but we have no reason to think they ever would or could have been discovered by the great mass of men.

Truths not suggested by nature — pardon of sin. — But there is, as already suggested, another class of truths, some of them fundamental and indispensable to be known, which are not, and could not be, suggested by nature. Such, particularly, first, is the truth that God can pardon sin on any terms. If there is any one primary doctrine of natural religion, it is, that God is just. This was so strongly felt by Socrates that he doubted whether God could pardon sin. To a sinner, as man is, it was indispensable that this fact should be known before any rational system of religion could be

5 *

framed, and, though some things in nature might lead to the hope that a remedy would be found for moral evil, as for so many others, yet these are too obscure to produce any practical results, and there seems every reason to believe that the general conviction that has prevailed on this subject has originated in revelation.

Conditions unknown — repentance insufficient. — But, secondly, if we were assured that God would pardon sin, it would be impossible for us to know on what conditions. Nothing can be more contrary to the history of all the past, than what is asserted by some modern deists, especially by Lord Herbert, that it is a dictate of natural reason that God will pardon sin on repentance. If it had been asserted that it is a dictate of natural reason that penance, and costly sacrifices, and self-torture, were the conditions of pardon, there would have been much in history to support it. But the deist may be challenged to show any heathen creed in which this was an article, or to bring forward any devotee of any other religion than the Christian, who holds to that doctrine now. Having the light of the Bible, we see distinctly that God can not properly pardon the guilty without repentance as a condition, meaning by repentance a thorough reformation, not only of the life, but of the principles of conduct, — of the motives and secret feelings of the heart. But who ever heard of such a repentance as this, as an article in the creed of other religions? And who, I may ask, ever heard of a deist as exercising such a repentance and continuing a deist? Instances are adduced, under other systems, of great natural goodness, in which it is supposed that no repentance was needed; but I know of none in which it has been supposed that a really vicious and abandoned man has repented in the high and only true sense of that term, except in connection with the motives of the gospel. Repentance, even as a condition of pardon, is peculiar to the gospel system; and as an historical fact, it is produced only by gospel motives. The truth is, deists have borrowed this partial truth from the Bible, and then used it to show that we do not need the very book from which they borrowed it. The question of the method or possibility of pardon, by a perfectly just God, involves the highest problem of moral government; and there is no analogy of the operation of human laws, and certainly nothing which we see of the inflexibility and severity with which the natural laws of God are administered, which could lead us to believe in the efficacy of repentance alone for the pardon of moral transgressions.

Divine assistance uncertain. — And thirdly, if man should endeavor to reclaim himself from the dominion of vice, he can not know whether God will regard him with favor, and will assist him, or whether he shall be left to struggle with the current by his own unassisted efforts. Grace, favor, the great doctrine of divine aid to the sinful and the tempted, so sustaining to the weakness, and so consoling to the wretchedness, of man, coming directly from God as a personal Being, it was impossible that nature should give any intimation of it. It is God's own hand stretched out to guide and sustain his benighted and feeble creatures.

Origin and end unknown. — Again, without revelation man could know nothing of the origin or end of the present state of things. Nearly all the ancient philosophers believed that matter was eternal; but of its forms, as indicating intelligence, and of the races of animals and of man, they could give no satisfactory account. And it is obvious, that a course of nature established, if it is ever to terminate, can, of itself, give no indication of that termination, either in respect to time or mode. Such knowledge would be highly satisfactory to man, and would alone enable him to direct his course in accordance with the purposes of God.

The result. — Now, when we consider the passions of men, the collisions of interest, the obtrusiveness of the objects of sense, the pressure of animal wants, the vices of society, and the shortness of life, who can believe, with this obscurity hanging over some points, and this total darkness resting upon others, that one in a million would sit down calmly to solve these great questions respecting God and his government, and human destiny? Who can believe that any speculative and problematical solution of one or all of them could introduce a religion that would effectually control the passions, and predominate over the senses, of men? No; it is exceedingly clear that, if any thing was to be done to enlighten man, it must be by a voice from heaven — a voice that should speak with "authority, and not as the scribes."

Moral ignorance and degradation. — And if mankind were thus benighted without revelation, it will follow, of course, that they were degraded. Moral darkness, voluntarily incurred, necessarily involves practical wickedness. Without an authoritative standard of morals, like the law of God, without a general system of moral instruction, without the motives drawn from the moral government of God and a future retribution, with a religion whose doctrines and rites were often at war with the dictates of the moral nature, we can not wonder at the tendency to deterioration that was every where manifest, nor at the general prevalence of falsehood, and cruelty, and nameless licentiousness. If some public and social virtues were cultivated, it was chiefly during certain periods of the rise of states, in the earlier and less corrupt stages of society, and never in connection with the worship of a spiritual and holy God, or with the cultivation of purity of heart and of life. Philosophy enabled its votaries rather to see and discourse about difficulties than to remove them. It did not even reform the lives of the philosophers themselves, and made no attempts either to instruct or reform the mass of the people. Quintilian says of the philosophers of his time, "The most notorious vices are screened under that name; and they do not labor to maintain the character of philosophers by virtue and study, but conceal the most vicious lives under an austere look and a singularity of dress." And when this could be said of the philosophers, we might believe, of the mass of the people, on less authority than that of inspiration, that they were "filled with all unrighteousness, fornication, wickedness, covetousness, maliciousness; full of envy, murder, debate, deceit, malignity; whisperers, backbiters, haters of God, despiteful, proud, boasters, inventors of evil things, disobedient to parents, without understanding, covenant-breakers, without natural affection, implacable, unmerciful." *

The extremity. — Here, then, we have a case the most melancholy of which we can conceive, in which the noblest faculties of a creature of God, those through which his highest perfection and happiness should be attained, have become the means of sinking him into the lowest forms of immorality, and of filthy, and cruel, and costly, and hideous superstition. The true God, the only object corresponding to the religious nature of man, being withdrawn, the faculties of man are not annihilated: he can not throw off his nature; he must have some religion; and superstition, and enthusiasm, and fanaticism come in, and every form of iniquity is perpetrated in the name of God, and the religious nature is used as an engine to crush human liberty and rivet the bonds of oppression. There is nothing that can adequately represent this dreadful mental and moral

* Rom. I. 29-31.

perversion but those forms of bodily disease in which the processes of life, that ought to build up a beautiful and perfect body, go on only to stimulate the activity of the fatal leprosy, only to minister to deformity, and make it more hideous. Here, then, the question is brought to an issue. In such a state of things, when it is obvious that nothing but a voice from heaven can bring deliverance, will that voice be uttered? Surely, if a case can occur in which, from the benevolence of God, we might hope for a special interposition, this is that case. On the question of such an interposition hung the destiny of the race; and to one who could bring his mind to the high conception of the possibility of mercy in God, it could not appear improbable that that interposition would be vouchsafed.

Revelation probable. — From what has been said, it appears that, if we regard man as in a state of innocence, we should naturally expect God would hold communications with him; that, if we regard him as guilty, and having lost the knowledge and moral image of God, such a communication would be absolutely necessary, if man was to be restored. We have, therefore, the same antecedent probability of a revelation as we have that God would interpose at all in behalf of the guilty, or that there would be any true religion upon earth. This probability, moreover, is strengthened by the general expectation of the race, shown by the readiness with which they have received accounts of supposed revelations, and by the natural tendency of man to crave aid directly from God.

If a revelation, then miracles. — But, whatever probability there was that there would be a revelation, the same was there that there would be miracles; because miracles, so far as we can see, are the only means by which it would be possible for God to authenticate a communication to man. It is true, he might make a special revelation to each individual, and certify him that it was a revelation, but that would not be analogous to his mode of proceeding in other things; and if his purpose was to make known his will to certain individuals, to be by them communicated to the rest of the race, it would seem impossible that they should exhibit any other seal of their commission than miracles. This is the simple, natural, majestic seal which we should expect God would affix to a communication from himself; and when this seal is presented by men whose lives and works correspond with what we might expect from messengers of God, it is felt to be decisive.

But though miracles are thus just as probable as a revelation, even though we should not choose to say that revelation itself is a miracle, and though the chief object of them is to give authority to a revelation, yet, as the main objections against revelation are made against it as miraculous, I wish to adduce here an additional consideration or two to show the probability that miracles would occur in a system like ours.

First effect of miracles. — The first consideration will be found in the effect miracles would have in producing a conviction of the being of a personal God. This is of the utmost importance. Let us suppose there had been no miracle, nor any supposition of one, as far back as history goes; that the uniform course of nature had moved on without any supposed intervention of a superior personal Power; that, in the language of the scoffer, all things had continued as they were from the beginning of the creation; that no flood had swept the earth, and no law had been given in the midst of thunderings and earthquakes, and no messenger from above, whose form was "like the Son of God," had walked with good men in the fire, and no other indications of a righteous administration and of future retribution had appeared than are connected with those unswerving laws that bring all things alike to all, — and who can estimate the tendency to practical, if not to speculative atheism, of such a state of things? It may even be questioned whether the common argument from contrivance, for the being of a personal God, when that stands alone, and is connected with such a uniform course of things, would be valid. If this rigid order could once be infringed for a good and manifest reason, it would obviously change the whole face of the argument. Could we once see gravitation suspended when the good man is thrown by his persecutors from the top of the rock, — could we see a chariot and horses of fire descend and deliver the righteous from the universal law of death, — could we see the sun stand still in heaven that the wicked might be overthrown, — then should we be assured of the existence of a personal Power, with a distinct will, whose agents and ministers these laws were. Such attestations of his being we might expect God would give, not merely to confirm a particular revelation, but with reference to this feeling of indefiniteness, of generality, of a want of personality in the supreme Power, which the operation of general laws, necessarily confounding all moral distinctions, has a tendency to produce.

Second effect. — The second collateral effect of miracles which I would adduce is, that they show that the laws of nature are subordinate to the higher laws of God's moral kingdom, and are controlled and suspended with reference to that. This supposes, of course, that the miracles are neither capricious nor frivolous, but are so wrought as to show this truth. The man, who has not yet seen that the moral government of God is that with reference to which the universe is constructed and sustained, is as far from the true system of God's administration as he would be from the true system of astronomy who should place the earth in the centre. This sentiment is involved in those extraordinary words of Christ, "It is easier for heaven and earth to pass, than one tittle of the law to fail," and might, indeed, be inferred from the nature of the case. What man of honor regards property at all, when his moral character is concerned? What wise man does not sacrifice property for the true good of rational and intelligent beings? So, if God has a moral character, and a moral government, then what we call nature and its laws, must hold the same relation to him that property does to the moral character of man. The power and wisdom of God may be seen in nature; but his justice, and truth, and mercy, in which his highest glory consists, can be seen only in his dealings with his moral creatures. If a law of nature were destroyed, it could be reëstablished; if a system of suns and planets were annihilated, another might be produced in its room; if heaven and earth were to pass away, they might be created again; but if the brightness of the moral character of God should be tarnished, that character would be lost forever. This distinction between mere nature and moral government is fundamental; and nothing could have a greater tendency to wake men up to a perception of it than to see God, as he moves on to the accomplishment of his moral purposes, setting aside those laws of nature which we had supposed were established like the everlasting hills — than to see the whole of visible nature, with all its laws, standing ready to pay its obeisance to the true embassadors of his moral kingdom. How else could God express to us the true relations to each other of his natural and moral government?

If, then, miracles were necessary to give authority to revelation, to give a practical impression of the existence of a personal God, and to indicate the true position of his moral government, who will say, on the supposition that he has a moral government, that they are improbable?

Import of a miracle. — There has, indeed, been a question raised, — and it is one of so much importance that it may be well to notice it here, — how far we are bound to receive any doctrine or command that may be confirmed by a miracle. But this depends on the further question, whether a miracle can be wrought by any being but God. If God, and God only, can work a miracle, then we are bound, both by reason and conscience, to believe every thing short of a known absurdity, and to do every thing short of essential wickedness, taught or commanded with that sanction. By essential wickedness, I do not mean any outward act, but positive malignity. To suppose God to command this, would be a contradiction, since he could not do it and be God. When God told Abraham to sacrifice his son Isaac, he was to do it though it might seem to contradict the dictates of natural affection, and what, without the command, would have been the dictates of conscience, and to be in direct opposition to the promises of God himself; and in doing it he honored God, and acted in accordance with the dictates of natural religion, and of the reason that God had given him. Not to believe and obey the direct word of God, would lead at once to absurdity and contradiction. It would involve the charge of falsehood and tyranny against God. But the moment you charge God with falsehood, there is an end to all ground of faith in any thing. If I can not believe God, I can not believe the faculties that come from God. By charging Him who gave me my moral nature with being false, I involve the probability that all the notices and indications of that nature are false, and all its distinctions baseless. Nothing could then save me from universal skepticism. Certainly natural religion, and reason itself, if it would not lose from under it the very ground on which it stands, would lead me to this. When God speaks, it is sufficient. His reason is the infinite reason, his authority is absolute authority, and nothing more dreadful, or more opposed to our most intimate convictions, could possibly occur than would be involved in disbelieving and disobeying him. Nor can I doubt that it is in the power of God so to authenticate his word to the soul of man as thus to set it in opposition to the utterances and promptings of every natural faculty; nor that it is only, as in the case of Abraham, when such an opposition occurs, that the most implicit confidence in God, and the highest grandeur of faith, can be seen.

Miracles real and pretended. — If, then, we suppose that God only can perform a miracle, its authority will be absolute. But may there not be a suspension or a reversal of the laws of nature caused by other beings than God? May not some malignant agent do that which, if it is not, must appear to us to be a real miracle? This is a question which I can not answer. It may be so. I know not what intermediate powers and agencies there may be between the infinite God and man. I know not but there may be created beings of such might that one of them could seize upon the earth, and hurl it from its orbit, or control its elements; nor do I know what range God may give to the agency of such, or of any other intermediate beings. I do not myself believe that any being but God can work a real miracle. Miracles are his great seal. This may be counterfeited; but if he should suffer it to be stolen, I see no possible way in which he could authenticate a communication to his creatures. A real miracle is to be distinguished from those feats and appearances which may be produced by sleight of hand, and by collusion when once a religion is established; and also from any effects of merely natural agents, however occult, under the control of science, but working according to their own laws. These, especially if science and deception are combined, and in an age of popular ignorance, may go very far; probably far enough to account for every thing in the Bible, seemingly miraculous, which we should not be willing to attribute to God. They may account for appearances and coincidences which, to the ignorant, must have seemed like miracles, and for extraordinary cures of a certain class, while the principle of life remained; but they can not account for a reversal of a law of nature, as when an ax is made to swim, or the shadow to go back on the dial; nor for an operation where the powers of nature have nothing to work upon, as when one really dead is raised to life. However, something like that of which I have spoken above is implied in the Bible, and provision is made for the state of mind which it must induce. This speaks of "signs and lying wonders." It was said to the Israelites of old, "If there arise among you a prophet, or a dreamer of dreams, and giveth thee a sign or a wonder, and the sign or the wonder come to pass, whereof he spake unto thee, saying, Let us go after other gods, which thou hast not known, and let us serve them; thou shalt not hearken unto the words of that prophet, or that dreamer of dreams; for the Lord your God proveth you, to know whether ye love the Lord your God with all your heart and with all your soul."

Faith and reason. — I would say, then, that an apparent miracle, performed by a creature of God, would not authorize me to receive what seemed to me to be contradictory to my natural faculties; and the voice of God himself would lay me under obligation to do this simply because the highest reason demands faith in him as an essential condition of faith in those faculties. It is, indeed, a contradiction to say that a man can believe what he knows to be an absurdity, or can be under obligation to do what is wrong; and, in general, I would say that no man is under obligation to believe what it is not more reasonable for him to believe than to disbelieve; but it may be reasonable to believe, on the authority of God, that that is not an absurdity which might otherwise seem to be so, and that the command of God would make certain outward actions right for us, which would otherwise not be so. If God should wish to make a communication to an individual that would seem in opposition to the dictates of his natural faculties, we might expect that he would, as in the case of Abraham, speak himself, and cause it to be known that the voice was certainly his; but when a creature of God appears as his messenger, then his character and the object of his mission must correspond with what we have a right to expect of a messenger from God; and no prodigy, no apparent miracle, ought to be received as a sufficient sanction for that which, without such sanction, would appear to be either absurd or vicious.

No practical difficulty. — But, however we may decide this question on the supposition of a conflict between the message confirmed by a miracle, and the intellectual, or the moral nature of man, there is no practical difficulty on this point when we speak of the Christian miracles. These are all worthy of God. They were wrought by men of pure and benevolent lives, and for the avowed purpose of confirming a message of the highest importance to man, and in entire conformity to his nature. And such miracles, wrought by such men, are, as I have said, the seal which we should naturally expect God would affix to their message. They are an adequate seal, and every fair-minded man responds to the sentiment uttered by

Nicodemus, "No man can do *these miracles that thou doest*, except God be with him."

The Christian religion or none. — I will simply say, in closing this lecture, that whatever probability there is that God has given a revelation at all, there is the same that Christianity is that revelation. We have now come to that point in the history of the world, in which the question among all well-informed men must be between the truth of Christianity and no religion. No man, surely, would advocate any form of idolatry or of polytheism, and there remain only the religion of Mohammed, and Deism, to be compared with Christianity. But I need not spend time in comparing, or rather contrasting, the religion of Mohammed, unsustained by miracles or by prophecies, propagated by the sword, encouraging fatalism, and pride, and intolerance, sanctioning polygamy, offering a sensual heaven, — a religion whose force is already spent, which has no sympathy or congruity with the enlarged views and onward movements of these days, and which is fast passing into a hopeless imbecility, — with the pure, and humble, and beneficent religion of Christ, heralded by prophecy, sealed by miracles, and now, after eighteen hundred years, going forth, with all its pristine vigor, to bless the nations.

Of Deism it may be doubted whether it should be called a religion. It has never had a priesthood, nor a creed, nor any book professing to contain the truths it teaches, nor a temple, nor, with the exception of a short period during the French revolution, an assembly for worship. If we mean, then, by religion, any such acknowledgment of God as recognizes our social nature, and binds mankind in one brotherhood of equality, while it presents them together before the throne of a common Father, Deism is not a religion. Those who profess to teach it have no agreement in their doctrines, and the doctrines themselves are, several of them, borrowed from Christianity, and then inculcated as the teachings of reason.

No; there is nothing on the face of the earth that can, for a moment, bear a comparison with Christianity as a religion for man. Upon this the hope of the race hangs. From the very first, it took its position, as the pillar of fire, to lead the race onward. The patriarchal, and Jewish, and Christian dispensations, all finding their identity in the true import of sacrifices, and in the inculcation of righteousness, have been one religion. The intelligence and power of the race are with those who have embraced it; and now, if this, instead of proving indeed a pillar of fire from God, should be found but a delusive meteor, then nothing will be left to the race but to go back to a darkness that may be felt, and to a worse than Egyptian bondage.

LECTURE III.

INTERNAL AND EXTERNAL EVIDENCE.—VAGUENESS OF THE DIVISION BETWEEN THEM.—REASONS FOR CONSIDERING THE INTERNAL EVIDENCES FIRST.—ARGUMENT FIRST: FROM ANALOGY.

In my first lecture, I attempted to show that, if God has given a revelation, we may certainly know it; and in the second, that there is no such antecedent improbability against a revelation, as to justify us in requiring proof different from that which we require for other events. There are laws of evidence according to which we judge in other cases, and I only ask that these same laws may be applied here.

If these points are established, we are ready to inquire whether God has in fact given a revelation.

On coming into life, we find Christianity existing, and claiming to be such a revelation. We wish to satisfy ourselves of the validity of that claim. How shall we proceed? The evidence by which its claims are sustained is commonly divided into two kinds, the external and the internal. This division is simple, and of long standing; but by it heads of evidence are classed together, having so little affinity for each other, and, in regard to some of them, it is so difficult to see on what principle they are classed under one rather than the other, that its utility may be doubted. Thus the evidences from testimony, from prophecy, from the mode in which the gospel was propagated, and from its effects, — topics resembling each other scarcely at all, — are classed under the head of the external evidences; while the various marks of honesty found in the New Testament, the agreement of the parts with each other, its peculiar doctrines, its pure morality, its representation of the character of Christ, its analogy to nature, its adaptation to the situation and wants of man, — topics still more diverse, — are classed under its internal evidences.

Chalmers and Wilson. — I notice the vagueness of this arrangement, because these two classes of evidence have often been opposed to each other, and the superiority of one over the other contended for; and because great and good men, as Chalmers formerly, have in some instances regarded it as presumptuous to study the internal evidences at all, as if it would be a sitting in judgment beforehand on the kind of revelation God ought to give; and others, as Wilson, have thought it arrogance to study the internal evidences first, as if the capacity to judge of a revelation after it was given implied an amount of knowledge that would preclude the necessity of any revelation at all.

Internal evidences — their study not presumptuous. — But of which of the internal evidences mentioned above can it be said to be presumptuous for man to judge without reference to external testimony? Certainly not of those natural and incidental evidences of truth spread every where over the pages of the New Testament; nor of the agreement of the several books with each other; nor of the morality of the gospel; nor of its tendency to promote human happiness in this life; and if there be some of the doctrines, of the probability of which we could not judge beforehand, that is no reason why we should be excluded from an immediate and free range in every other part of this field. There is what has been called, by Verplanck, a critical, as well as a moral internal evidence. Of the first we are competent to judge, and, in determining the question of our competency to judge of the second, we are not to overlook a distinction made by the same able writer. It is that "between the power of discovering truth, and that of examining and deciding upon it when offered to our judgment." "In matters of human science," he goes on to say, "to how few is the one given, and how common is the other! Look at that vast mass of mathematical invention and demonstration which has been carried on by gifted minds, in every age, in continued progress, from the days of the learned priesthood of ancient Egypt to those of the discoveries of La Place and La Grange. Who is there of the mathematicians of this generation who could be selected as capable of alone discovering all this prolonged and continuous chain of demonstration? If left to their own unaided researches, how far would the original and inventive genius of a Newton or a Pascal have carried them? Yet we know that all this body of science, this magnificent accumulation of the patient labors of so many intellects, may be examined and rigorously scrutinized in every step, and finally completely mastered and familiarized to the understanding, in a few years' study, by a student who, trusting solely to his own mind, could never have advanced beyond the simple elements of geometry.

"This reasoning may be applied, either directly or by fair analogy, to every part of our knowledge of the laws of nature and of mind; and it therefore seems to be neither presumptuous nor unphilosophical, but, on the contrary, in strict accordance with the soundest reasoning, to maintain that though 'the world by wisdom knew not God,' yet, so far forth as he reveals himself to men, and calls upon them to receive and obey that revealed will, he has given to them faculties, by no means compelling, but yet enabling them to understand his revelation; to perceive its truth, excellence, and beauty; and to become sensible of their own want of its instruction, as well as to estimate that extrinsic human testimony by which it may be supported or attended."*

Certainly, there are many things in which we perceive a fitness and an excellence, when they are made known, of which we should never, of ourselves, have formed any conception. Thus the Newtonian system comes before the eye of the mind as a great mountain does before that of the body, and we see at once that it is worthy of God. No timid disclaimer of our right to judge of the works of God can prevent this effect. Its simplicity, and beauty, and majesty, speak with a voice more pleasing, and scarcely less satisfactory, than that of mathematical demonstration. I will not say how much of this perceived excellence, or whether any, must belong to a revelation which we are under obligation to receive. Certainly, that of the Jews had to them far less of this than ours to us. But I will say that it is the natural impulse of the mind to examine any thing claiming to be a revelation by such tests; and if it is done in a proper spirit, and with those limitations which good sense must always put to human inquiries, it is neither presumptuous nor dangerous. It is not judging beforehand of what God ought to do; it is judging of what it is claimed that he has done; and the same spirit that would prevent us from doing this would debar us from any study of final causes in the works of God. If the gospel is to act upon character, it must be received with an intelligent perception of its adaptation to our wants, and of its excellence. The message, not less than the minister of God, might be

---

* Verplanck's Evidences of Revealed Religion.

expected to commend itself "to every man's conscience in the sight of God."

Standards and tests in the mind. — I would not claim for reason a place which does not belong to it. So far as the Christian religion rests on facts, it must rest on historical evidence; but so far as it is a system of truth and of motives intended to bear on human character and well-being, it must be judged of by that reason and conscience which God has given us. There are in the mind, as God made it, standards and tests which must ultimately be applied to it. Men may be uncandid or irreverent in applying these tests, and so they may be in examining historical proof; and I have no more fear in one case than in the other. In arguing for, or against such a system as Christianity, we of course take for granted the being and perfections of God; we have a previous knowledge of his works, of his providence, of the difference between right and wrong, and of the beings for whom the system is intended. Let, now, a candid man find in the system nothing absurd or immoral, but many things that seem to him strange, and little accordant with what he would have expected, and he will be still in doubt. He will make due allowance for the imperfection of his knowledge, and the limitation of his faculties, and he will hold his mind open to the full force of historical proof. But let him be shown a system which, though he could not have discovered it, he can see, when discovered, to be worthy of a God of infinite wisdom and goodness, — let him find it congruous with all he knows of him from his works, coincident with natural religion, so far as that goes, containing a perfect morality, harmonizing with the highest sentiments of man, and adapted to his wants as a weak and guilty being, — and he may find in all this a ground of rational conviction that such a system must have come from God, and so, that those facts which are inseparably connected with it must be true. The historical testimony may then be to him much as the testimony of the woman of Samaria was to her countrymen after they had seen and heard the Saviour for themselves. And this is the natural course when any system on any subject is presented to us. We inquire what it is, and how far it agrees with our previous knowledge; we come up to it, and examine it, and then, if necessary, we investigate the history of its origin.

This proof logical. — Nor is this proof from internal evidence, as some seem to suppose, merely the result of feeling. If God has given us a religion which we are to receive in the exercise of our reason, and which is to act on us through our affections and in harmony with our natural faculties, I can not conceive that there should not be found in it such congruities and adaptations to man, — such a fitness to promote his individual and social well-being, — as to show that it came from Him who made man; and the proof arising from a perception of this congruity is as purely intellectual, as strictly argumentative, as that from historical evidence. In such a case, we do not believe the religion to be true because we feel it to be so, but because we see in it a divine wisdom, and the adaptation of means to an end.

Arrangement hitherto — reasons for a change. — It has been some feeling of the kind, mentioned above as manifested by Chalmers and Wilson, that has determined the arrangement of every treatise I know of, published either in England or this country, in which the external and internal evidences are considered together. The external are treated of first, are regarded as settling the question, and then the internal are brought in as confirmatory. Certainly, I think the historical evidence conclusive, and it is indispensable, because the Christian religion is not a mere set of dogmas, or of speculative opinions, but has its foundation in facts. It is, indeed, a manifestation of principles, but not by verbal statement and injunction merely; those principles are imbodied in acts, and it is only as thus imbodied that they have their effective power. That Jesus Christ lived, and was crucified, and rose from the dead, are facts as necessary to the Christian religion as the foundation to a building; and no one but a German neologist could possibly think otherwise. But if the external evidences are thus indispensable and conclusive, so also are the internal. What would have been the effect and force of Christ's miracles, without his spotless and transcendent character? If I am to say which would most deeply impress me with the fact that he was from God, the testimony respecting his miracles, or the exhibition of such a character, I think I should say the latter; and I think myself as well qualified to judge in the one case as in the other; and, as I have said, I think this is the evidence which now first presents itself.

At first, when the religion was every where called in question, when miracles were wrought to sustain it, before it had had time to show fully its adaptation to the wants of the individual man and of society, it was natural to refer first to miracles and to testimony for its divine authority; but now, when the religion is established, it is quite as natural to pass, without any particular attention to the historical evidence, to the consideration of the religion itself, its suitableness to what we know of God, and to our own wants. It is, in fact, in this way that most men who embrace Christianity are led to do it, and I do not think it either "presumptuous or unphilosophical" to follow, in presenting the evidence, the course which has been followed by most Christians in attaining that ground of faith on which they now rest.

Let us, then, instead of going first through a long line of historical testimony, come directly to the Christian religion itself. Let us examine it, with candor indeed, but with perfect freedom. Let us compare it with, and test it by, whatever we know of God or his works, or of man. It courts such an examination. It is because it is not thus examined, that it is so little regarded. We know that any system that comes from God must be worthy of him; that it must be in harmony with all his other works and with all other truth; that the ends proposed by it must be good, and that it must be adapted in the best manner to accomplish those ends. We know, I say, that such a system must really *be* all this; and, in proportion to our knowledge, we shall *see* it to be so. If we can not understand it fully, as indeed, if it be what it claims to be, we ought not to expect to do, we may yet know in part. We live in an age of light. The religion has been long in the world, and has come in contact with God's natural providence, and with human institutions, at many points. It was intended to act upon us; and, if it be really from God, it would be strange if we could not find upon it some impression of his hand.

ARGUMENT I.

ANALOGY.

General statement. — We say, then, first, that we find evidence of the divine origin of the Christian religion in its analogy to the works and natural government of God. There is a harmony of adaptation, and also of analogy. The key is adapted to the lock: the fin of the fish is analogous to the wing of the bird. Christianity, as I hope to show, is adapted to man: it is analogous to the other manifestations which God has made of himself.

The works of God are divided into different departments, each of which has its laws, which are in some sense independent of the others; yet there is such a correspondence manifest between them, that we recognize them, at once, as having proceeded from the same hand. Scientific research impresses upon us the conviction that God is one, and that he is uniform and consistent in all his works; and leads us to expect, if he should introduce a new dispensation, that there would be, between it and those which had preceded it, an analogy similar to that which had been found to exist between the other departments. Now, we affirm that the gospel contains that code of laws which God has given for the regulation of the moral and spiritual department of his creation in this world, and that there is between it and the other works of God the analogy and correspondence which were to have been expected.

The Bible coincident with nature. — 1. I observe, that the Bible is coincident with nature, as now known, in its teachings respecting the natural attributes of God. The New Testament seldom dwells upon the natural attributes of God; but when it does to any extent, as in the ascription of Paul, "To the King eternal, immortal, invisible, the only wise God," it plainly recognizes and adopts the doctrines of the Old, and they may, therefore, for this purpose, be fairly taken together. Let us go back, then, to those ancient prophets. If we exclude the idea of revelation, nothing can be more surprising than the ideas of God expressed by them. These ideas, of themselves, are sufficient to give the stamp of divinity to their writings. Surrounded by polytheists, they proclaimed his unity. Living in a period of great ignorance in regard to physical science, they ascribed to God absolute eternity, and that unchangeableness which is essential to a perfect Being, and they represented all his natural attributes as infinite. Accordingly, it is when these attributes are their theme, that their poetry rises to its unparalleled sublimity. "Who," says Isaiah, "hath measured the waters in the hollow of his hand, and meted out heaven with the span, and comprehended the dust of the earth in a measure, and weighed the mountains in scales and the hills in a balance?" Even now, when science has brought her report from the depths of infinite space, and told us of the suns and systems that glow and circle there, how can we better express our emotions than to adopt his language, and say, "Lift up your eyes on high, and behold who hath created these things, that bringeth out their host by number: He calleth them all by names, by the greatness of his might, for that he is strong in power; not one faileth." And when science has turned her glass in another direction, and discovered in the teeming drop wonders scarcely less than those in the heavens; when she has analyzed matter; when she has disentangled the rays of light, and shown the colors of which its white web is woven, when the amazing structure of vegetable and animal bodies is laid open; what can we say of Him who worketh all this, but that he is "wonderful in counsel, and excellent in working"! "There is no searching of his understanding." And when, again, we can look back over near three thousand years more, in which the earth has rolled on its appointed way, and the mighty energies by which all things are moved have been sustained, what can we do but to ask, "Hast thou not known, hast thou not heard, that the everlasting God, the Lord, the Creator of the ends of the earth, fainteth not, neither is weary?" With them we find no tendency, as among the ancient philosophers, to ascribe eternity to matter; they every where speak of it as created; nor, with the pantheists, to identify matter with God; nor, with the idolater, to be affected with its magnitude, or forms, or order, or brightness, or whatever may strike the senses. But, with them, all matter is perfectly subordinate and paltry when compared with God. They represent him as sustaining it for a time in its present order, and then as folding up these visible heavens as a vesture is folded, and laying them aside. Nothing could more perfectly express the absolute infinity of the natural attributes of God, or the entire separation and disparity between him and every thing that is called the universe, or its complete subjection to his will.

Now, that men, undistinguished from others around them by learning, in an age of prevalent polytheism and idolatry, and of great ignorance of physical science, should adopt such doctrines respecting the natural attributes of God, as to require no modification when science has been revolutionized and expanded as it were into a new universe, does seem to me no slight evidence that they were inspired by that God whose attributes they set forth.

Perfection of natural and moral law. — 2. I observe, that there is an analogy between the laws of nature, as discovered by induction, and the moral laws contained in the New Testament, not only as implying the same natural attributes in God, but as they are carried out to the same perfection. It is the great and sublime characteristic of natural law, especially of the law of gravitation, that, while it controls so perfectly such vast masses, and at such amazing distances, it yet also controls equally the minutest particle that floats in the sunbeam; and that, however wildly that particle may be driven, — wherever it may float in the infinity of space, — it never, for one moment, escapes the cognizance and supervision of this law. It never can. This implies a minuteness and perfection of natural government, of which science, as known in the time of Christ, could have given no intimation. But now, how natural does it seem that the same God, who, in the universal control of his natural law, no more neglects the minutest particle than the largest planet, should also, in his moral law, take cognizance of every idle word, and of the thoughts and intents of the heart! Yes; I find, in the particle of dust, shown by the greatest expounder of God's natural law to be constantly regarded by him, and in the idle word declared by Christ to come under the notice and condemnation of his moral law, — I find, in the minuteness and completeness of the government of matter, as revealed by modern science, and even shown to the eye by the microscope, and in that interpretation of the moral law which makes it spiritual, causing it to reach every thought and intent of the heart, — a conception of the same absolute perfection of government, both in the natural and moral world; and I find the same infinite natural attributes implied as the sole conditions on which such a government in either of these departments can be carried on.

This idea of the absolute universality and perfection of government in any department — the only one, however, worthy of a perfect God — is not an idea, especially in its moral applications, which I should think likely to have originated with man. In the department of nature we know that he did not originate or suspect it till it was forced on his observation. And how comes it to pass that this absolute perfection of moral government, this notice of the particle of dust there, this judgment of every idle word, of every secret thing, of the minutest moral act of the most inconsiderable moral being that ever lived, should have been discovered and announced thousands of years before its more obvious counterpart in the natural world was even suspected?

And here I can not but notice, though I will not put

it under a separate head, how coincident all that science has discovered is with the Scripture doctrine of the universal and particular providential government of God. We all know how slow men have been to receive this; and yet it would seem that no theist, with a clear perception of the mode in which natural law operates, could doubt it. Does God control constantly immense masses of matter through natural law? How? Why, by causing the law to operate, not upon the mass as a whole, but upon every individual particle composing that mass; that is, he governs the vast through his government of the minute. And if he does this in matter, who will deny the probability of a providential care, proceeding on precisely the same principles, which numbers the hairs of our heads, and watches the fall of the sparrow? Shall God care for the less and not for the greater? "If he so clothe the grass of the field, shall he not much more clothe you, O ye of little faith?"

Kind and limit of knowledge. — 3. I observe, that there is an analogy, both in their kind and in their limit, between the knowledge communicated by nature and that by Christianity. Nature is full and explicit in her communication of necessary practical facts, but is at no pains to explain the reasons and methods of those facts. She gives us the air to breathe, and we are invigorated; but she does not teach us that it is composed of oxygen and nitrogen, and that our vigor comes from the oxygen alone. She gives us the light, and we see; but how long did the world stand before she whispered to any one that that light was composed of the seven primary colors? She instructs us in the uses of fire; but she does not teach us how the process of combustion is carried on. Men have boiled water equally well from the beginning; but it was left to this age, and to Faraday, to discover that flame is the product of electrical agency. She teaches us the facts; she enables us to go through the practical processes; and then she leaves us to find our way as we best may through the philosophy of those facts.

And so it is with the knowledge communicated by Christianity. There is not a great practical fact which a moral being can ask to know, concerning which it does not speak with perfect distinctness. The fact of a full and a perfect accountability, and of a future retribution, — the fact of immortality, of the resurrection of the dead, of a particular providence, of the freedom of man, of his dependence upon God, and of the mercy of God to returning penitents, — each of these is made known with entire fullness and explicitness; but very little is said respecting the philosophy of these facts, or the mode in which they may be reconciled to each other. The Bible gives the information that is needed, and there it stops. It communicates practical, and never speculative knowledge as such.

Now, when we consider that Christianity solves, in its own way, all the great questions relating to human destiny, it must be regarded as remarkable, that, in communicating this information, it should thus stop precisely where nature stops. When we consider how strong the tendency must have been to unaided human nature to gratify and excite man by particular descriptions of other worlds and of things unseen, so naturally to be expected from a messenger from those worlds; when we consider how strong a hold the fanatic and the impostor gain upon the imagination of their followers by such means, and that, without miracles and without evidence, this is, indeed, the chief hold they can have upon them; and when we observe the course taken at this point by all others who have pretended to revelation, we shall not estimate this argument lightly.

Christianity and other systems. — How different the course of Christ and his apostles, in this respect, from that of the writers of the Shasters, and of Mohammed! When Christ and his apostles speak of a future world of reward and of punishment, it is, indeed, in such terms as to produce a strong moral impression, but it is still with a severe and cautious reserve. Those terms are general. There is no dwelling upon particulars, as if for the purpose of gratifying curiosity, or giving a loose rein to the imagination. They speak of "the kingdom of heaven," of "everlasting life," of "a crown of glory that fadeth not away," of "life and immortality," of "many mansions," and a "Father's house;" but then they say, "Eye hath not seen, nor ear heard, neither have entered into the heart of man, the things which God hath prepared for them that love him." So, on the other hand, they speak of "the fire that never shall be quenched," "where their worm dieth not, and the fire is not quenched;" of the "everlasting fire, prepared for the devil and his angels;" of "everlasting destruction from the presence of the Lord, and from the glory of his power;" of "the blackness of darkness forever;" but they descend into no minute descriptions. Not so Mohammed. Speaking of heaven, he says, "There are they who shall approach near unto God. They shall dwell in gardens of delight. Youths, which shall continue in their bloom forever, shall go round about to attend them with goblets and beakers, and a cup of flowing wine,—their heads shall not ache by drinking the same, neither shall their reason be disturbed; and with fruits of the roots which they shall choose, and the flesh of birds of the kind which they shall desire. And there shall accompany them fair damsels, having large black eyes resembling pearls hidden in their shells, as a reward for that which they have wrought."* "But as for the sincere servants of God, they shall have a certain provision in paradise, namely, delicious fruits; and they shall be honored; they shall be placed in gardens of pleasure, leaning on couches, opposite to one another; a cup shall be carried round unto them, filled from a limpid fountain, for the delight of those who drink, — it shall not oppress their understanding, neither shall they be inebriated therewith. And near them shall lie the virgins of paradise, refraining their looks from beholding any besides their spouses, having large black eyes, and resembling the eggs of an ostrich covered with feathers from the dust."† So, also, speaking of the world of punishment, he says, "Those who believe not have garments of fire fitted to them; boiling water shall be poured on their heads; their bowels shall be dissolved thereby, and also their skin; and they shall be beaten with maces of iron. So often as they shall endeavor to get out of hell because of the anguish of their torments, they shall be dragged back into the same, and their tormentors shall say, 'Taste ye the pains of burning.'"‡ "It shall be said unto them, Go ye into the punishment which ye denied as a falsehood: go ye into the smoke of hell, which shall arise in three volumes, and shall not shade you from the heat, neither shall it be of service against the flame; but it shall cast forth sparks as big as towers, resembling yellow camels in color."§ We can now see that the stern refusal on the part of Christ and his disciples to lift the vail and show us the invisible world was not only analogous to the course of nature, but that it was the only course compatible with good sense and sound philosophy. But why have these men, of all those who have made pretensions to inspiration,

---

* Koran, chap. lvi. Sale's edition.   ‡ Koran, chap. xxii.
† Koran, chap. xxxvii   § Koran, chap. xxvii.

thus kept upon that difficult line which so commends itself to the sober judgment of the thinking part of mankind?

Christianity and nature — relation to the infinite and mysterious. — And not less striking is the analogy between the limits of that knowledge which is obtained from nature and that which is obtained from the Bible; or, to express my thought more exactly, between the mode in which what is made known in both cases, runs out into an infinite unknown. However long, and in whatever department the student of nature may labor, he finds himself no nearer the completion of his knowledge; and, as he passes on, he is ready to exclaim, with Burke, "What subject is there that does not branch out into infinity!" Even when most successful, he compares himself to a "child picking up pebbles upon the beach, while the great ocean of truth is still before him." The intellectual vision of one man may extend further than that of another; he may have a wider horizon; but to both alike the sky closes down upon the mountains, and what is known stretches off into the infinity that is unknown. Nature places us in the midst of infinity. She intimates a probable connection between our planet and the myriads of worlds which float in space; she suggests, by analogy, the probability of a moral and intellectual system corresponding in extent to the greatness of the physical universe; she awakens our curiosity respecting the forms and modes of being of those who dwell in the stellar worlds; but she gives us no means of gratifying our curiosity. The language of nature to man is, 'You are a pupil, upon one form, in the great school of God's discipline. You are permitted to conjecture that there are other and higher forms, but to know nothing of what is taught there. Your business is to learn the lessons which are taught here, and be content, though you can not but see that all known truth has relations with much more that is unknown.' And just so it is with the Bible. It does not present us with a defined system of truth, squared by the scientific rule and compass, which the human mind can master and comprehend. Its truths take hold on the eternity that is past, and stretch on into that which is to come. Does nature lead us into deep mysteries? So does the Bible. Does she leave us there, to wonder and adore? So does the Bible. We claim mysteries as a part of Christianity. We say that a religion coming from the God of nature could not be without them. We are nothing moved by the sneer of the infidel when he asks, "What kind of a revelation is the revelation of a mystery?" We say to him that it is the revelation of a fact, all the modes and relations of which are not known, or which may seem to conflict with something already known; and that, in the revelation of portions of an infinite scheme to a finite mind, facts thus related would be naturally expected. Is no revelation of any value but that which is clear, full, and distinct? What kind of a revelation is that which nature makes of the starry heavens — dim, remote, obscure, suggesting a thousand questions, and answering none? And yet even this is of infinite value to man. And thus it is that the Bible takes it for granted that there are other orders of intelligent beings, angels and archangels, principalities and powers, heavenly hosts innumerable — just such an intellectual and moral system as we might suppose from our present knowledge of the works of God; but no particulars are given; it merely shows them as the night shows the stars, and, like nature, it leaves us standing in the midst of infinity, with a thousand questions unanswered. Now, I can not help thinking, if the Bible had been made by man, that it would either have been a system perfectly defined, with the clearness, and at the same time, the shallowness, of the human intellect; or it would have been wild, and extravagant, and vague; or it would have pretended to lay open minutely the secrets of distant and future worlds.

Temper of mind required. — 4. I observe, that there is an analogy or correspondence between the works of God and the Bible, such as we had a right to expect, if both came from him, because a similar temper and attitude of mind is required for the successful study of both. The identity of that spirit, which Christ inculcates as the essential prerequisite to the proper understanding and reception of the great truths which he taught, with the true philosophic spirit, was first noticed by Bacon. He says, in very remarkable words, "The kingdom of man, which was founded on the sciences, can not be entered otherwise than the kingdom of God, that is, in the condition of a little child." The meaning and the truth of this will be manifest from a moment's attention to the history of science. So long as man attempted to theorize, and to sit in judgment upon God, to determine what he ought to have done, instead of taking the attitude of a learner before the book of nature, nothing can exceed the puerilities and absurdities into which he fell. But the moment he laid aside the pride of theory, and took the humble attitude of a learner and observer, an interpreter of nature, science began to advance. Man talked of rearing the temple of science, as if it were to be constructed by him. But, as far as there is any temple, it has stood, as it now stands, in its imposing majesty, since the creation of the works of God; and all that man can do is to unvail that temple, and show its fair proportions. The true philosopher does not think of rearing any thing of his own. He feels that he is a learner, and a learner only at the feet of nature. He represses entirely the imagination, however beautiful and enticing may be the theories which it would form; rejects all prejudice and preconceived opinion; and follows fearlessly wherever observation, and experiment, and facts, may lead him.

Is it said that there have been great philosophers who have been infidels, and have not had this spirit? I answer, no. There have been second-rate philosophers, who have distinguished themselves by following out the discoveries of greater men; but all the great discoverers, those whose minds have sympathized most intensely with nature, have been distinguished for this spirit.*

But that this spirit and temper are required by the gospel in order to a knowledge of that, it is hardly necessary to show. There we find the original requisition to become as a little child. It requires every imagination to be brought down, and every high thing that exalteth itself against the knowledge of God; and that every thought should be brought into captivity to the obedience of Christ. No progress can be made in religion, or in science, till the pride which exalts itself to judge over God, and to decide what he ought to have done, is repressed, and till the man takes his place as a learner at the feet of Jesus, as the philosopher takes his place at the feet of nature. So coincident is the spirit of true religion and of true philosophy; so perfectly did our Saviour express the true spirit of both eighteen hundred years ago. Wonderful indeed is it that, when the great expounder of method in natural science would express the true spirit of the true method, he should find no fitter words than those used by Christ, before the inductive philosophy was dreamed of, to express the proper method of study in a higher department of the kingdom and government of God. If, then, nature and revelation are thus similarly related to the human mind, they must be analogous to each other.

* See Whewell's Bridgewater Treatise.

Mode and results of teaching. — In close connection with this head, I observe that, so far as nature teaches natural religion and moral truth, there is an analogy between both the mode and the results of her teaching and those of Christianity. Nothing can be more evident than that the condition in which God intended man should be placed, in this world, is that of a probation, in which there should be no overwhelming force, or preponderance of motives, on either side; in which a wrong choice should be possible, and a right one often difficult. No other supposition accords with the limited knowledge of man, or with the mixed and balanced motives in the midst of which he must often act. Accordingly, while the moral and religious teachings of nature are real and valid, and he that has ears to hear may hear, they are yet never obtrusive. The voice of those teachings is a still, small voice, easily drowned by the roar of passion or by the din of the world, but sweet and powerful in the ear of those who are willing to listen. Accordingly, nothing is easier, or more common, than for men " to quench the light of natural virtue by a course of profligacy, and to acquire contempt for all goodness by familiarity with vice." This is the method in which nature teaches moral and religious truth, lifting up always the same quiet voice, whether men will hear or whether they will forbear; and these are the results. Christianity keeps to the principle of that method, nor are the results different in kind. Whether we consider the evidence for its divine origin, or the moral truths which it inculcates, we find that, while it has such evidence as to be satisfactory to those who will attend to it, yet that it does not force that evidence upon the attention of any. Here the voice is indeed a louder voice, and he that hath ears may hear; but it does not compel the attention of men. Accordingly, as we find men disregarding the teachings of natural conscience, and the general maxims of virtue, so also do we find them remaining in ignorance, and consequent contempt, of God's revelation.

I know that this feature of revelation has been made an objection against it. It has been said that, if God had given a revelation, he would have accompanied it with evidence that must have forced conviction upon every mind — that he would have written it upon the heavens; but the objector does not consider that, in that case, this would have been no longer a place of probation, and the revelation of the gospel not at all in keeping with the revelation of nature. Are the great truths of natural religion written upon the heavens? Are the common maxims of temperance, and integrity, and benevolence, forced upon the attention of all? Instead, therefore, of finding, in the unobtrusive nature of the evidence and claims of Christianity, an argument against it, I find, in these very circumstances, an argument that it is from that God who has caused the light of natural religion, and even the light of science, to exist in the world under precisely the same conditions.

A system of means. — 5. I observe, that Christianity is in harmony with the works of God, because it is a system of means.* It is asked, by some, if God wishes the holiness of men, why he does not make them holy at once; and that he should take a long course of means, to accomplish his wish, is objected to as derogatory both to his power and to his wisdom. But, surely, I need not say that all nature is a system of means — that the end to be accomplished never is accomplished without the means, and that those means often require the lapse of ages before this end is obtained. No doubt God could create a tree at once in its full perfection; but, instead of this, he causes it to germinate from a

* Butler's Analogy, part 2, chap. 4.

little seed, and makes his sun shine upon it, and waters it with showers, and subjects it to the vicissitudes of the seasons, (during portions of which it seems to make no progress,) till, at length, it towers toward heaven, and defies the storms of ages. So the kingdom of heaven in the soul is like a grain of mustard-seed, which is indeed the least of all seeds; but God causes it to spring up, and shines upon it with the light of his countenance, and waters it with the dews of his grace, till it becomes a plant bearing fruit in the garden of God. And yet those who believe that nature is of God, object to the gospel because of the very circumstances in which it harmonizes with his other works.

And here I mention a ground of misapprehension which is common to nature and to Christianity. A system of means implies the gradual development of a plan, and of course the plan must present very different aspects to those who view it in its different stages. There are some processes in nature that could not have been understood in the first ages of the world. Thus the periods and motions of some of the heavenly bodies were so obscure and complicated, that it required the observation and study of near six thousand years to understand and reduce them to system; and the eye of the philosopher who scanned those bodies before such observations could be made, must have remained unsatisfied and perplexed. He saw the light of the bodies, and walked in it; but he could not understand the philosophy and harmony of their motions. So it is with Christianity. While it gives freely the practical light which is necessary to our guidance, men have been very differently situated in regard to their opportunities of judging of its philosophy. Respecting this they have judged, and still judge, very differently, and probably none of them, in all points, correctly. They are not yet in the right position. Place a man in the sun, and he will be an astronomer at once. His position will enable him to see the motions of the planets just as they are. And Christianity speaks of just such a point, in relation to itself and the moral government of God, where every man will hereafter be placed. It speaks of a "day of the restitution of all things." In the mean time, those who refuse to be governed by the practical light of Christianity, because they can not understand certain points of its philosophy, pursue the same course as those philosophers who lived before the time of Newton would have done, if they had shut their eyes upon the light of the moon because they could not understand its motions.

A remedial system. — 6. I observe, that Christianity is analogous to the system of nature because it is a remedial system.* When the body is diseased, when a limb is broken, when gangrene commences, nature does not certainly leave the man to perish. She has provided a remedial system; and if the proper remedies are applied in season, the man may be restored. Now, what this remedial system is in the course of nature, Christianity is in the moral government of God. It comes to us in the same way, not as to the whole, but as to the sick, and offers us assistance upon similar conditions. The man who is sick must have sufficient faith in the remedy to give it a fair trial, and so must he who would be benefited by Christianity. The remedial system of nature often requires the suffering of great present pain, that greater future pain may be avoided; and Christianity requires self-denials and sacrifices which are so difficult, that they are compared to the cutting off of a right hand, and the plucking out of a right eye. The remedial system of nature does not free the sick man at once from all the painful consequences of his disease. He suffers, and, it may be,

* Butler, part 2, chap. 3.

lingers long under it, in spite of the best remedies. So he who receives Christianity does not escape at once all the painful consequences of sin. He suffers and dies on account of it; but the remedy is sovereign, and through it he shall finally be delivered from sin altogether, and restored to perfect moral soundness. Nature makes no distinctions. The pains which she inflicts are as severe, and the remedies which she offers are as bitter, to one as to another. Christianity, also, is entirely impartial. All who receive it must receive it on the same humbling terms, and upon all who will not receive it, it denounces the same fearful punishment. Under this head, therefore, we find a very close analogy between the mode of administration in nature and that which is revealed by Christianity.

A mediatorial system. — 7. I observe, that Christianity is analogous to the system of nature because it is a mediatorial system. In mentioning this, I do not intend to enter upon any controverted ground, for all admit that, through the sufferings and death of Christ, voluntarily undergone, we receive at least great temporal benefits; and what I contend for is, that, whether we confine his interposition and mediation to this low sense, or suppose it the sole ground of pardon, still the principle, as one of mediation, is not changed, and is in accordance with what constantly passes under our notice in the natural government of God. " The world," says Butler, " is a constitution, or system, whose parts have a mutual reference to each other; and there is a scheme of things gradually carrying on, called the course of nature, to the carrying on of which God has appointed us in various ways to contribute. And when, in the daily course of natural providence, it is appointed that innocent people should suffer for the faults of the guilty, this is liable to the very same objection as the instance we are now considering. The infinitely greater importance of that appointment of Christianity, which is objected against, does not hinder, but it may be, as it plainly is, an appointment of the very same kind as that which the world affords us daily examples of." "Men, by their follies, run themselves into extreme distress and difficulties, which would be absolutely fatal to them were it not for the interposition and assistance of others. God commands, by the law of nature, that we afford them this assistance, in many cases where we can not do it without very great pains, and labor, and suffering to ourselves, And we see in what variety of ways one person's sufferings contribute to the relief of another, and how this follows from the constitution and laws of nature which come under our notice ; and, being familiarized to it, men are not shocked with it. So that the reason of their insisting upon objections of the foregoing kind against the satisfaction of Christ, is, either that they do not consider God's settled and uniform appointments as his appointments at all, or else they forget that vicarious punishment is an appointment of every day's experience." As therefore evils, and great evils, and such as we could not of ourselves avoid, are so often averted from us, in the providence of God, by the interposition of our fellow-creatures, so it is in perfect harmony with that providence to suppose that greater evils, otherwise unavoidable, might be averted by the interposition of the Son of God.

In these, and other particulars which might be mentioned, we find an analogy between Christianity and nature, such as to show that they came from the same hand. Here is a test — its general correspondence and harmony with the works of God and with the natural and providential government of God — which no false system can stand. And more especially remarkable is it that Christianity can sustain this test, when we consider it in contrast with that to which it was subjected at its first appearance in the world. With the presentation of this contrast I shall close this lecture.

The early and later test contrasted.— Christianity and Judaism.— Christianity, at its commencement, recognized the Jewish religion as from God; and it was a ground of its rejection by the Jews, that it destroyed their law or ritual. Hence it became necessary — and this was the main object of the apostle in the Epistle to the Hebrews — to show that it was in perfect harmony with the Jewish religion when rightly understood, and was, indeed, necessary to its completion. Did the Jews insist that Christianity had no priesthood? The apostle affirms that it had such a high priest as became us, "who is holy, harmless, undefiled, separate from sinners, and made higher than the heavens." Did the Jews affirm that Christianity had no tabernacle? The apostle asserts that Christ was the minister "of the true tabernacle, which the Lord pitched, and not man;" that he had "not entered into the holy places made with hands, which are the figures of the true, but into heaven itself." Was it objected that Christianity had no altar and no sacrifice? The apostle affirms that "now, once in the end of the world, Christ had appeared to put away sin by the sacrifice of himself." Thus did the apostle show that the Jewish religion, having dropped its swaddling-clothes of rites and ceremonies, was identical in spirit with Christianity. The same correspondence was either attempted to be shown, or taken for granted, by all the New Testament writers. But when we remember that Christianity is a purely spiritual religion, encumbered by no forms, and that the Jewish was apparently the most technical and artificial of all systems; when we remember that there was not only to be preserved a correspondence with the types and ceremonies, but also that there was to be the fulfillment of many prophecies, we may see the impossibility that any human art should construct a system so identical in its principles, and yet so diverse in its manifestations. Nor, indeed, could there have been any motive to induce such an attempt; for, besides its inherent difficulty, Christianity so far dropped all the peculiarities of the Jews as to forfeit every hope of benefit from their strong exclusive feelings, while at the same time it came before other nations subject to all the odium which it could not fail to excite as based on the Jewish religion. We accordingly find that, in point of fact, it was equally opposed by Jews and Gentiles. But such was the system — exclusive, typical, ceremonial, external, magnificent, addressed to the senses — between which and Christianity, simple, universal, without form or pomp, it was necessary to show a correspondence; and this the apostle Paul, and the New Testament writers generally, did show.

Christianity and nature — extent and grandeur. — How different the test to which Christianity is now put! The works of God are acknowledged to be from him, and, as now understood, how simple in their laws, how complex in their relations, how infinite in their extent! And can the same system, which so perfectly corresponded with the narrow system of the Jews, correspond equally with the infinite and unrestricted system and relations of God's works? Is it possible that the religion once embosomed in the ceremonies of an ignorant and barbarous people, which received its expansion and completion in an age of the greatest ignorance in regard to physical science, should yet harmonize, in its disclosures respecting God and his government, with those enlarged conceptions of his nature and kingdom which we now possess? Could Newton step from the study of the heavens to the study of the Bible, and feel that he made no descent? It is even so. The God whom the Bible discloses, and the moral system which it reveals, lose nothing when compared with the extent of nature, or with the simplicity and majesty of her laws; they seem rather worthy to be enthroned upon, and to preside over, such an amazing domain. The material universe, if not infinite, is indefinite in extent. We see in the misty spot which, in a serene evening, scarce discolors the deep blue of the sky, a distant milky way, like that which encircles our heavens, and in a small projection of which our sun is situated. We see such milky ways strown in profusion over the heavens, each containing more suns than we can number, and all these, with their subordinate systems, we see bound together by a law as efficient as it is simple and unchangeable. "They stand up together . . . not one faileth!" But long before this system was discovered, there was made known, in the Bible, a moral system in entire correspondence with it. We see at the head of it, and presiding in high authority over the whole, one infinite and "only wise God," "the King eternal, immortal, invisible." Of the systems above us, angelic and seraphic, we know little; but we see one law, simple, efficient, and comprehensive as that of gravitation, — the law of love, — extending its sway over the whole of God's dominions, living where he lives, embracing every moral movement in its universal authority, and producing the same harmony, where it is obeyed, as we observe in the movements of nature. We find here none of the puerilities which dwarf every other system. The sanctions of the law, the moral attributes revealed, the destinies involved, the prospects opened up, — all take hold on infinity, and are in perfect keeping with the solemn emotions excited by dwelling upon the illimitable works of God. "Deep calleth unto deep."

LECTURE IV.

ARGUMENT SECOND: COINCIDENCE OF CHRISTIANITY WITH NATURAL RELIGION.—ARGUMENT THIRD: ITS ADAPTATION TO THE CONSCIENCE AS A PERCEIVING POWER.—PECULIAR DIFFICULTIES IN THE WAY OF ESTABLISHING AND MAINTAINING A PERFECT STANDARD.—ARGUMENT FOURTH: IF THE MORALITY IS PERFECT, THE RELIGION MUST BE TRUE.

IF, as was attempted in the last lecture, a distinct analogy can be shown between Christianity and the constitution of nature, it will afford a strong presumption that they both came from the same hand. But if such an analogy can not be shown, it will not be conclusive against Christianity, because there is such a disparity between the material and the spiritual worlds, and the laws by which they must be governed, that a revelation concerning one might be possible, which yet should not seem to be analogous to the other.

ARGUMENT II.
COINCIDENCE OF CHRISTIANITY WITH NATURAL RELIGION.

Not so, however, with the argument which I next adduce, which is drawn from the coincidence of Christianity with natural religion. Truth is one. If God has made a revelation in one mode, it must coincide with what he has revealed in another. If, therefore, it can be shown that Christianity does not coincide with the well-authenticated teachings of natural religion, it will be conclusive against it. Nature is from God. Her teachings are from him, and I should regard it as settling the question against any thing claiming to be a divine revelation, if it could be shown to contradict those teachings. If, on the other hand, it can be shown that Christianity coincides perfectly with natural religion, and indeed teaches the only perfect system of it ever known, it will furnish a strong argument in its favor, especially when we consider how the religion originated.

Natural religion defined. — By natural religion, I mean that knowledge of God and of duty which may be acquired by man without a revelation. So far as this phrase is made to imply, as it sometimes is, that revealed religion is not natural, it is objectionable; for I conceive that the original and natural state of man was one of direct communication with God, and even now, that revelation is, in the highest sense, natural. It ought to be used simply to contradistinguish the knowledge, which man might gain from nature, from that which revelation alone teaches. Of natural religion the ideas of many are exceedingly indefinite; but that the definition now given is the true one is obvious, because it is the only one that can give it any fixed and definite meaning. It can not mean what men have actually learned from nature, for this has varied at different times. We should be doing injustice to the teachings of nature if we were to call that knowledge of God and of duty, which has been attained by the most enlightened heathen, the whole of natural religion. We mean, by revealed religion, not the partial and perverted views of any sect, but that system which God has actually revealed in the Bible, and which the diligent and candid can discover to be there. And so we mean, by natural religion, not what indolent, and biased, and selfish men have discovered, but that which nature actually teaches, and which a diligent and candid man could discover in the best exercise of his powers.

Teachings — how made known. — If this, then, be natural religion, how are its teachings made known? Its mode of teaching concerning God, and concerning duty, is not the same. Its teachings concerning God and his attributes are made known chiefly by reasoning from effects to their cause. In addition to this, it is supposed by some that all men have certain intuitive and necessary convictions concerning the being of a God. But, however this may be, I think that the being of a God, and the perfection of most of his natural attributes, might be inferred from nature as now known. That nature and Christianity agree in their teachings concerning these attributes, I have already shown; concerning the moral attributes of God, it is more difficult to say what nature does teach. Certain it is that man has never so learned them, from her light alone, as to lay the foundation for any rational system of religious morality; or so as to free the best minds from great and distressing uncertainty.

Her mode of teaching duty is by the tendencies and results of different actions, and courses of action. We can not doubt — at least natural religion does not permit itself to doubt — that the object of God, in the constitution of things, and in the relations established by him, is the good of man. If, therefore, we see any course of conduct tending to, and resulting in, the good of man, individually and socially, we infer that it is according to the will of God. If we see a course of conduct tending to, and resulting in, the unhappiness of the individual and of society, we infer that it is contrary to his will. It is in this way, solely, by the tendencies and results of actions, that natural religion teaches us our duty.

Not adapted to the common mind. — But it must be

conceded that this mode of teaching, by relations, and tendencies, and results, is not well adapted to the common mind. Even to comprehend these relations and tendencies fully, much more to trace them out originally, requires a philosophic mind of the highest order. In some cases, indeed, the tendency of actions, or courses of action, is obvious, and the will of God, when we believe in his being and perfections, is thus as clearly indicated as it would be by a voice from heaven; but in others, nothing can be more complex or difficult of determination even after an experience somewhat extended. After all their experience, men are still divided on the tendencies and results of a protective tariff, which we should think it would be perfectly easy to test to the satisfaction of all; but so varied are the interests involved, and so complex are the causes at work, that men seem now no nearer an agreement respecting them than ever. And if this is so on a subject to which attention is stimulated by immediate interest, and which appeals to interest alone, how much more must it be so with those courses of action in which moral tendencies and results, so obscure and tardy, are to be considered, and in which the strong natural feelings of the heart are at work to bias the judgment? Accordingly, though the teachings of nature have been open to all, and have influenced all to some extent, yet it has been only among the enlightened few, and at favored periods, that a *system* of natural religion could be said to exist at all, or that its teachings have exerted any considerable influence. Nor, when we consider how complex are the tendencies of actions, and how remote are often their completed results,—how plausible are some courses of action, which yet experience shows to be injurious,—when we consider the eagerness of passion, the blinding power of selfishness, how opposed some of the virtues are to the strongest feelings of men, and how evil practices, when once adopted, perpetuate themselves and become fixed by custom and association in the community, can we wonder that nothing like a perfect system of natural religion was ever discovered by man.

Teaching by inference, too, without any immediate sanction to the laws she could establish, and without any certain knowledge of a future retribution, there was very little in the voice of natural religion to arrest the attention of man. Accordingly, we find that her teachings were overlooked and disregarded by the great mass of men. They have been entirely drowned and superseded by systems of idolatry, and superstition, and fanaticism. Far, very far, therefore, have even the wisest heathen been from listening to all the voices uttered by nature, from reading all the lessons of wisdom and virtue inscribed on her pages.

It is, indeed, often difficult to know precisely how much we ought to attribute to natural religion. It seems certain that there was a primitive revelation communicating the idea of sacrifices, and modifying the religious and moral views of after times; rays of light from the Jewish and Christian revelations may have been more widely dispersed than we suppose, and many things, when once made known, so commend themselves to reason as to cause it to be felt that they might have been discovered. Hence deists have claimed several principles as discovered by reason, as the pardon of sin on repentance, which are unquestionably due to revelation alone. But whatever natural religion might teach, we do know that it can not teach facts, but only laws and tendencies. However complete, therefore, we may suppose it, it never could have taught those great *facts* which lie at the foundation of a system of mercy; but precisely how much of duty it might have taught, we can not say. We know, also, that the whole of the system never was reasoned out, nor is there the least reason to suppose it ever would have been.

The thing to be done. — Now, if a system purporting to come from heaven, comprises incidentally and naturally a perfect system of natural religion, gathering up all the obscure voices that nature utters, tracing out the indistinct lines which she has written; if its precepts are often in opposition to the common judgment and to the strong feelings of men, and yet, when tested by tendencies and results, are universally found to be sustained by these sanctions of natural religion; if it originated among a people who had manifested no tendency to philosophical studies, and from men without education, then we may well inquire, "Whence had these men this wisdom?" The more we consider the extreme difficulty of tracing out these tendencies, the minute and comprehensive knowledge both of man and of nature which it must require to do it perfectly, together with the blinding influence of selfishness and passion in such inquiries, the more highly shall we estimate the marvelous sagacity that could gather up and imbody every utterance and law of nature as declared by results.

Christianity has done it. — But this Christianity has actually done. Here we feel that we stand on firm ground. At this point, we challenge the scrutiny of the infidel. We defy him to point out a single duty even whispered by nature, which is not also inculcated in the New Testament; we defy him to point out a single precept of Christianity, a single course of action inculcated by it, which does not, in proportion as it is followed, receive the sanction of natural religion as declared by beneficial consequences. In fact, moral philosophy, and political economy, and the science of politics, the sciences which teach men the rules of well-being, whether as individuals or as communities, are, so far as they are sound, but experience and the structure of organized nature echoing back the teachings of Christianity. What principle of Christian ethics does moral philosophy now presume to call in question? What are the general principles of political economy, but an imperfect application, to the intercourse of trading communities, of those rules of good neighborhood, and of that spirit of kindness, which Christianity inculcates? What is the larger part of political science but a laborious and imperfect mode of realizing those results in society which would flow spontaneously from the universal prevalence of Christian morals and of a Christian spirit? Does Christianity command us to be temperate? Science, some eighteen hundred years afterwards, discovers that temperance alone is in accordance with what it calls the natural laws; and political economy reckons up the loss of labor and of wealth resulting from intemperance; and then, after an untold amount of suffering, what do they do but echo back the injunction, "Add to knowledge temperance." Does the Bible command men to do no work on the seventh day, and to let their cattle rest? It is now beginning to be discovered that this is in accordance with an organic law, and that, thus doing, both men and animals will be more healthy, and will do more work. And so, in regard to every course that would lead men to unhappiness, Christianity has stood from the first at the *entrance* of the paths, and uttered its warning cry. The nations have not heard it, but have rushed by, and rushed on, till they have reaped the fruit of their own devices in the corruption of morals, in the confusion of society through oppression and misrule; and then philosophy has condescended to discover these evils, and, if it has done any thing for the permanent relief of society, it has brought it back to the letter or spirit of the gospel.

The stern teachings of experience are making it manifest, — and they will continue to do it more and more, — that the Bible is God's statute-book for the regulation of his moral creatures, and that the laws of the Bible can no more be violated with impunity than the natural laws of God.

The system completed. — If Christianity had contained all the teachings of natural religion known at that day, had gathered up all that the great and wise men of all previous time had reasoned out, and had made some additions of its own, it would have been most extraordinary, and would have required for its production the greatest philosopher of the age. But while it adopted many things that were then taught, and rejected nothing that was good, it completed the system for all ages, leaving nothing for philosophy to do but to apply and verify its principles. And in doing this, it promulgated many things that were entirely contrary to all the tastes and all the teachings both of the Jews and of the Gentiles. Several of the fundamental principles of Christian morality — such as, if adopted, would change the face of society — were original with Christ, at least in their practical enforcement, and were so opposed to every thing taught among the Jews, that it was with great difficulty and slowness that the disciples themselves were made to understand them, or to conceive the possibility of their adoption. Such, for example, were its condemnation of war, and private retaliation, and of polygamy, and of divorce except for a single cause; such its inculcation of purity of heart, of meekness and humility, of the love of enemies, and of universal benevolence. Such was its estimation of the poor as standing on the same level of immortality with the rich; such its principle of self-denial for the good of others, its supreme regard to the will of God, and its regard for the interests of the soul rather than those of the body. So that Christ did not merely make some improvements, such as a great genius might be supposed to do; nor did he, as Linnæus in botany, discover a new method or system, which gave him a clew to vast stores of new knowledge; but, standing precisely where other men had stood, with no education, with no knowledge of Greek or Roman literature in the ordinary way, he adopted all that was good in the prevalent systems, but still introduced so much that was new, that the system, as a whole, was not only perfect, but was a new and an original system. The adoption of it was opposed by every selfish principle, and seemed to require, and often did require, the renunciation of life itself. But the system was original in its motives as well as in its principles. Many were led to adopt it, and now we see that it is through these principles, and these alone, that individuals and society can be made happy, and we bow with humble reverence before that wisdom by which they were promulgated. Let these principles be adopted and carried out, and we have an entirely different world from that which could exist on any others — a world from which the chief causes of unhappiness are removed.

And is it possible that any human sagacity could have adopted so much that was new, and yet have excluded every thing that was injurious, or excessive, or unbalanced? "With such an agent as man," says Bishop Sumner, "and in a condition so complicated as that of human society, it is no less dangerous than difficult to introduce new modes of conduct and new principles of action. What extensive and unforeseen results have sometimes proceeded from a single statute, like that which provides for the support of the poor in England; a single institution, like the trial by jury; a single admission, like that of the supremacy of the Roman pontiff; a single principle, as Luther's appeal to the

Bible!"* And yet, here is a new system, involving all the relations of human society, the results of which are invariably confirmed by those of experience.

The only possible objection to the morality of Christianity is, that it is too perfect; that, though it may fit men for heaven, it will subject those who adopt it to injury and depredation here. But, whatever injury may be done in this way is the result, not of Christianity, but of a system of wickedness which it forbids; and surely it ought not to be made responsible for the results of disobeying its precepts. It claims to be a universal system. Let it be universally obeyed, and the objection vanishes.

ARGUMENT III.
CHRISTIANITY TESTED BY THE CONSCIENCE.

But there is another test to which the morality of Christianity may be brought; it may be tested, not only by its tendencies, but by the conscience of man. The utility of an action is one thing, its rightness is another. The understanding judges of the utility, the conscience of the rightness, of actions. That the conscience is not an infallible test in all cases, must be conceded. It is liable to be both blunted and perverted. Still, with the light we now have, it is not difficult to determine, respecting any system, whether it does commend itself to the conscience of the race. Let it stand before men from age to age, so as to come in contact with the conscience, — and the more intimately, the more the conscience is developed, — and if it is found to teach that system, and those rules of conduct, in favor of which the conscience gives its verdict as founded in the eternal rules of right, then either it must have come from God, or it must be precisely such a system as God would reveal, — for, plainly, he would reveal no other.

---
* Sumner's Evidences, chap. 8.

Does, then, Christianity, whether we consider it as a system of doctrines or of morals, fully meet the demands of the conscience as a discriminating power? We say, Yes. We say that there is not a single principle of moral government, not a single course of action, not a temper of mind, approved by it, which an enlightened conscience does not also approve as right, and suitable to the relations in which man is placed. This, so far as the morality of Christianity is concerned, I may safely say, because it is conceded by infidels. There is no candid and well-informed man who does not now concede that the morality of Christianity, whether tested by tendencies or by conscience, is perfect; that, if it were fully carried out, it would promote happiness in all the relations of life, and that it is the only system that can do so to the same extent.

Task difficult. — But, in meeting this test, Christianity has had a task to perform, the difficulty of which is seldom appreciated. It was necessary that it should do four things, neither of which has ever been done by any other system.

Perfect standard, and perfect application. — And, first, it was necessary, not only that it should assume a standard absolutely perfect, — which, however far from any thing that man has ever done, would be comparatively easy, — but that it should apply a perfect law to those complex and infinitely diversified cases which arise when law is violated. A perfect moral government of perfect beings must require a perfect law. If Christianity is to meet the demands of the conscience that has once recognized such a law, it must utter no precept opposed to it — nothing opposed to the highest standard of which we are capable of conceiving. So long as a perfect state remained, the simple law of perfection would be the only precept required, and it would be comparatively easy to obey it. The substance of the perfect law of God is the love of God and of our neighbor; and where this law is perfectly observed, nothing can occur to provoke ill-will. Hence there is in heaven no precept that, when they are smitten on the one cheek, they shall turn the other also. But Christianity lays down a multitude of precepts intended to regulate, in the spirit of a perfect rule, the intercourse of beings inclined to inflict upon each other injury and depredation. Does it, then, in order to meet the apparent exigencies of the case, to conciliate to itself human prejudice or passion, ever, in any of these subordinate precepts, depart from its high requisitions, or abate any thing from the integrity of its original and fundamental principle? We know the opposition it encountered, and that the true ground of that opposition was the high standard it assumed. If it had been of the world, the world would have loved its own. There was, then, the strongest temptation, if not to Christ himself, yet to those who succeeded him, to dilute this original principle, and soften down their requirements, lest they should incur the charge of inculcating an impracticable morality. Have they done this? In no case have they done it. There are no Jesuitical exceptions or reservations. Not only was Christ consistent with himself in his minor precepts, but the apostles were in every instance true to their trust, and no stronger proof could be given, not only of integrity, but of wisdom. Nothing but the most perfect integrity could have adhered to the law in all its breadth, and nothing but a divine wisdom could have accommodated it to the very peculiar circumstances of man in this world. The minor precepts of Christianity are all consistent with its fundamental and its perfect law.

Treatment of the injurious. — And here I may remark that not only does Christianity sustain the authority of a perfect law, but, in the line of conduct it lays down toward the injurious, it has adopted the very principle which, according to the laws of mental operation discovered in later times, must tend in the greatest possible degree to diminish injury. It is a well-ascertained fact, that the most powerful mode of inculcating and exciting any quality, or temper, is the distinct and vivid manifestation of that temper. The manifestation of anger toward another excites anger in him; and the manifestation of a meek and forgiving spirit has a tendency to disarm hostility, and does all that can be done to prevent ill-feeling. If, therefore, a man were to inquire how, according to principles of mental philosophy alone, he could do most to banish the malignant and selfish passions from the earth, and make it like heaven, he would be obliged to adopt the very course prescribed by the New Testament.

New revelations and duties. — But, secondly, Christianity, as I have already shown, agrees with nature, so far as that goes, in its teachings concerning the natural attributes of God, and concerning morality; but it reveals some things concerning God peculiar to itself; and it imposes upon man some new duties. The question, then, is, whether the additional revelations concerning God are in keeping with those of nature, and whether they satisfy the demands of the conscience for a perfect Being, in the moral attributes which they reveal; and, also, whether the duties it imposes are agreeable to reason and conscience. So far as Christianity coincides with nature, I take it for granted that it satisfies the demands of the conscience. Does it do this equally when it passes on beyond nature to those independent and fuller revelations which it makes of God and of duty, so that the transition from the one to the other is only as that from the dim twilight to the full blaze of day? We know something of God from nature, just as we know something of the heavens from the naked eye. Are, then, the revelations of Christianity respecting him in keeping with those of nature, only more imposing and magnificent, just as the revelations of the telescope concerning the heavens are in keeping with those of the naked eye, while they so far transcend them?

We are so accustomed to contemplate God as invested with all those paternal and perfect moral attributes with which Christianity clothes him, — to see him in that amazing attitude of holy sovereignty and paternal goodness in which it represents him, — that this perfect combination of moral attributes, this completeness of moral character, in the Sovereign of the universe, such that we should as soon think of adding to infinite space as of adding any thing to its perfection, seems as a matter of course, and we do not remember how difficult it must have been to carry out the fragmentary revelation of nature to its absolute completeness, and to combine with those tremendous natural attributes, shadowed forth in the agencies of nature, the benignity and mercy, the justice and compassion, that form the character of our Father in heaven. We forget that Nature has her terrific and fearful aspects, her barren wastes, her regions of wild disorder, her lightning and thunder, her tornadoes and earthquakes, and her breath of pestilence, as well as her glad voices, and her quiet sunshine that rests like a smile on the face of creation, and her waving harvests, — and that it is by her terrific aspects that men are most impressed, and that hence they have been led to form gloomy ideas of God, and not unfrequently to impersonate the principle of evil into a sovereign divinity whose wrath they were chiefly desirous of propitiating. We forget the distressing perplexity in which the greatest and best men of antiquity were respecting the moral attributes of God, and the important fact that *they never so conceived of him as to make the love of God a duty.* All this, I say, we seem to forget, and to think it was a matter of course that Christianity should thus carry out, into all conceivable perfection, the dim revelations of nature concerning God. This indeed it does with such ease, so incidentally, so little with the pride or in the forms of philosophic disquisition, that we scarcely give it credit for what it does, though all this but renders it the more remarkable. It is related of a palace built by genii, that all the treasures of a great monarch were inadequate to complete one of the windows purposely left unfinished. And when I see how fragmentary the structure of religious knowledge was left by nature, — when I see how inadequate all the labors of man had proved for its completion, — and when I look at the glorious and completed dome reared by Christianity, I can not but feel that other than human hands have been employed in the structure. The first and fundamental condition of a perfect religion — of one which can do all for the moral powers that can be done for them — is a perfect character in the object of worship. The mind is naturally assimilated to the object which it contemplates with delight, and especially which it worships; and it is demonstrable, on principles of reason, that, unless the character of the God of Christianity is absolutely perfect, then that character not only will not meet the demands of the conscience, but can never do for man, in the elevation and perfection of his character, all that could be done for him. But, the more we dwell on it, the more we shall see that the character of the God of the Bible is absolutely perfect, and therefore, either the God of Christianity is the true God, or there can be no being who shall be God to us — none who shall meet that conception of absolute perfection which we form in our minds, and feel that we must transfer to him.

New duties not arbitrary. — Of the new duties demanded by Christianity, it may be said that they are in no case arbitrary and capricious, but are exactly those which grow out of the new relations in which we are placed by Christianity, and which the conscience can not but approve the moment these relations are perceived. Thus, if God has shown us new evidence of love through Christianity, then are we under new obligations of gratitude to him. If Christ has signally interposed in our behalf, then we are under obligations to him in proportion to what he has done for us. If we are intrusted by Christianity with good tidings of great joy, then we are under obligation to publish them to all people.

Thus, whether we consider the additional revelation of Christianity respecting God or duty, we find that it perfectly meets the demands of an enlightened conscience.

Lenity and law. — But, thirdly, in neither of the particulars just mentioned do we find the most difficult task which Christianity had to perform, if it would meet the demands of conscience. Its professed object was to introduce a system of lenity. And was it possible it should do this, and still cause that perfect law, which, if it meet the demands of the conscience, it must sustain, to appear as strict and binding as if no such system had been introduced? This it must do if it meets the demands of the conscience; for, when once that has obtained the conception of absolute moral perfection, nothing can satisfy it which would weaken the obligation of that. Here is a fundamental difficulty. Whatever Christianity may profess, does not lenity, in the nature of the case, tend to weaken the sanctions of law, and to deduct from its binding force? Is it possible to conceive of a lawgiver who remits the *just* penalty of crime, and, at the same time, manifests the same abhorrence of it, and the same anxiety to guard against its commission, as he would have done if he had caused the penalty to be executed? All good men agree in the essential principle, that the full authority of God's law must be sustained. But how can this be done while pardon is granted? This is a difficulty which if Christianity has not removed, it is not because it has not perceived it, and made the attempt. "That he might be just, and the justifier of him which believeth in Jesus," is declared by the apostle to be the great object of all that had been done by God in introducing the Christian revelation. This is the very centre and soul of Christianity; and, if it has not accomplished this, then has it failed of the very end proposed by itself. This is a question which is not stated even, in any false religion, because that all-important conception of the holiness of God, out of which it grows, has not been sufficiently distinct to produce it. If men have offered sacrifices, and submitted to torture, it has been under the impression that God might be moved like an earthly monarch, and never under the idea of him as having an impartial and inflexible adherence to rectitude, or with the purpose of bringing forgiveness within the range of any great principle. But this question a religion that would deal fairly with an enlightened mind must meet. This problem it must solve. Standing where I do, it would not become me to state the method in which I suppose Christianity has solved this problem. I intend to enter upon no disputed doctrines. I take it for granted that all Christians suppose the mercy of God to be entirely compatible with his perfect holiness. Let individuals adopt what views they choose in respect to the method in which this is accomplished. I wish solely to draw attention to the difficulty of the problem, to the fact that this difficulty was fully understood by the original writers on Christianity, and that they profess to have solved it. If they have done this, then how divine the wisdom which could so perfectly meet the demands of the most enlightened conscience by sustaining law, and at the same time provide for the wants of the guilty! Problems so high, human systems do not attempt to solve; wisdom so divine as must be involved in the solution of this, they do not manifest.

Justice and the disorders of the world. — There is one thing more which it behooved Christianity to do, if it would meet the demands of conscience as a discriminating power. It was, to satisfy our natural sense of justice with reference to the disorders of this present world. These disorders, in the height to which they have risen, have always presented a great moral enigma to those who have reasoned concerning the providence and moral government of God. This was strongly felt and strongly stated as long ago as the time of Job. "Some," says he, "remove the landmarks; they violently take away flocks, and feed thereof. They drive away the ass of the fatherless. They take the widow's ox for a pledge. They cause the naked to lodge without clothing, that they have no covering in the cold. They pluck the fatherless from the breast, and take a pledge of the poor. Men groan from out of the city, and the soul of the wounded crieth out: yet God layeth not folly to them." "Wherefore do the wicked live, become old, yea, are mighty in power? Their seed is established in their sight with them, and their offspring before their eyes. They spend their days in wealth, and in a moment go down to the grave." "The earth," says he, "is given into the hand of the wicked; he covereth the faces of the judges thereof; if not," — as much as to say, this must be allowed whether we can reconcile it to the righteous government of God or not, — "if not, where and who is he?" Thus was this wise and good man perplexed before the light of Christianity. The Psalmist found no relief under the same difficulty until he went to the sanctuary of God, and there saw the end of the wicked. Solomon, too, says, " Moreover I saw under the sun the place of judgment, that wickedness was there ; and the place of righteousness, that iniquity was there. I said in mine heart,"— then he said, when he saw this, as furnishing the only solution of the difficulty, — " God shall judge the righteous and the wicked." Nor does the picture assume a brighter hue as we come down the ages. History is full of multiplied, and aggravated, and unredressed wrongs, inflicted by man upon man. Look at the slave-trade. Look at slavery as it exists now. Look at the peasantry of Europe. Look at Poland. Or, if we turn from the contemplation of open and high-handed violence, to consider the triumphs of injustice; the success of fraud; the spoliations and heartless atrocities which are effected under the forms of law ; the wrongs, and cruelties, and petty tyrannies, that are exercised in families, and imbitter the lives of thousands, our difficulties will not be diminished. Surely, to a thoughtful man, without revelation, this world must present a most perplexing and discouraging spectacle. He must see that there are injuries for which there is no redress upon earth, questions unsettled for which there is no adjudication here ; and, while he has no satisfactory evidence that a time of adjudication will ever come, he must feel that a violence is done to his moral nature if these questions are to be cut short by death, and left unsettled forever. To this state of perplexity, so natural and so universal, Christianity furnishes complete relief. It gives us the most positive assurance that these questions shall be carried up to an impartial tribunal. It makes known to us the Judge and the rules of the proceedings of that great " day of the restitution of all things ; " — yes, " the restitution of all things." When it is known that this is to be, then the perplexed and agonized heart is set at rest. Then, and not till then, there is felt to be a congruity between the course of events, as they shall ultimately terminate, and our moral frame and the demands of the conscience are fully met.

Recapitulation.—What I would say, then, is, that Christianity commends itself to a conscience fully enlightened, not only in its morality, but by uniformly adhering to a perfect standard of rectitude, and under circumstances which, to mere human wisdom, would seem to be incompatible with it. Man is capable of forming the idea of moral perfection; and, having once formed it, his moral nature requires that a religion claiming to come from God should neither command nor reveal any thing incompatible with that idea. The necessity of meeting this requisition, whether man is regarded as possessed of discriminating powers simply, or as a being to be elevated and assimilated to something higher and better than himself, Christianity, and that alone, has fully perceived; and it will be seen that it was this very necessity which created the difficulty in each of the cases that I have stated. In the first case, it was necessary that precepts should be laid down which should be compatible both with a perfect law, and with the state of things in this world, so that the conduct required should be neither wrong nor impracticable. Who but Christ and his followers has ever done this? Who else has ever attempted it without conceding much to human weakness and frailty? In the second case, the difficulty lay in carrying out the moral character of God, to the perfection required by the conscience, from the imperfect and often seemingly contradictory revelations of nature. In the third case, it consisted in reconciling a system of lenity with the claims of this same perfect standard; and, in the fourth case, in revealing a method by which, in the administration of God, the disorders of this world are reconciled with the present existence and ultimate triumph of a perfect law. In each of these cases, therefore, the principle is the same. That there must be a perfect standard established and maintained, both in the character and law of God, is settled. That is taken for granted; and the difficulty lay in reconciling other things with that, which apparently only a divine wisdom could have reconciled.

To my mind, the argument from these cases is of great weight. But, leaving them aside, I lay my finger upon the morality of Christianity, whether tested by consequences or by the conscience, and I claim that it is perfect — "that the virtues inculcated in the gospel are the only virtues which we can imagine a heavenly teacher to inculcate." Is, then, this claim allowed? It has been allowed by infidels, and I feel confident it must be by every candid man. But if so, who does not see that a perfect system of duty must come from God? Who does not see the absurdity of supposing that it should be originated in connection with a system of falsehood and imposture?

Morality not the primary object. — And this morality is the more remarkable, because the great and primary object of Christianity is not to regulate the relations of earthly society, or to provide for the welfare of man in this life. It is to bring "life and immortality to light," and to prepare men for that immortality. In its spirit, we must indeed suppose this morality to belong to the heavenly state; but in many of the forms of its manifestation, it is but the *earthly* garment of Christianity — but as the mantle of the ascending prophet, which fell from him when he was translated. Great, then, as is the work, and the blessing of a perfect system of morality, it is only incidental; it is only as a branch from the main stem of that species of the palm-tree well known in India, which still passes on upward, and produces its fruit from a single magnificent blossom at the top. This morality is an infinite blessing; it is the fruit of Christianity; but it is borne, as it were, only by its lower branches, while it is the great doctrine of salvation, of "life and immortality brought to light," that expands at its top, and sheds its fragrance over the nations.

Men, then, may say what they please of the power of the human mind to make discoveries in moral science; but to me it seems that to suppose a system like this, thus perfectly coinciding with all the teachings of natural religion and with the requisitions of conscience, to have originated with peasants and fishermen of Galilee, requires nothing less than the capacious credulity of an infidel.

ARGUMENT IV.

A PERFECT MORALITY CAN NOT BE FROM A FALSE RELIGION.

The morality of Christianity, as tested both by natural religion and by the conscience, being thus perfect, the question arises whether it is inseparably connected with the religion; and if so, whether it is possible that a perfect morality should come from a false religion.

Separation of morality and religion.—That a system of morality and of religion should coexist, and yet not be necessarily connected, is very conceivable. The morality may be correct, as was much of that taught by Cicero, in his book *De Officiis*, and yet the religion with which it is associated may be entirely false. The precepts may have no connection with the facts, or doctrines, or rites of the religion. This has been the case with all false religions. There has been no tendency in the doctrines or facts of the religion to form men to the precepts of moral virtue. The morality has often been better than the religion, and might be easily separated from it. And if this has been so with other religions, why may it not be so with Christianity?

Concession of infidels. — This question I am bound to notice, because infidels have not been backward in conceding to the morality of Christianity all that we ask. They speak in terms of high eulogy of the Sermon on the Mount; they eagerly claim whatever they can of its peculiar doctrines as the teachings of nature, and seem to perceive no difficulty even in admitting that the morality is perfect, and yet rejecting the religion.

But that the two are inseparable, and must be received or rejected as one whole, appears, —

True morality must be from God. — First, because we can not otherwise account for the morality. It seems to me, as I have already attempted to show, that man could not have originated such a system of morals. When I stand between two cliffs rent asunder by a convulsion of nature, I do not need to be told that that passage was not opened by a human arm. When I see the bow spanning the heavens, I do not need to be told that no human hand has bended it. So, when I compare such a system with the intellectual and moral power, not merely of unlettered fishermen, but of man, and especially with all the attempts he has actually made, I feel that there is an utter disparity between them. I feel that the morality must have come in connection with the religion of which it forms a part.

An attempt to deceive incredible. — But, secondly, it is incredible and contradictory, contrary to all the known laws of mind, to suppose that men whose moral discrimination and susceptibilities were so acute — who could originate a system so pure, so elevated, so utterly opposed to all falsehood — should, without reason or motive that we can see, deliberately attempt to deceive mankind concerning their highest interests. If they had a system of morality to communicate, why did they not, like honest men, communicate it as an abstract system, unencumbered with doctrines which were, and which they must have foreseen would be, to the Jews a stumbling-block and to the Greeks foolishness? Why did they connect with it a narrative of facts which, if false, might have been easily disproved? How much more safe and dignified to have delivered the system in its abstract form, after the manner of the philosophers! The combination of folly and wickedness, which such a course would involve, with those high qualities, both of the intellect and of the heart, in which alone such a system could have originated, seems to me impossible.

The morality grows out of the facts and doctrines. — Once more, thirdly, the peculiar morality of Christianity can not be separated from it, because it so grows out of its facts and doctrines, and so derives its power from them. It does not lie in the religion, as the gem does in the rock, but is an organized part of one vital whole. It is as the hands and the feet to the heart and the brain. And surely nothing but a divine wisdom could cause all the great doctrines and facts of such a religion to bear, either in the way of instruction or motive, upon the formation of a right moral character. How difficult — I may say how impossible — that a writer of fiction should introduce an extraordinary person, like Christ, possessed of high supernatural powers, and yet not attribute to him one wild or fanciful adventure, such as we find in every account of heathen gods; not one capricious, or selfish, or unworthy exertion of his miraculous powers; but that he should make all the exertions of those powers, and all the events of his life, such that they bear powerfully as motives on the practice of a then unheard-of and perfect morality!

New motives. — As I have already said, there are

many new duties growing out of the new relations in which we are placed by the facts of Christianity; but not to these only, to every duty, those facts furnish new and powerful motives, without which the system, as a practical whole, has no power. Certainly, it is from the character of God as revealed by Christianity, and from the new relations assumed by him toward us, that the most effective motives are drawn for the performance of many of our duties toward our fellow-men. The paternal relation of God to man, as a practical doctrine, is made known only by Christianity. It is true — what was said by Madame De Stael — that, if Christ had simply taught men to say, "Our Father," he would have been the greatest benefactor of the race. If the heathen had some notion of the beneficence of the supreme power, from the operation of general laws, yet there was a difference heaven-wide between that and all that is involved in the doctrine of a particular providence and of paternal regard and supervision. Yet how effectively does Christ himself use this doctrine, and those high moral qualities revealed in connection with it, to enforce practical duty! Does he command us to love our enemies, and bless them that curse us? It is that we may be the children of our Father which is in heaven, who "maketh his sun to rise on the evil and on the good." Does he teach us the duty of forgiveness? It is because God forgives us. If the master forgives the debt of ten thousand talents, the servant should forgive his fellow-servant the debt of a hundred pence. Does he teach that the pure in heart are blessed? It is because "they shall see God." Does he teach the duty of letting our light shine? It is that we may glorify our Father which is in heaven. Would an apostle teach men the duty of mutual love? "Herein," says he, " is love; not that we loved God, but that he loved us, and sent his Son to be the propitiation for our sins. Beloved, if God so loved us, we ought also to love one another." And in the same way are the character and acts of Christ referred to. Would Peter teach us to bear injuries patiently? He tells us of Him "who, when he was reviled, reviled not again; when he suffered, he threatened not; but committed himself to Him that judgeth righteously." Would Paul teach us lowliness of mind, and to esteem others better than ourselves, what is his argument? He says, "Let this mind be in you, which was also in Christ Jesus; who, being in the form of God, thought it not robbery to be equal with God, but made himself of no reputation, and took upon him the form of a servant." Indeed, the more we examine this point, the more we shall be surprised to see how almost exclusively the motives to Christian morality are drawn from the Christian religion, and how its doctrines, and facts, and motives, and precepts, all coalesce and become indissolubly united in one harmonious and perfect whole.

The morality proves the religion. — The morality and the religion being thus blended as one whole, the inquiry arises, whether it is possible that such a morality should either originate in, or be thus incorporated with, a false religion.

A common faculty for both. — There are those, I know, who say that the foundations of morality in man are different from those of religion; and I am not disposed to deny that certain faculties are called into high activity in religion, which are excited slightly, if at all, in the duties of morality. Still, so far as duty is concerned, which is the whole of morality, and which is the central and indispensable part of any true religion, they both appeal to the same conscience, and to that alone. Depending thus upon a common faculty, a true religion and a true morality must have an essential unity.

A perfect religion involves a perfect morality. — That a perfect religion must comprise a perfect morality, is certain, because a perfect religion must include every religious duty; and we are under obligation to perform our duty to our fellow-creatures, not simply from our relations to them, but because the performance of that duty is the will of God. Hence every moral duty is, and must be, also binding as a religious duty; and hence no man can be truly religious further than he is moral.

Perfect morality impossible from a false religion. — But a true religion, carried out, would thus certainly bear as its fruit a perfect morality. Is it possible that a false religion should bear the same fruit? Then truth would be no better than error; the true God no better than an idol. Then a corrupt tree might bring forth good fruit; "a clean thing might come out of an unclean." The question is not simply to what extent a true morality and a false religion may coexist, but whether such a morality can be the necessary outgrowth and fruit of such a religion. That it can be, is opposed to our primary and intuitive convictions.

It is not conceivable that a perfect system of moral duty should coalesce and harmonize with the religious duty taught by a system of falsehood, such as the Christian system must be, if it did not come from God. But in the Christian system, the moral and religious duties do thus coalesce, and form a part of one independent whole. The religious morality of the Bible, if I may call it so,—that which relates to God,— is quite as extraordinary as that which relates to man; it is quite as far elevated above that of any other system; and these, when united and interwoven as they are in the Bible, form one whole, perfect and complete. Besides, a perfect system of morality could not be laid down, even in an abstract, or tabular form, in connection with a false religion; because many of our duties to our fellow-men, as well as the motives by which they are enforced, arise out of our relations to them as the children of a common parent, and a knowledge of these relations can come only from a true religion.

Conclusion. — Our conclusion then is, that if the morality is what we claim it to be, the religion must be true; and infidels must either — as they can not — deny that the morality is perfect, or accept the religion. Christianity is no heterogeneous mass, promiscuously thrown together. It is one, an organic whole, and must be accepted or rejected as such. From the nature of the case, therefore, we might expect — what all experience shows has happened — that any attempt to separate this morality from this religion, and yet give it power, would be like the attempt to separate the branch from the parent stock, and yet cause it to live. We might expect, if we were ever to see a perfect morality coming up from the wilderness of this world, that she would come, not walking alone, but, "leaning upon her Beloved."

LECTURE V.

ARGUMENT FIFTH: CHRISTIANITY ADAPTED TO MAN.—DIVISION FIRST. ITS QUICKENING AND GUIDING POWER.—ITS ADAPTATION TO THE INTELLECT, THE AFFECTIONS, THE IMAGINATION, THE CONSCIENCE, AND THE WILL.

CHRISTIANITY is analogous to nature; it coincides with natural religion: it meets the demands of the conscience as a discriminating power; and, as embosoming a perfect morality, it must be from God.

We next inquire after its adaptation to man. What are its capacities to quicken and guide those leading faculties in the right action of which his perfection and happiness must consist. Those faculties are the Intellect, the Affections, the Imagination, the Conscience, and the Will.

Christianity and the intellect. — *Information and reflection.* — By the adaptation of Christianity to the intellect, I mean its tendency to give it clearness and strength. I mean by it just what is meant when it is said that nature is adapted to the intellect. The intellect is enlarged and strengthened by the exercise of its powers on suitable subjects. This exercise can be induced in only two ways — by furnishing it with *information*, or by leading it to *study* and *reflection;* and whichever of these we regard, we need not fear to compare Christianity with nature as adapted to enlarge and strengthen the intellectual powers.

Information. — And, first, of information. If we consider the Christian revelation, as we fairly may in this connection, as it recognizes, includes, and presupposes the Old Testament, there is no book that can compare with it for the variety and importance of the information it gives; nor can it be exceeded by nature itself. From this, and from this alone, do we know any thing of the origin of the world and of the human race; of the introduction of natural and moral evil; of the history of men before the deluge; of the deluge itself, as connected with the race of man; of the early settlement and dispersions of the race; of the history of the Jews; and of the history of the early rise and progress of Christianity. Without the Bible, an impenetrable curtain would be dropped between us and the whole history of the race further back than the Greeks, or certainly the Egyptians; and who does not feel that the letting down of such a curtain would act upon the mind, not simply by the amount of information it would withdraw, but with the effect of a chill and a paralysis, from the necessity of that information to give completeness to knowledge as an organized whole? It would be like taking the hook out of the beam on which the whole chain hangs. And, again, what information gained from nature can be more interesting than that which the Bible gives concerning God as a Father, concerning his universal providence, our accountability, a resurrection from the dead, the second coming of Christ, and an eternal life? Who would substitute the mists of conjecture for this mighty background, piled up by revelation along the horizon of the future?

Philosophic spirit required. — But — to say nothing of information, as it is not from that that the mind gains its chief efficiency — I infer that Christianity is adapted to the intellect, 1. From the fact of the identity of its spirit with that of true philosophy. Of this I have already spoken.

Indirectly favorable. — 2. Christianity is indirectly favorable to the intellect by bringing men out from under the dominion of sensuality, and of those low vices by which it is checked and dwarfed in its growth. The temperance and sobriety of life which it enjoins are essential, as conditions, to the full expansion and power of the intellect.

Its estimate of truth. — 3. That Christianity is favorable to the intellect, is obvious from the place which it assigns to truth. Truth, in this system, lies at the foundation of every thing. It is contradistinguished from every other system, pretending to come from God, by this. Christ said that he came into the world to bear witness of the truth. He prayed that God would sanctify men, but it was through the truth. It seems to have been the object of Christ to place his disciples in a position in which they could intelligently, as well as affectionately, yield themselves to him, and to the government of God. How remarkable are his words! "Henceforth," says he, "I call you not servants; for the servant knoweth not what his lord doeth; but I have called you friends; for all things that I have heard of my Father I have made known unto you." Christ is spoken of as a light to lighten the Gentiles. The object of Paul was to turn men from darkness to light, as well as from the power of Satan unto God. He spoke the words of truth as well as of soberness. If he was strongly moved by the conduct of a church, it was because it did not obey the truth. Does the beloved disciple exhort the elect lady not to receive some into her house? It is those who do not teach the truth. Light in the understanding is scarcely less an object, with Christianity, than purity in the affections. Its whole scope and tendency is to magnify the importance of truth. The enemies of Christianity can not point out any thing, either in its letter or spirit, which would restrict knowledge or cramp the intellect. We are, indeed, required to have faith; but we are also required to "add to faith knowledge." We are to adopt no conviction on the ground of any blind impulse; we are always to be able to give a *reason* of the hope that is in us. We glory in Christianity, as a religion of light not less than a religion of love.

Freedom of opinion required. — 4. Christianity is favorable to the intellect, because, wherever it exists in its purity, there must be freedom of opinion, and this is one great condition of vigorous intellect. Recognizing truth as the great instrument of moral power and of moral changes in the soul, making no account of any forms, or external conduct not springing from conviction, Christianity claims truth as the right of the human soul. What was the fundamental principle of the Reformation, but the right of the people to the truth, and the whole truth — access for themselves to its fountain-head in the Bible? And whence did that principle spring, but from the Bible itself, from that Bible found and read by Luther? It is to the very book he abuses that the infidel owes that freedom by which he is permitted to abuse it; for where, except where the Bible has influence, do you find opinion free? The fact is, that Christianity gives to God and truth a supremacy in the mind which unfits man for becoming either the dupe or the tool of designing men; and hence, chiefly, their attempts to corrupt it, and to take it from the people.

Adapted as nature is. — 5. But I have intimated that Christianity is adapted to the intellect in the same way that nature is. I wish to show this. How is it, then, that nature improves the mind? Evidently only as it contains thought. Mind can not commune with chaotic matter, but only with mind; and therefore the study of nature can improve the intellect only as we gain from it the thought of its Author. It would seem to be plain that nothing, whether a book, or a machine, or a work of art, or of nature, can be a profitable object of study, except for the thought it contains; and that when the whole of that thought is grasped by the mind, there can be no longer any improvement in the study of that object. And nature seems to be so constructed, in almost all her departments, (perhaps for the very purpose of training the intellect,) as to render it difficult to discover the controlling thought according to which they were constructed. On the surface, all seems confused and irregular; but as we penetrate deeper, perhaps by long processes of observation and induction, we find a principle of order and harmony running through all. What more confused, apparently, than the motions and appearances of the heavenly bodies? See, now, the ancient astronomer studying these appearances. How does he grope in the dark! How fanciful and inadequate are his hypotheses! Plainly, he is but groping after the true idea or thought of the system, as it lay in the mind of God. Give him this carried out into its details, and he has the science of astronomy completed. It has nothing more to say to him. So the heavens are constructed; so they move. Not less confused to the eye of man, for ages, was the vegetable creation; but at length, running like a line of light through all its species and genera, the true principle of classification was found. So it was in chemistry; so in geology, if, indeed, the true thought there be yet found.

It would appear, then, that nature is adapted to the intellect of man only, first, as it contains the thought of God; and, secondly, as it is so constructed as to stimulate and task the powers of the intellect in the attainment of that thought. Now, I have no right to assume, here, that the Bible contains the true thought of God; but I do say that its thoughts are not less grand and exciting than those of nature, and that there is between its construction and that of nature a singular analogy, as adapted to the intellect. There is the same apparent want of order and adjustment, and the same deep harmony, running through the whole. An individual truth, revealed in one age for a particular purpose, and, by itself, adapted to the use of man, lies imbedded here, and another there. By comparison, it is seen that they may come together, as bone to its fellow-bone, till, at length, the mammoth framework of a complete organization stands before us. Does the Bible contain a system of theology? Yes, a complete system; but it contains it as the heavens contain the system of astronomy. Its truths lie there in no logical order. They appear at first like a map of the apparent motions of the planets, whose paths seem to cross each other in all directions; but you have only to find the true centre, and the orbs of truth take their places, and circle around it like the stars of heaven. And I venture to say that the efforts of thought, the struggles of intellect, that have been called forth for the adjustment of this system, have done more for the human mind than its efforts in any other science. Its questions have stirred, not the minds of philosophers alone, but every meditative human soul. Does the Bible contain a system of ethics? Yes; but it is as the earth contains a system of geology; and long might the eye of the listless or unscientific reader rest upon its pages without discovering that the system was there,— just as men trod the earth for near six thousand years without discovering that its surface was a regular structure, with its strata arranged in an assignable order. And after we have reason to suppose there is a system, whether in nature or the Bible, we often find facts that seem to contradict each other, that can be reconciled only by the most patient attention; perhaps, in the present state of our knowledge, can not be reconciled at all. How strong, then, is the argument, drawn from this structure of the Bible, that it did not originate in the mind of man! The mind loves unity; it seeks to systematize every thing. It is in finished systems that great minds produce their works, never leaving truths, seemingly incompatible, lying side by side, and requiring or expecting us to adopt them both. But so does the Bible, and so does nature. Our conclusion, therefore, is that, if nature is adapted to the mind of man, so, and on the same principle, is the Bible.

A higher kind of knowledge given. — 6. Once more, Christianity is adapted to the intellect because it puts it in possession of a higher *kind* of knowledge than nature can give. It solves questions of a different order, and those, too, which man, as an intellectual being, most needs to have solved. There are plainly two classes of questions which we may ask concerning the works of God; and concerning one of these, philosophy is profoundly silent. One class respects the relation of the different parts of a constituted whole to each other and to that whole. The other respects the ultimate design of the whole itself. In the present state of science, questions of the first class can generally be answered with a good degree of satisfaction. Man existing, the philosopher can tell the number of bones, and muscles, and blood-vessels, and nerves, in his body, and the uses of all these. He may, perhaps, tell how the stomach digests, and the heart beats, and the glands secrete; but of the great purpose for which man himself was made, he can know nothing.

But this knowledge Christianity gives. It attributes to God a purpose worthy of him; one that satisfies the intellect and the heart; and the knowledge of this must modify our views of all history, and of the whole drama of human life. It gives us a new *stand-point*, from which we see every thing in different relations and proportions. We had seen the river, before, on which we were sailing; now we see the ocean. Entirely different must be the relation of man to God, both as an intellectual and a practical being, when he knows his plans and can intelligently coöperate with him. He now comes, in the language of our Saviour, into the relation of a friend. Surely no one can think lightly of the influence of this on the intellect!

Testimony of facts. — From the arguments now stated, we infer that Christianity is adapted to the intellect; and these arguments are confirmed by fact. No book, not nature itself, has ever waked up intellectual activity like the Bible. On the battle-field of truth, it has ever been around this that the conflict has raged. What book besides ever caused the writing of so many other books? Take from the libraries of Christendom all those which have sprung, I will not say indirectly, but directly from it, — those written to oppose, or defend, or elucidate it, — and how would they be diminished! The very multitude of infidel books is a witness to the power with which the Bible stimulates the intellect. Why do we not see the same amount of active intellect coming up, and dashing and roaring around the Koran? And the result of this activity is such as we might anticipate. The general intellectual, as well as moral superiority of Christian nations, and that, too, in proportion as they have had a pure Christianity, stands out in too broad a sunlight to be questioned or obscured. Wherever the word of God has really entered, it has given light — light to individuals, light to communities. It has favored literature; and by means of it alone has society been brought up to that point at which it has been able to construct the apparatus of physical science, and to carry its investigations to the point which they have now reached. The instruments of a well-furnished astronomical observatory presuppose accumulations of wealth, and the existence of a class of arts, and of men, that could be the product only of Christian civilization. Accordingly, we find, whatever may be said of literature, that physical science, except in Christian countries, has, after a time, either become stationary, or begun to recede; and there is no reason for supposing that the path of indefinite progress which now lies before it, could have been opened except in connection with Christianity. Individual men who reject Christianity, and yet live within the general sphere of its influence, may distinguish themselves in science; they have done so; but it has been on grounds and conditions furnished by that very religion which they have rejected. Christianity furnishes no new faculties, no direct power to the intellect, but a general condition of society favorable to its cultivation; and it is not to be wondered at, if, in such a state of things, men who seek intellectual distinction solely, rejecting the moral restraints of Christianity, should distinguish themselves by intellectual effort.

Objection.—But if there is this adaptation of Christianity to the intellect, ought not those who are truly Christians to distinguish themselves above others in literature and science? This does not follow. Up to a certain point, Christianity in the heart will certainly give clearness and strength to the intellect; and cases are not wanting in which the intellectual powers have been surprisingly roused through the action of the moral nature, and of the affections, awakened by the religion of Christ. But when we consider that the change produced by Christianity is a moral change; that the objects it presents are moral objects; that it presents this world as needing not so much to be enlightened in the more abstract sciences, or to be delighted with the refinements of literature, as to be rescued from moral pollution, and to be won back to God; — perhaps we ought not to be surprised if it has caused many to be absorbed in labors of an entirely different kind, who would otherwise have trodden the highest walks of science.

Distinguished piety not unfavorable to intellectual cultivation. — And here, precisely at this point, I think we may see how an impression has been originated in the minds of some that distinguished piety is even unfavorable to the highest cultivation of the sciences and arts and to refinement of taste. If this were so, — as it is not, — it would prove nothing against Christianity; nor would it invalidate at all the position I have taken, that it is favorable to the intellect. There are things more important than science, or literature, or taste. Nor is it in these that the true and the highest dignity of man consists. Perhaps Paul, if he had not been a Christian, might have shone as a philosopher. He did not become less a philosopher by being a Christian; but the energies of his mind were given neither to philosophy nor to literature, but to something far higher. In a noble forgetfulness of self, he strove to turn men "from darkness to light, and from the power of Satan unto God." And so, now, many of the finest spirits of our race are diverted from science by the practical calls and self-denying duties arising from the spiritual wants of the world. But does this dwarf the intellect? Far from it. It leads it to grapple practically with questions higher than those of science, though it may be not so as to gain the admiration of men;

and hence we often find in a humble Christian a breadth of mind which we should look for in vain in many professed votaries of literature. Can that dwarf the intellect which shows it realities more grand than those of science; which, with a full comprehension of the nature, and processes, and ends of science and of literature, yet gives them their rightful, though subordinate place? Never; even though it should sometimes lead to the general feeling expressed by one who said that he would attend to his more immediate duties here, and study the science of astronomy on his way up to heaven. No; men may do what they please in disseminating school libraries, and scattering abroad cheap publications; but, for energy and balance, I would rather have the intellect formed by the Bible alone, — by grappling with its mighty questions, by communing with its high mysteries, by tracing its narratives, by listening to its matchless eloquence and poetry, — than to have that formed by all the light and popular literature, and by all the scientific tracts, in existence; and if these efforts should practically exclude the Bible, and prevent a general and familiar acquaintance with it on the part of the young, instead of being a blessing, they would bring only disaster.

The Bible adapted to all. — Before leaving this subject, perhaps I ought to advert to the manner in which the teachings of the Bible are given, as a book adapted to the instruction of all classes, and of all ages. This, though a minor point, is one of great interest. In this respect, again, the Bible is like nature, and is indeed a most wonderful book. What a problem it would be to prepare a book now, which should be equally adapted to the young and to the old, to the learned and to the unlearned! Man could not do it. But such a book is the Bible. It has a simplicity, a majesty, a beauty, a variety, which fit it for all; and, as the eye of the child can see something in nature to please and instruct it, while the philosopher can see more, and yet not all, — so does the youngest and most ignorant person, who can read its pages, find, in the Bible, narratives, parables, brief sayings, just suited to his comprehension; while the profoundest theologian, or the greatest philosopher, can never feel that he has sounded all its depths. And here we may perhaps see one great reason why the revelation of God was written by so many different persons, at different times, and with such different habits of thought and of feeling. It was because it was intended to be a book for the instruction of the race, and this it could not be if it were written in any one style, or were stamped with the peculiarities of any one human mind. In order to this, it must embrace narratives, poetry, proverbs, parables, letters, profound reasoning, — which, while they all harmonized in doctrine and in spirit, should yet be as diversified as the hills and valleys of the green earth; should yet refract the pure light of inspiration in colors to catch and fix every eye. Wonderful book! If some of its parts seem to *us* less interesting, let us remember that nature too has many departments, and that it was made for all; and the more we study it in this point of view, the more ready shall we be to join with the apostle in saying, that "*all* scripture is given by inspiration of God."

We say, then, that Christianity is adapted to the intellect, because its spirit coincides with that of true philosophy; because it removes the incubus of sensuality and low vice; because of the place it gives to truth; because it demands free inquiry; because its mighty truths and systems are brought before the mind in the same way as the truths and systems of nature; because it solves higher problems than nature can; and because it is so communicated as to be adapted to every mind.

Christianity adapted to the affections. — But, if Christianity is adapted to the intellect, as a religion of light, it is not less adapted to the affections, as a religion of love. The affections are that part of our being from which we are most susceptible of enjoyment and of suffering. They are the source of all disinterested action, of all cheerful and happy obedience. They are, to the other faculties of man, what the light is to the body of the sun, what its leaves and blossoms are to the tree; and the system in which they are not regarded, and put in their proper place, can not be from God.

Affections — how elicited. — The affections, as we all know, are not under the immediate control of the will; that is, we can not love any object we choose, simply by willing to love it. We may act toward an unworthy being — a tyrant, for example — as if we loved him; but, unless we see in him qualities really excellent and lovely, it is impossible we should love him. The natural affections, so far as they are instinctive, have their own laws. Laying them, then, aside, the first condition on which it is possible for us to love a moral being, as such, is a perception of some excellence in his character. If we are rightly constituted, we shall love him on the perception of such excellence, whether he has any particular relation to us or not. But the whole strength of our affections can be elicited only when goodness is manifested toward us individually. That which should call forth our strongest affections would evidently be a being of perfect moral excellence, putting forth effort and sacrifice on our behalf. To be adapted to the affections, then, any system must first recognize and encourage them; and, secondly, it must present suitable objects to call them forth.

Support in trials. — I observe, then, first, that Christianity is adapted to the affections, because it encourages and supports them in the relations and trials of the present life. And here, perhaps, I ought to mention that the domestic constitution, which Christianity, and that alone, enjoins and maintains in its purity, is fundamental to a pure and healthful state of the natural and social affections. It is impossible there should be, under any other system or conditions, the same conjugal, and parental, and filial affection as there will be when the domestic constitution, as enjoined by Christianity, is strictly regarded. Here we see the far-reaching wisdom of Christ in casting up an inclosure, the materials of which we now see were provided in the nature of things, which should be to the affections as a walled garden, where their tendrils and blossoms might put forth secure from any intruder. Accordingly, who can estimate the blessings of peace, and purity, and hallowed affection, which have been enjoyed through this constitution, and which are now enjoyed around ten thousand firesides in every Christian land? But, besides this, Christianity encourages directly the natural affections of kindred and of friendship; it never condemns grief as a weakness; and it affords the most effectual consolation when these relations are sundered by death. In this respect, it is contrasted not only with the selfish Epicureanism and sensual indulgences by which the heathen became "without natural affection," but especially with the proud spirit of Stoicism — a spirit far from having become extinct with the sect. Stoicism would fain elevate human nature, but it really dismembers it. It was an attempt to destroy that which they knew not how to regulate. To do this, they were obliged to deny their own nature, and to affect insensibility, when it was impossible that man should not feel. It was, indeed, a hard task which this system imposed, — to feel the cold hand of death grasping those warm affections which are so deeply rooted in the heart, and withering them up, and tearing them away, and yet shed no tear. They were driven to this because they could find no consolation in death. They knew not the rod, or Him who appointed it; but assumed an attitude of sullen defiance, and steeled themselves as well as they were able against the bolts of what they deemed a stern necessity. This system, indeed, was not favorable to the growth of the natural affections at all; and many who adhered to it refused to suffer them to expand, or to enter into any intimate alliances. But Christianity neither destroys those affections in which we find the beauty and the fragrance of existence, nor does it nourish those which must bleed, without furnishing a balm to heal the wound. It is indulgent to our weakness, and never sneers at the natural expression of sorrow. "Jesus wept." Surely, if we except our own death-bed, there is no place where we so much need support as at the death-bed of a friend, a wife, a child; and the religion or the system, the Stoicism or the Skepticism, which fails us there, is good for nothing. How desolate often the condition of those

> Who "to the grave have followed those they love,
> And on th' inexorable threshold stand;
> With cherished names its speechless calm reprove,
> And stretch into th' abyss their ungrasped hand"!

But just here it is that Christianity comes in with its strong supports. This it does, 1. By the sympathy which it provides; for it not only supposes those who are afflicted to weep, but it commands others to weep with them. 2. By teaching us that our afflictions are brought upon us, not by a blind fate, but by a wise and kind Parent. 3. By the blessed hopes which it enables us to cherish. We sorrow not as those who have no hope; "for, if we believe that Jesus died and rose again, even so them also which sleep in Jesus will God bring with him." 4. And by encouraging and enabling us to fix our affections upon a higher and better object. So long as we have something to love, the heart is not desolate. Christianity furnishes us with an object that can not fail us. It suffers the affections to shoot out their tendrils here upon the earth as vigorously as they may; but it trains them up, and trains them up, till it fixes them around the base of the eternal throne. Then, if these lower tendrils are severed, they do not fall to the dust to be trampled on, and wither, and decay, till our hearts die within us; they fix themselves the more firmly to their all-sufficient and never-failing support. It is easy to see that all these circumstances must make the valley of affliction far less dark than it once was. To the true Christian there is light all the way through it, there is light at the end of it.

Thus Christianity aims at no heights of Stoicism. It neither uproots nor dwarfs the affections, on the one hand, nor does it, on the other, leave them to the wild and aimless paroxysms of a hopeless sorrow; but it encourages their growth, and, in affliction, gives them the support which they need.

Presents an adequate object. — And this leads me to observe, secondly, that Christianity is adapted to the affections because it presents them with an object, upon which they can rest, that is infinite, perfect, and unchangeable. Here we find the transcendent excellence of this religion, in that it presents God as the object of our affections; and I know of nothing in it more amazing than the union that it presents, in God, of those infinite natural attributes which raise in the mind the highest possible emotions of awe and sublimity, — and of those holy moral attributes which cause the angels to vail their faces, — with the pity, and condescension, and love, which Christianity represents him as manifesting toward the guilty creatures of a day. Here was a difficult point. Beforehand, I should have thought it impossible that the infinite and holy God should so reveal himself, to a creature so insignificant and guilty as man, as to lead him to have confidence in him, and to look up and say, "My Father!" Yet so does Christianity reveal God. It is a revelation adapted, not to angels, but to just such a being as man, guilty, and having the distrust that guilt naturally engenders, yet seeking assurance that a God so holy, and so dreadful, and so infinitely exalted above him, could yet love him and be the object of his love. Certainly it abates nothing of the infinite majesty or purity of God. It enthrones him with the full investment of every high and holy attribute, and yet nothing can exceed the expressions of tenderness and compassion with which he seeks to win the confidence of his creatures. He is represented as having an unspeakable affection for the race of man; as watching over all in his universal providence; as the Father of the fatherless, and the widow's God and Judge; as strengthening men upon the bed of languishing, and making all their bed in their sickness; as hearing the groanings of the prisoner and the cry of the poor and needy, when they seek water and there is none, and their tongue faileth for thirst; as the God that hears the faintest whisper of true prayer; as the God upon whom we may cast all our cares, because he careth for us; the God who comforteth those that are cast down; who shall wipe away all tears from all faces; who is more ready to give to man the Holy Spirit (the greatest of all gifts) than earthly parents are to give good gifts to their children; who so loved the world that he gave his only-begotten Son, that whosoever believeth on him should not perish, but have eternal life. If such expressions, and such a pledge, do not satisfy men of the love of God, and lead them to him, nothing can. Well might the apostle say,

"He that spared not his own Son, but delivered him up for us all, how shall he not with him also freely give us all things!" Well might he invite men to "come boldly unto the throne of grace," that they may "obtain mercy and find grace to help in time of need." Nothing can be more tender or winning, more calculated to secure the confidence of men, more unspeakably touching and affecting, than the mode in which God is revealed to us in the gospel of his Son.

Holiness and happiness provided for. — But, in thus offering himself as the object of affection to man, we can not fail to see that God has made provision, in the very nature of things, both for his holiness and his happiness. It is impossible that we should truly love Him, without being conformed and assimilated to his character. The moment the first throb of affection is felt, that process must begin, spoken of by the apostle, where he says, "We all, beholding as in a glass the glory of the Lord, are changed into the same image from glory to glory, even as by the Spirit of the Lord." And when this process is once commenced, through the operation of the great principle that we become morally conformed to that which we contemplate with delight, it will go on to its consummation. Nor, if we can contemplate them separately, is provision less made in this way for happiness than for holiness — since the happiness derived from the affections must arise from their exercise, and since the highest conceivable happiness would arise from the perfect love of such a being as God. It is in this way only that God can become the portion of the soul; and thus he may become its infinite and only adequate portion. Let the affections rest upon a perfect being, and happiness, so far as it can be derived from them, will be complete; but when their object is not only perfect, but infinite and unchangeable, then is there provision both for perfect happiness, and for its perpetuity and augmentation forever.

God must be presented as an object of love. — Here, then, we find a mark which must belong to a religion from God. From our present knowledge of the faculties of man, and of their relations to each other, and of the conditions on which alone they can be improved and perfected, we see that a religion which is to elevate man, and make him either holy or happy, must present God as the object of love, and provide for the assimilation of the character of man to his character.

No other religion does this. — But what of this love do we find provided for, or possible, out of Christianity? Absolutely nothing. The love of God never entered as an element into any heathen religion; nor, with their conceptions of God, was it possible it should. The affections, as already stated, are drawn forth by moral excellence, especially when manifested in our behalf. Was it possible, then, on either of these grounds, that the Jupiter, or Pluto, or Bacchus, of old, should be *loved?* Were their moral characters even reputable? Did they ever make disinterested sacrifices for the good of men? Is it possible that the present Hindoos should love, on either of these grounds, any being or thing that is presented for their worship? According to the very constitution of our minds, it is impossible. The objects of worship are neither in themselves, nor in their relations to man, adapted to draw out the affections. Again, is it possible that the affections should be strongly moved by the God of the deist, who manifests himself only through general laws that bring all things alike to all, who never speaks to his creatures, or makes himself known as the hearer of prayer? I think not. Who ever heard of a devout deist? Who ever heard of one who was willing to spend his life in missionary labor for the good of others? It is not according to the constitution of the mind that such a system should awaken the affections. And what is true of these systems is true of every false system. All such systems leave the heart cold, and, accordingly, exert very little genuine transforming power over the life.

Love made the governing principle. — And this, again, leads me to observe, thirdly, that Christianity is adapted to the affections, from the place it assigns to *love* as the governing principle of action. Moral order requires obedience to God. But what is that obedience which can honor God and make him who renders it happy? Plainly, it is not a selfish, external obedience, which would be wicked; not an obedience from fear, — for all "fear hath torment;" but it can be only an intelligent and an affectionate obedience. Such an obedience would honor God, and make him who rendered it happy. There is in it no element of degradation or slavish subjection. On the contrary, as the whole intellect, and conscience, and heart, conspire together in such an act, performed with reference to the will of such a Being, it must elevate the mind. It is the only possible manner in which we can conceive a rational creature to act so as to honor God, and make himself happy; and, therefore, that system of religion which is so constructed, with reference to the human mind, as to produce intelligent and affectionate obedience in the highest degree, must be the true religion; and no other is possible. Now, we certainly can see that no heathen system can produce such obedience, and that the Christian system is adapted to produce it in the highest possible degree.

Its representation of a future state. — But I observe, once more, that Christianity is adapted to the affections from its representations of a future state. It does not, like Hindooism, or Pantheism, represent man as absorbed into the Deity, nor, like Mohammedanism, as engrossed in sensuality; but it represents heaven as a social state of pure and holy affection. It does not, indeed, tell us that we shall recognize there our earthly kindred, though it leaves us no ground to doubt this; but it tells us of a Father's house, and of the one family of the good who shall be gathered there, and to whom we shall be united in nearer bonds than those of earth. What possible representation could be better adapted to a being endowed with affections? — the one infinite Father and Redeemer of his creatures, and the united family of all the good!

The imagination. — We next proceed to the imagination. And I observe that Christianity is no less adapted to this than to the conscience, the intellect, or the affections. The imagination is a source of enjoyment, a spring of activity, and an efficient agent in molding the character; and any system may be said to be adapted to it which is calculated to give it the highest and purest enjoyment, and so to direct the activity which it excites as to mold the character into the finest form.

As a source of enjoyment. — Looking at the imagination simply as a source of enjoyment, that system will be best adapted to it which contains the most elements of beauty and sublimity, and which leaves for their combination the widest range. And in this respect, certainly nothing can exceed Christianity. There are no conceivable scenes of grandeur equal to those connected with the general judgment and the final conflagration of this world; no scenes of beauty like those connected with the new Jerusalem — with the abodes and the employments of those who shall be sons and heirs of God, and to whom the whole creation will be given, so far as it may be subservient to their enjoyment. And if the present scene is filled up with so much of beauty and sublimity, what imagination can conceive of the splendors of that world whose external decorations shall correspond with its spiritual glory? Let no one say, then, that Christianity would repress the imagination; or that God did not intend that imagination, and poetry, and the exertion of every faculty which brings with it what is beautiful and pleasing, should be connected with it. He did intend it; he has made provision for it, and that not in this life only. There will be poetry in heaven; its numbers will measure the anthems that swell there. There will be imagination there. This is no impertinent faculty, given, as some seem to suppose, only to be chided and repressed. No; its wing, however strong, will always find room enough in the illimitable universe and the unfathomed perfections of God.

As prompting to activity. —But it is chiefly of the imagination as prompting to activity that I would speak. "The faculty of imagination," says Stewart, "is the great spring of human activity, and the principal source of human improvement. As it delights in presenting to the mind scenes and characters more perfect than those which we are acquainted with, it prevents us from ever being completely satisfied with our present condition or with our past attainments, and engages us continually in the pursuit of some untried enjoyment, or of some ideal excellence." Again he says, "Tired and disgusted with this world of imperfection, we delight to escape to another of the poet's creation, where the charms of nature wear an eternal bloom, and where sources of enjoyment are opened to us suited to the vast capacities of the human mind. On this natural love of poetical fiction Lord Bacon has founded a very ingenious argument for the soul's immortality; and, indeed, one of the most important purposes to which it is subservient is to elevate the mind above the pursuits of our present condition, and to direct the views to higher objects." *

With this representation of the office and importance of this faculty I agree in the main; but, instead of a world of the poet's creation for it to range in, I would have one of God's creation. Certainly we can, by means of this faculty, form to ourselves models of individual excellence, and of what we may conceive to be a perfect state of things, which shall essentially guide our activity and affect our character and influence. But here, no less than in the intellect, does all experience show that we need to find the thought of God as a model and guide to this formative power. Left to itself, how many false standards of character has it set up! How many Utopian schemes has it originated! How little has it ever conceived of individual excellence, or of an ultimate and perfect state of things, worthy of God or having a tendency to exalt man! Witness the heathen gods and representations of heaven; the classic fables; the speculations of Plato, even, respecting a future state; the Hindoo mythology, and transmigration; and the Mohammedan paradise. These are to that future, and to that heaven which God has revealed, what the conjectures and systems of ancient astronomers were to the true system of the physical heavens. Not more do the heavens of true science exceed those imagined by man,—not more does the actual Milky Way, composed of a stratum of suns lying rank above rank, exceed that conception of it from which its name is derived,—than the glory of the millennial day, and the purity and grandeur of the Christian heaven, exceed any future ever imagined by man, and adopted as the basis of a religion invented by him. In both cases, in the moral no less than in the

* Elements, vol. i. chap. 7.

physical heavens, we need to have given us the outline as sketched by God, and then it is the noblest work of the imagination to fill it up.

Ideal excellence. — Christianity alone furnishes the model of a perfect manhood, and the true elements of social perfection; it alone furnishes to the imagination a representation of a perfect state on earth; and it unfolds the gates of a heaven, at whose entrance it can only stand and exclaim, "Eye hath not seen, nor ear heard, neither have entered into the heart of man, the things which God hath prepared for them that love him!" It is therefore perfectly adapted to the imagination, so far as that is a faculty which leads to activity by setting before us ideal excellence which we may attempt to realize in actual life.

How attained. — Before leaving this point, I may just say that Christianity does not, like systems of philosophy, present us with an ideal excellence without showing us how to attain it. The obedience of its precepts would realize the excellence it portrays; and it is a remarkable fact that thus, and thus only, can there be brought out, into the bold relief of actual life, the visions of those ancient prophets whose imaginations were fired by these scenes of grandeur and of beauty.

The conscience. — The excellence above spoken of could be realized only by obedience, under the guidance of an enlightened conscience. Is, then, Christianity adapted to quicken and exalt the action of the conscience?

Force of the argument. — This is a point of the first importance; for if it can be shown that the moral powers are quickened and perfected in proportion as the mind comes under the action of any system, that system must be from God. That a false system should tend to perfect the conscience in its discriminating, and impulsive, and rewarding, and punishing power, would be not only impossible, but suicidal. It would purge the eye to a quicker perception of its own deformities, and nerve the arm for its own overthrow. Other systems act upon men through prescription, through awe and reverence, through hope and fear, and not by commending themselves, as righteous, to every man's conscience, in the sight of God.

Provides a perfect standard. — But Christianity provides for quickening the conscience, first, by the perfect standard which it sets up. This is found in the character and law of God. In training the conscience, nothing can countervail the absence of a right standard. In every community, the tendency is to try actions by the public sentiment, the usages and customs of that community. These will vary according to the supposed interests of each; and in the use of such tests, conscience must remain in abeyance, and become dwarfed. It can be trained and perfected only by a full activity, in the light of a perfect law; and this is furnished by Christianity.

Doctrine of responsibility. — Secondly, Christianity is adapted to the conscience by its doctrine of responsibility. Than this, nothing can be more entire. As was said in the second lecture, the moral law, which Christianity imbosoms, is as universal and pervading as that of gravitation. Under it there can be no concealment, or evasion; for it reveals a future judgment, and an omniscient and righteous Judge. This must tend to a careful scrutiny of all moral acts, and so to the full activity and perfection of the conscience.

Sanctions and pardon. — Thirdly, Christianity is adapted to the conscience, on the one hand by the force of its sanctions, and on the other by its provision for pardon. These are brought together as equally manifesting that which is the central element of Christianity, and the source of its power over the moral nature. This is its intense regard for the moral quality of action. This being the centre and life of the system, it can not fail to give life.

Only needs to be applied. — It is thus that Christianity does all that we can conceive any system should do, to quicken and to perfect the powers of moral perception and of action. The adjustments of the system are made; they are perfect; it only needs to be applied. Accordingly, we find that an efficient and an enlightened conscience exists just in proportion to the prevalence of pure Christianity; and we must see that its full influence would banish moral evil as the sun disperses the darkness. It is by the light and strength drawn from Christianity itself that we are able to apply many of those tests which we now apply in judging of it; and the more fully we are under its influence, the more competent shall we be to apply such tests, and the more convincing will be the evidence derived from their application.

The will. — *Two modes of adaptation.* — It now only remains to speak of Christianity as adapted to the will. A system may be adapted to the will of man by flattering his pride, by taking advantage of his weaknesses, by indulging his corruptions; and in this sense false systems have been adapted to it with great skill. But, properly speaking, a system is adapted to the will of a rational and moral being when it is so constructed that it must necessarily control the will in proportion as reason and conscience prevail. This is a point of high importance, because, the will being that in man which is personal and executive, nothing is effected till this is reached; and the system which can not legitimately control this may have every other adaptation, and yet be good for nothing.

Provides for pardon and aid. — I observe, then, first, that Christianity is adapted to the will because it provides for the pardon of sin, and for divine aid in the great struggle in which it calls upon us to engage. I remarked, when speaking of the intellect, that Christianity was adapted to it because it relieved it from the incubus of vice. It is much in the same way that it acts here in reference to the will. The will of man never acts when the attainment of his object is absolutely hopeless; and a sense of pardoned sin, and a hope of divine aid, if not immediate motives, yet come in as conditions on which alone the will can be brought up to the great struggle of the Christian warfare. Without these, a mind truly enlightened would rest under a discouragement that would forever paralyze effort.

Adapted to the affections. — I observe, secondly, that Christianity is adapted to the will because it is adapted to the affections. I do not, as some have done, regard the will and the affections as the same. They are, however, intimately connected; and the affections being, as I have said, the only source of disinterested action and of happy moral obedience, it is evident that, just in proportion as any system takes a strong hold of them, it must be adapted to move the will. It is not enough to know our duty, and to wish to do it simply as duty. We need to have it associated with the impulses of the affections, with that love of God, and of man, implanted in the heart, which are the first and the second great moral precepts of Christianity, and which, where they reign, must induce a happy obedience.

Because of its sanctions. — I observe, thirdly, that Christianity is adapted to the will from the grandeur of those interests which it presents, and from its amazing sanctions. Here it is unrivaled. Here every thing takes hold on infinity and eternity. Here the greatness of man as a spiritual and an immortal being assumes its proper place, and throws into the shade all the motives and the interests of time. Its language is, "What shall it profit a man, if he shall gain the whole world, and lose his own soul; or what shall a man give in exchange for his soul?" It makes the will of God our rule; it places us under his omniscient eye; it points us forward to the tribunal of an omnipotent Judge, to a sentence of unmixed justice, and a reward of matchless grace. Nothing can be more alluring, on the one hand, or more terrific, on the other, than its descriptions of the consequences of human conduct. It speaks of "eternal life;" of being the "sons and heirs of God;" of a "crown of life;" of "an inheritance incorruptible, and undefiled, and that fadeth not away." It speaks, also, of "the blackness of darkness forever;" of "the worm that dieth not, and the fire that is not quenched." Laying aside, then, the affections, and looking solely at the direct motives of duty and of interest which it presents, surely no other system can be so adapted to move the will as this, when it is really believed.

Teachings not abstract. — I observe, finally, that Christianity is adapted to the will, and to the whole emotive nature of man, because its teachings respecting the character of God and human duty are not by general and abstract propositions, but by facts, and by manifestations in action. At this point Christianity is strongly contrasted with natural religion, and with every thing that tends towards pantheism. "It is indeed," says Erskine, "a striking, and yet an undoubted fact, that we are comparatively little affected with abstract truths in morality." "A single definite and intelligible action gives a vividness and a power to the idea of that moral character which it exhibits, beyond what could be conveyed by a multitude of abstract descriptions. Thus the abstract ideas of patriotism and integrity make but an uninteresting appearance when contrasted with the high spectacle of heroic worth which was exhibited in the conduct of Regulus, when, in the senate of his country, he raised his solitary voice against those humbling propositions of Carthage, which, if acquiesced in, would have restored him to liberty, and which for that single reason had almost gained an acquiescence; and then, unsubdued alike by the frantic entreaties of his family, the weeping solicitations of the admiring citizens, and the appalling terrors of his threatened fate, he returned to Africa, rather than violate his duty to Rome and the sacredness of truth." "In the same way, the abstract views of the divine character, drawn from the observation of nature, are, in general, rather visions of the intellect than efficient moral principles in the heart and conduct; and, however true they may be, are uninteresting and unexciting when compared with the vivid exhibition of them in a history of definite and intelligible action. To assist our weakness, therefore, and to accommodate his instructions to the principles of our nature, God has been pleased to present us a most interesting series of actions, in which his moral character, as far as we are concerned, is fully and perspicuously embodied."

So great is this difference, as ideas are presented in different modes, that an idea or a principle may be apparently received, and approved, in its abstract form, which shall not be recognized as the same when it takes the form of action. "A corrupt politician, for instance, can speculate on and applaud the abstract idea of integrity; but when this abstract idea takes the form of a man and a course of action, it ceases to be that harmless and welcome visitor it used to be, and draws on itself the decided enmity of its former apparent friend." "In the same way, many men will admit the abstract idea of a God of infinite holiness and goodness, and will even take delight in exercising their reason or their taste in speculating on the subject of his being and attributes; yet these same persons will shrink with dislike and alarm from the living energy which this abstract idea assumes in the Bible."* The great object of Erskine is to show, first, that there is this difference between ideas thus presented; and, secondly, that God has made in action such manifestations of himself as must, if they are believed, bring the character into conformity with his. Whatever we may think of the second proposition, there can be no doubt of the principle involved in the first; nor of the fact that the emotive nature of man is addressed, in accordance with it, both in the Old Testament and in the New. All that series of mighty acts which God performed in behalf of the Israelites — the deliverance from Egypt, the giving of the law, the passage through the wilderness and through Jordan — could not but affect their hearts and wills infinitely more than they could have been by any description of God, or by any mere precepts. Probably it was better adapted than any thing else could have been to give that people correct ideas of God, and to lead them to a full and joyful obedience of his commandments. And so the great fact of the New Testament, that "God so loved the world, that he gave his only-begotten Son," and the example of our Saviour, "who loved us and gave himself for us," have ever been among its most powerful and constraining motives. They have, in fact, been those without which no others would have been of any avail.

Whether, then, we consider its offers of pardon and of aid; its connection with the affections; the power of its direct motives; or its mode of appeal by facts and manifestations in action, — we see that Christianity is perfectly adapted to the will of man.

* Internal Evidence.

LECTURE VI.

ARGUMENT FIFTH, CONTINUED. DIVISION SECOND: CHRISTIANITY AS A RESTRAINING POWER.—ARGUMENT SIXTH: THE EXPERIMENTAL EVIDENCE OF CHRISTIANITY.—ARGUMENT SEVENTH: ITS FITNESS AND TENDENCY TO BECOME UNIVERSAL.—ARGUMENT EIGHTH: IT HAS ALWAYS BEEN IN THE WORLD.

MAN is a complex being. He has been called the microcosm, or little world, because, while he has a distinctive nature of his own, he is a partaker and representative of every thing in the inferior creation. In him are united the material and the spiritual, the animal and the rational. He has instincts, propensities, desires, passions, by which he is allied to the animals; he has also reason, conscience, free-will, by which he is allied to higher intelligences and to God. Hence the ends he is capable of choosing, and the principles by which he may be actuated, are very various. Body and soul, reason and passion, conscience and desire, often seem to be, and are, opposing forces, and man is left

> "In doubt to act or rest,
> In doubt to deem himself a god or beast,
> In doubt his soul or body to prefer."

"The intestine war of reason against the passions," says Pascal, "has given rise, among those who wish for peace, to the formation of two different sects. The one wished to renounce the passions, and be as gods; the other to renounce reason, and become beasts."

Excitement, guidance, restraint — difficulty of. — With this wide range of faculties, and consequent variety of impulses and motives, in the individual, and especially when we consider the variety of his social relations, we may well say that, if any problem was beyond human skill, it was the choice of ends, and the arrangement of means and motives, — the contrivance of a system of excitement, and guidance, and restraint, — which should harmonize these jarring elements, and cause every wheel in the vast machinery of human society to move freely and without interference. Accordingly, whether we look at the faculties excited, or at the ends to which they have been directed, or at the restraints imposed, we find in all human systems a great want of adaptation to the nature of man. *Excitement, guidance, restraint,* — these are what man needs; and a system which should so combine them as to lead him, in its legitimate influence, to his true perfection and end, would be adapted to his whole nature. I have already spoken of the power of Christianity to excite and to guide some of the principal faculties. I now proceed to make some observations upon it as a restraining power.

No natural principle to be eradicated. — There is no natural principle of action which requires to be eradicated, but there are many which require to be directed, subordinated, and restrained. There are principles of our nature, which conduce only to our well-being when acting within prescribed limits, which become the source of vice and wretchedness when those limits are overstepped. But to put the check upon each particular wheel, precisely at the point at which its motion would become too rapid for the movement of the whole, requires a skill beyond that of man.

The appetites — too much or too little restraint. — To fix, for example, the limits within which, for the best interests of the individual and of society, the appetites should be restrained, requires a knowledge of the human frame, and of the relations of society, which no philosopher, unenlightened by the Bible, has ever shown. I need not say how essential it is to the well-being of any community that these limits should be rightly fixed. If there is too much restraint, society becomes secretly, and often hopelessly, corrupt; to other sins the guilt of hypocrisy is added, and sanctimonious licentiousness — the most odious of all its forms — becomes common. If there is too little restraint, vice walks abroad with an unblushing front, and glories in its shame. The state of the ancient heathen world is described by the apostle in the first of Romans. The accuracy of that description is remarkably confirmed by testimony from heathen writers, and, according to the testimony of all impartial travelers, that chapter is true, to the letter, of the heathen of the present day. The tendency of human nature to sensuality, in some form, is so strong that no false religion has ever dared to lay its hand upon it, in all its forms. Mohammed, it is well known, did not interfere essentially with the customs of his country in this respect; and, in fact, all his rewards and motives to religious activity were based on an appeal to the sensitive, and not to the rational and spiritual part of man. In instances not a few, the grossest sensuality has been made a part of religion; and, in almost all cases, the voluptuary has been suffered to remain undisturbed, or has been led to commute, by offerings, for indulgence in vice.

Ascetic tendency. — Those, on the other hand, who have recognized the higher nature of man, and have felt that there was something noble in the subjugation of the animal part' of the frame, have been excessive.

Instead of regulating the appetites, they have attempted to exterminate them; and the mass of their followers have been ambitious, corrupt, and hypocritical. "Nothing," says Isaac Taylor, "has been more constant in the history of the human mind, wherever the religious emotions have gained a supremacy over the sensual and sordid passions, than the breaking out of the ascetic temper, in some of its forms; and most often in that which disguises virtue, now as a spectre, now as a maniac, now as a mendicant, now as a slave, but never as the bright daughter of heaven." *

Sensuality and self-torture. — But not only have men framed systems of religion which allowed of sensuality, — not only have they attempted to subdue the animal nature altogether, — they have also ingrafted sensuality upon self-torture. There is in man a sense of guilt; and, connected with this, the idea has been almost universal that suffering, or personal sacrifice, had, in some way, an efficacy to make atonement for it. Hence the costly offerings of heathen nations to their gods; hence their bloody rites, the offering up of human victims, and even of their own children. But when once the principle was established that personal suffering could do away sin, then a door was opened for license to sin; and hence the monstrous, and apparently inconsistent spectacle, so often witnessed, of sensuality walking hand in hand with self-torture.

The Christian method. — In opposition to these corruptions and distortions, how simple, how clearly in accordance with the original institutions and the evident intentions of God, are the principles of Christianity! Christ assumed no sanctity in indifferent things, such as that by which the Pharisees sought to distinguish themselves. He swept away, without hesitation or compromise, the rabbinical superstitions and slavish

---

* Lectures on Spiritual Christianity.

exactions which had been ingrafted on the Jewish law. He came "eating and drinking." He declared that that which entereth into a man doth not defile him. He sanctioned marriage, and gave it an honor and a sacredness little known before, by declaring it an institution of divine origin, which was appointed in the beginning. "The superiority of the soul to the body was the very purport of his doctrine; and yet he did not waste the body by any austerities! The duty of self-denial he perpetually enforced; and yet he practiced no factitious mortifications! This teacher, not of abstinence, but of virtue, — this reprover, not of enjoyment, but of vice, — himself went in and out, among the social amenities of ordinary life, with so unsolicitous a freedom as to give color to the malice of hypocrisy in pointing the finger at him, saying, 'Behold a gluttonous man and a wine-bibber; a friend of publicans and sinners!'"* But, while he did this, he did not yield at all to the prejudices and vices of the age, but forbade all impurity, even in thought. The teaching and course of the apostles was marked by the same wisdom. Paul asserts, in relation to meats, that every creature of God is good, and to be received with thanksgiving; and says of marriage, that it is honorable in all; while, at the same time, he ranks drunkenness, and gluttony, and impurity, among those sins which will exclude a man from the kingdom of heaven. He was a preacher of temperance, as well as of righteousness and of a judgment to come, and insisted upon that temperance in all things.

Malevolent and selfish passions. — Nor are the prohibitions and restraints of Christianity laid with less discrimination upon the malevolent and selfish passions, — as anger, malice, envy, revenge, of the first; and vanity, pride, and ambition, of the second. These, with the exception of anger, it absolutely prohibits;

* Lectures on Spiritual Christianity.

and it prohibits that, so far as it is malevolent. It distinguishes between the holy indignation which must be excited by wickedness, and any mere personal feeling, or desire to inflict pain for its own sake; and hence it speaks of Christ as looking on men "with anger, being grieved for the hardness of their hearts," and it commands us to " be angry and sin not."

To be prohibited. — Of the propriety of an absolute prohibition of the malevolent feelings, probably few at this day will doubt. They are dissocial, and are destructive alike of the happiness of him who indulges them and of those against whom they are indulged. It is impossible that a man, in whose breast they bear sway, should be happy; and, so far as their influence extends to others, they produce unhappiness of course. We can not conceive of them as entering heaven, which would no longer be heaven if they were there, nor of their having a place in a perfect society on earth.

Nor, if we analyze them fairly, can there be more room to doubt the propriety of prohibiting what I have called the selfish passions — as vanity, pride, and ambition. Vanity, notwithstanding the commendation of it by Hume as a virtue, will be condemned by all as weak, if not wicked; and if we regard pride and ambition as the love of superiority for its own sake, and of ruling over others, we must see that they are both selfish and mischievous. By confounding pride with true dignity, and ambition with the love of excellence, some have been led to suppose that these were necessary elements in an efficient and elevated character. But Christianity fully recognizes the distinction between these qualities; and while it asserts, far beyond any other system, the true dignity of man, — while it sets before him the pursuit of an excellence, and the objects of an ambition, which must call forth every energy, though their attainment implies no inferiority on the part of others, — it prohibits, and, by its doctrines and very structure, eradicates every selfish element of what are usually called pride and ambition. It is, indeed, a great distinction and glory of Christianity, that its objects of pursuit and its sources of enjoyment are like the sunlight and the air, which are free to all; and that the highest attainments of one have no tendency to diminish the happiness of others.

The desire of property. — I mention another strong principle of action — the desire of property, which Christianity regulates wisely. Recognizing the inadequacy of property to meet the wants of a spiritual being, it prohibits covetousness as idolatry, and exhorts the rich not to trust in uncertain riches, but in the living God. At the same time it forbids indolence, requiring industry and frugality; and when, by means of these, or by any other means, property is acquired, it commands us to do good, to be "ready to distribute, willing to communicate." He that stole is to steal no more, but is to labor, working with his hands, that he may have to *give* to him that needeth. Thus would Christianity transform every lazy, thievish pest of society into an industrious, useful, and liberal man. It is also worthy of remark how careful Christianity is to guard its ministers against the love of money, and how entirely free it is, as we find it in the New Testament, from holding out any inducement to the people to build up rich and pompous religious establishments. Its ministers are to take the oversight of the flock, not for filthy lucre, but of a ready mind. In instructing both Timothy and Titus whom to ordain, Paul mentions the love of "filthy lucre" as a disqualification. And while such a motive on the part of the minister is prohibited, and would be contrary to the entire spirit of Christianity, it never speaks of the giving of money to him as *peculiarly* meritorious. It provides for his support, and makes provision for that, simply, a common duty. Its exhortations would all lead men to works of general beneficence, — to give to him that *needeth*, whoever he may be, — and would thus cause money to become a means of spiritual culture to him who has it, as well as of blessing to him to whom it is given.

Three remarks. — *Prohibitions on the source of acts.* — I need not speak further of the particular things which Christianity prohibits and regulates. Respecting them all, three remarks, of much importance, are to be made. The first is, that these prohibitions are laid, not upon the outward act, but, in all cases, upon the spirit or temper from which outward acts spring. Nothing can be more evident than that Christianity legislates for man as a spiritual being, and the subject of a kingdom in which every secret thought is known, and every malicious, and covetous, and impure desire is a crime. This has often been mentioned as a proof of the wisdom and superiority of the Christian system of morals, because the only possible way of regulating the external act is to regulate the spirit. But, however wise and necessary this might be in a system of morals, it was not adopted by Christianity as a system of morals, but because it recognizes man as a member of a spiritual kingdom, in which volition itself is action, and character itself, and not its outward manifestation, is the object of legislation. It is far enough from striking at the principle of wickedness because this is necessary to restrain the outward act; but because it deals with realities, and not with appearances, and is at war with wickedness itself, which has no existence in act as distinguished from its principle.

A religion of principles. — The second remark, intimately connected with the first, is, that Christianity, considered as prohibitory, is not a religion of mere precepts, but of principles. "The New Testament," says Taylor, "contains vital principles; not always defined; but which, as they are evolved one after another, and are successively brought to bear upon the opinions and manners of Christianized nations, do actually remove from them those flagrant evils which had accumulated in the course of time, and which, so long as they are prevalent, abate very much the religious sensibilities even of those who are the most conscientious." He says, further, "that the New Testament, considered as embodying a system of morals for the world, — a system which is slowly to develop itself, until the human family has been led by it into the path of peace and purity, — effects this great purpose, not by prohibiting, in so many words, the evils it is at length to abolish, but by putting in movement unobtrusive influences, which nothing, in the end, shall be able to withstand." * It is thus that Christianity has wrought the revolution in favor of woman; that it abolished the ancient games and gladiatorial contests; that it has mitigated the horrors of war; that it has, over a large portion of the earth, abolished slavery, and that it is now hastening to bring it to a full end. This peculiarity of Christianity gives it a power of expansion, and of adaptation to all circumstances, which fits it for man as man.

Prohibits only as it excites and guides. — The third remark is, that Christianity is a system of prohibition and restraint only as it is a system of excitement and guidance. Plainly, there are two kinds of self-denial: the one from fear — formal, slavish, barren; the other from love — blessing the spirit, and strengthening it in virtue. So far as Christianity requires self-denial, it is uniformly and only of this latter kind. It does not call men off from the world, that they may sit sullenly by and envy others the pleasures which they can not share.

* Lectures on Spiritual Christianity.

If it calls them at all, it calls them to something higher, purer, nobler, happier. Its self-denial is that of a son who is laboring for the support and comfort of a mother; of a mother who denies herself that she may educate a son; of a soldier who is marching on to do battle for liberty; of a racer who is speeding to the goal. It is the self-denial of the great Howard, traversing Europe, and diving into dungeons to "take the gauge of human misery," with his heart too much interested in this service to spend much time even to look at the masterpieces of art. And who will say that he did not find a satisfaction higher, and more consonant to his nature, than any work of art could have given? Christianity excludes man from no enjoyment that is compatible with his highest good. It can not, indeed, reconcile incompatibilities. It can not make a man a soldier on duty, and let him be at the same time enjoying himself by his fireside; it can not make him a racer, and at the same time permit him to sit down at his ease by the side of the course. It does call men to be soldiers, but it is in the army of the Captain of their salvation; it does make them racers, but it sets before them an immortal crown. Utterly do they misapprehend the religion of Christ who regard it as gloomy and austere — as a system of formal prohibitions and restraints. No; its self-denial is from love. It is a system of prohibition and restraint only as it is a system of excitement and guidance. Let Christians be fully inspired with the great positive ideas and motives of their religion, and it is impossible there should be in their deportment any thing austere, or sanctimonious, or gloomy, more than there was in the deportment of Christ and of his apostles. It is only under the influence of self-denial from love that the highest character can be formed.

Balance of motives. — Nor, in speaking of Christianity

as a system of excitement and restraint, ought we to omit its wonderful balance of motives, and the manner in which every weak point is guarded. Of particular instances of this I have spoken incidentally; but the system is full of them. Thus, in the case recently mentioned, while a selfish pride is guarded against and destroyed, the true dignity of man is secured; while the ambition of superiority and comparison is repressed, the ambition of excellence is cherished; while the deepest reverence toward God is demanded, it is made compatible with an affectionate and filial confidence; while humility, that virtue so peculiarly Christian, is promoted, there is no approach toward meanness or servility. It is "sorrowful, yet always rejoicing;" it requires active beneficence, yet represses all self-gratulation; it insists strongly on the duties of piety and of devotedness to God, but it excludes mysticism and monachism, by insisting equally upon our duties to man; it inculcates universal benevolence, but weakens no tie of family or of country.

Christian manhood and Christian society. — If, then, there is this adaptation of Christianity to man; if it is adapted to his conscience, his intellect, his affections, his imagination, his will, — exciting and guiding them aright; if it represses only evil, and that at its source; if its motives are wonderfully balanced, so that the character produced by them would be one of great loveliness and symmetry, — then it will follow that it must carry the individual to the highest state of perfection, not simply as a Christian, but as a man. There are, indeed, manly traits which are not distinctively Christian; but no man can become a Christian without becoming a better man, or can improve as a Christian without improving in manhood, and the ideal of true manhood will find its completion only in the perfection of the Christian character. And what is thus true of the individual must, for that very reason, be true of the community. If we may suppose Christianity to have done its work upon all the individuals of a community, they would be like the stones and the beams prepared by the workmen of Solomon in the mountains, and would be ready to go up into the magnificent temple of a perfect society, without the sound of the ax or the hammer. And, moreover, the same process which would perfect individuals as such, and at the same time fit them to coalesce in an harmonious society here, would, of course, fit them for that perfect state of society which is represented as existing in heaven. In this respect, Christianity commends itself to our reason. It does not, like other religions, care for rites, and forms, and ceremonies, except as they bear upon character. It lays down no arbitrary rules, to the observance of which it offers a reward in the form or on the principle of wages, but it goes to form a definite character; and we can see that the *character* it forms is precisely such as must be a preparation for the *heaven* which it promises. It speaks of a holy heaven, and its great object is to make men holy here that they may be fit to enter there. This is its great object; but, in doing this, it would bring the individual man, considered as an inhabitant of the earth, to the highest perfection, and would adjust, in the best possible manner, the relations of society.

Would accomplish all that can be accomplished. — This is a point upon which I insist that we are competent to judge. It is a vital point to all who would do any thing to advance society beyond its present state. We know something of man; and we certainly can tell what would be the effects upon the individual, and upon society, if the law laid down in the Bible — the great law of love — were universally obeyed, and if the principles there insisted on were universally regarded.

We know what the representation of heaven is, as made in the Bible, and we certainly can tell whether the following of Christ would be a natural and necessary preparation for such a state. My object has been to compare Christianity with the nature of man; to observe their adjustments to each other, and to see what that nature would become, if yielded wholly to its influence. And if, imperfectly as this has been done, I yet find that the powers of the individual man come forth, in their true strength and proportion, only under its influence; if I find that there can be no perfect state of society except in accordance with its laws; if I see that it would fit man for a heaven of purity and love, involving the highest activity and fullest expansion of every power,—then I am prepared to say that, if this religion be not from God, it must yet be true; and that, if God should reveal a religion, it could neither propose nor accomplish any thing higher or better.

ARGUMENT VI.
THE EXPERIMENTAL EVIDENCE OF CHRISTIANITY.

I have now brought to a conclusion the argument from a comparison of Christianity with the constitution of man. There is another, usually termed the experimental evidence of Christianity, which is intimately connected with this; for, if this religion is indeed adapted to act thus fully and powerfully upon the mind, it can not but be that he who yields himself to its influence, will find, growing out of that very influence, a deeply-wrought conviction of its wisdom, and of its adaptation to his nature and wants. Of the validity of this argument there have been various opinions. Some have objected to it altogether, as fanatical; while others have supposed that it might be valid for the Christian himself, but neither ought to be, nor could be, any ground of conviction for another. What, then, is the nature of this argument? What ought to be its force, first, upon the minds of Christians, and, secondly, upon the minds of others? An answer to these inquiries would exhaust the subject.

Nature of the argument. — What, then, is the nature of this argument, and the consequent force which it ought to have upon the mind of the Christian himself? The Christian contends that he has a knowledge of Christianity, and a conviction of its truth, which he did not acquire by reasoning, and which, therefore, reasoning can not, and ought not, to shake. Can he have such a knowledge and conviction in a rational way? By confounding reasoning with reason, many have been led to suppose that we could have no rational conviction of any thing which we could not prove by reasoning. Than this no mistake could be greater; for a very large part of our knowledge is neither acquired by reasoning nor dependent on it. This is so with all the intuitions of reason, and with all the knowledge acquired by sensation and by experience. The very condition of knowledge at all is a direct power of perception; and where this does not exist, there can be no reasoning. Thus, no one can know what it is to live, but by living; what it is to see, but by seeing; what it is to feel, but by feeling; nor, in general, can any one know what it is *to be* any thing, but by *becoming* that thing. Direct knowledge, thus gained, is the condition of all reasoning, and it is not within the proper province of reasoning to call it in question. The knowledge is not gained by reasoning, but it is in the highest degree rational to admit it and act upon it. The question is, whether there is a knowledge of Christianity which is obtained in this way; whether, in order to be a Christian, a man is simply to believe something, or whether he is to become something.

Essential to the system. — And here I observe that,

if Christianity be true, there must be such a knowledge. It claims to be, not a mere system of rites and forms, nor a system of philosophical belief, but a *life;* and, if so, that life can be known only by living it; if so, there must be gained, by living it, immediate perceptions and experimental knowledge, such as we gain by living our natural life. Without these it would be merely a form, or a creed in the understanding, or an external rule — something dead and formal; and not as "a well of water springing up into everlasting life." Without these, it is impossible that the words of Christ should be "spirit and life."

Moral and physical maladies. — The analogy is often drawn in this respect, and, so far as I can see, properly, between Christianity, as a remedy for the moral maladies of man, and remedies for bodily disease. It is plain that he who takes a remedy for bodily disease may have an evidence and conviction of its efficacy entirely independent of any testimony or reasoning, and more convincing than either or both of these could give. He may try the remedy in such a variety of forms, may so watch the symptoms as he takes or omits it, that he can have no more doubt of its effect than he has of the rising and setting of the sun. Here is something which comes within the province of consciousness and of direct knowledge, and it is in vain that you attempt to destroy a conviction thus produced. You may tell him that he is not sick, and never was; that the dose was minute, or the medicine inert, and therefore could not have done him any good; but he may have had experience of such a kind that it would be practically irrational, and the height of folly, for him to lay aside his medicine on the ground of any reasoning, or previous estimate of probabilities. And so, when the mind is awakened to the realities of its spiritual condition, if, as the conscience is quickened and the moral eye is purged, it is perceived that there is a wonderful correspondence between the discoveries which a man makes concerning himself and the delineations of the heart which he finds in the Bible; if this correspondence is the same in kind with that which he finds in the writings of those who have best described human character, but is more perfect; if it is such that an uncultivated man, to whom the Bible becomes a new book, may well say, as one recently did say, "I see now that a man's history may be written before he was born;" if he finds in himself wants, hungerings and thirstings of spirit, for which Christianity, and nothing else, makes provision, and feels that that provision is precisely adapted to his wants; if he finds himself engaged in a conflict for which Christianity furnishes the only appropriate armor; if he obtains answers to prayer, and finds grace to help in time of need, so that his evil tendencies are overcome and his virtues are strengthened, — then it would be no more rational for him to doubt the truth of the Christian religion than to doubt the testimony of his senses. Of such correspondences between his heart and the Bible, of such wants and their supplies, of such helps and of such conquests, we might naturally suppose the Christian would have an experimental knowledge, if Christianity be true; and I venture to say that no religion could do for man what Christianity proposes to do without furnishing to those under its influence this kind of evidence.

Christianity promises it. — And not only might we rationally expect such a ground of conviction, but Christianity itself, understanding its own nature and the grounds on which it would be believed in, promises to give it to all who will put themselves in a position to avail themselves of it. "If any man," says Christ, "will do his will, he shall know of the doctrine."

"He," says John, "that believeth on the Son of God, hath the witness in himself." "The Spirit itself," says Paul, "beareth witness with our spirit that we are the children of God." This evidence Christianity regards as indispensable. It counts itself to have done nothing till this is given. Till then, it is like the physician who stands by the bedside and exhibits the evidences of his skill, but accomplishes nothing, if the patient so dislikes the remedy that he prefers to suffer the pain, and risk the consequences of the disease, rather than to take that remedy. Here, indeed, is the great point of difficulty. It is not so much that men are not speculatively convinced of the truth of Christianity, as that they defer applying it to themselves, and thus fail of the highest of all possible grounds of conviction — that of experience.

Possessed by all Christians. — And as this evidence might be anticipated from the nature of the case, and is promised in the Scriptures, so we find it possessed by all true Christians, though in a degree by no means proportioned to their learning or talents, but to the sincerity of their faith and the fullness of their obedience. Hence, unlike those species of evidence which require learning, it is open to all, and forms, for Christians of every age and of every variety of attainment, a ground of conviction, which they do not perhaps state as an argument, but which is rational, and satisfactory to all. To the philosopher it is satisfactory, because he can trace it up to its principles, and can feel that, in resting on it, he is resting on precisely the same kind of evidence which commands assent in all other cases of consciousness; and it is not less satisfactory to the unlettered man through that healthy assent, unaccompanied by any reflex act of the mind, by which we gain all our primary knowledge. "Merely literary men," says Wilson, taking the thought from Verplanck, "are slow to admit that vulgar minds can have any rational perception of truths involving great and high contemplation. They overlook the distinction between the nice analysis of principles, the accurate statement of definitions, logical inferences, and the solution of difficulties, and *the structure of our own thoughts and the play of the affections.* They discern not between the theory of metaphysical science and the first truths and rational instincts which are implanted in the breasts of all, and which prepare them to see the glory of the gospel, to feel its influence, and to argue from both for the divinity of Christianity. The one is an elevating employment of the intellect; the other, the germs and seeds of all intellectual and moral knowledge, which lie dormant till they are called forth by occasions, and then burst forth into life and power." *

Ground of martyrdom. — And this evidence, being thus universal, shows us the true reason of that hold which Christianity has upon the minds of men, and of the place which it holds in the earth as a leavening and extending power. It is through this that the weak are made strong and the timid brave; that persons of every description have become martyrs, equally in the first freshness and power of the religion, and near the seat of its origin, and, in these last days, in the remote island, and among the semi-barbarous people, of Madagascar. I know it is said that all religions can claim their martyrs, and that for a man to die for his religion only shows that he is sincere, and not at all the truth of the religion. But it seems to me that the Christian religion is peculiar in this respect, on the ground we are now considering, and that its martyrdoms do show something more. As between *Christian* sects, martyrdom can, indeed, show nothing concerning the truth of particular tenets; and it may be doubted whether other

* Wilson's Evidences.

religions have had their martyrs, in the strict sense of that word. In confirmation of what other religion can it be shown that any considerable number of persons have laid down their lives solely from their belief in the religion, unconnected with ambition, or the revolution of parties? I know of none. What other religion could go to the Island of Madagascar, and, not only without any temptation of honor or gain, but in opposition to every motive of this kind, and to the entreaties of friends, could induce persons to change their religion, and then lead them, solely for the sake of the new religion, to wander about destitute, afflicted, tormented, and finally to lay down their lives? And here we see only the operation of the same principle that led persons of all descriptions, under the Roman emperors, to submit to the loss of all, and to martyrdom. Such martyrs, — the most enlightened philosophers and scholars, multitudes of the common people, women, and even children, evidently upheld by the same convictions, — I contend, are peculiar to the Christian religion. The history of the world can show nothing like them; and whoever will consider them candidly, must confess that they show, not merely the sincerity of those who suffered, but the adaptation of the religion to take a deep hold of the human mind, and its power to produce conviction, in the manner of which I am now speaking. In this power we rejoice. We point it out to the infidel. We say to him that, as long as this power remains, his warfare against Christianity must be in vain. We tell him that he may argue, may ridicule, may scoff; may think, with the mild Pliny, that "such inveterate obstinacy ought to be punished;" and he may persecute and kill; — but that he can never cause the true Christian to yield his faith, or prevent the working of those secret but mighty affinities by which he becomes more attached to it than to kindred, or wealth, or life.

Satisfactory to Christians. — If, then, this evidence is of a nature so unexceptionable; if it is promised in the Scriptures; if we find such evidence of it in the lives of Christians, — we may well conclude that it must be, to *them*, a rational and satisfactory ground of conviction that the religion is true.

Should be to others. — But the unbeliever may say, This may be all very well for the Christian himself, but it can be no evidence to me. Let us see, then, whether it would be no evidence to a candid man; whether an attempt is not made in this, as in so many other cases, to judge of religion in a way and by a standard different from those adopted in other things. To me it seems that the simple question is, whether this kind of evidence is good for the Christian himself; for if it is, then the candid inquirer is as much bound to take his testimony as he is to take that of a man who has been sick, respecting a remedy that has cured him. If a large number of persons, whose testimony would be received on any other subject, should say that they had been cured of a fever by a particular remedy, there is no man who would say that their testimony was of no account in making up his mind respecting that remedy, though he had not himself had the experience upon which the testimony was founded. If it is said that the evidence to the Christian himself is not well founded, and is fanatical, very well. Let that point be fairly settled. But if it be a good argument for him, then we ask that his *testimony* should be received on this subject as it would be on any other. The testimony is that of many witnesses; and I am persuaded that a fair examination of facts, and a careful induction, after the manner of Bacon, would settle forever the validity of this argument, and the proper force of this testimony. Every circumstance conspires to give it force. It is only from its truth that we can account for its surprising uniformity,

I may say identity, in every age, in every country, and when given by persons of every variety of talent and of mental culture. Compare the statements given, respecting the power of the gospel, by Jonathan Edwards, by a converted Greenlander, a Sandwich Islander, and a Hottentot, and you will find in them all a substantial identity. They have all repented, and believed, and loved, and obeyed, and rejoiced; they all speak of similar conflicts, and of similar supports. And their statements respecting these things have the more force, because they are not given as testimony, but seem rather like notes, varying, indeed, in fullness and power, which may yet be recognized as coming from a similar instrument touched by a single hand. If I might allude here to the comparison, by Christ, of the Spirit to the wind, I should say that in every climate, and under all circumstances, that divine Agent calls forth the same sweet notes whenever he touches the Æolian harp of a soul renewed. And this uniform testimony does not come as a naked expression of mere feeling; it is accompanied with a change of life, and with fruits meet for repentance, showing a permanent change of principle. This testimony, too, is given under circumstances best fitted to secure truth — given in affliction, in poverty, on the bed of death. How many, how very many, have testified in their final hour to the sustaining power of the gospel! And was there ever one, did any body ever hear of one, who repented, at that hour, of having been a Christian? Why not, then, receive this testimony? Will you make your own experience the standard of what you will believe? Then we invite you to become a Christian, and gain this experience. Will you be like the man who did not believe in the existence of Jupiter's moons, and yet refused to look through the telescope of Galileo for fear he should see them? Put the eye of faith to the gospel, and if you do not see new moral heavens, I have nothing more to say. Will you refuse to believe that there is an echo at a particular spot, to believe that the lowest sound can be conveyed around the circuit of a whispering gallery, and yet refuse to put your ear at the proper point to test these facts? Put your ear to the gospel, and if you do not hear voices gathered from three worlds, I have nothing more to say. Will you refuse to believe that the colors of the rainbow are to be seen in a drop of water, and yet not put your eye at the angle at which alone they can be seen? Or, if you think there is nothing analogous to this in moral matters, — as there undoubtedly is, — will you hear men speaking of the high enjoyment they derive from viewing works of art, and think them deluded and fanatical till your taste is so cultivated that you may have the same enjoyment? Surely, nothing can be more unreasonable than for men to make their own experience, in such cases, a standard of belief, and yet refuse the only conditions on which experience can be had.

Conclusion. — I have thus endeavored to show, first, that there is in Christianity a self-evidencing power, and that the experimental knowledge of a Christian is to him a valid ground of belief; and, secondly, that a fair-minded man will receive his testimony respecting that knowledge as he would respecting the colors in a drop, or the echo at a particular point, or the pleasures of taste, or any other experience which he had not himself been in a position to gain.

ARGUMENT VII.
FITNESS AND TENDENCY OF CHRISTIANITY TO BECOME UNIVERSAL.

There is one argument more, intimately connected with the adaptation of Christianity to the constitution of man, to which I now proceed. A fitness and tendency to become universal must be discernible in a religion coming from God, and claiming to be given for the race; and if there is the adaptation for which I have contended, then Christianity must have this fitness and tendency.

What it is not — its object as related to human institutions. — The fitness, however, of Christianity to become universal, arises as much from what it is not as from what it is, and can be fully appreciated only by looking at the relation of its object to all human institutions. That object is a moral object, with no taint of any thing earthly about it; and, in pursuing it, Christianity keeps itself entirely aloof from all political and local questions. It regards man solely as a moral and spiritual being, under the government of God; and its object, distinctly announced from the first, is to save men from the consequences of transgression under that government. "His name shall be called Jesus," said the angel, "for he shall save his people *from their sins;*"— not from the Roman yoke — not primarily from any earthly evil — but from their sins. Upon this one object Christianity steadily keeps its eye. The Son of man came "to seek and to save that which was lost." It is simply a system of salvation from sin, and its consequences under the government of God; and whatever may be his age, or language, or country, or the form of government under which he lives, it is equally adapted to every child of Adam who is led to ask the question, "What must I do to be saved?" It comes with pardon and hope to every one who feels the guilt of sin, or who is subject to bondage through fear of death. There are certain great moral interests which are common to the race, — certain chords in the human heart which vibrate whenever they are struck; and it is remarkable that Christianity concerns itself only with those interests, and strikes only those chords. It has to do with individuals as guilty under the government of God, without respect to their earthly relations; and hence it has the power to enter in as a new element, and to pervade and enlighten every form of society, as the sunlight enters into and pervades the body of the atmosphere. Hence, in its original diffusion, regarding man simply as man, it swept as freely as the breeze of heaven past all territorial and national limits. All other religions are adapted to particular climates; are upheld, like that of the Jews, by association with particular places; but, since Christ has entered into the true tabernacle above, incense and a pure offering may go up from every place. All other religions are connected with the government, and we have no evidence that without such connection they could be sustained. But "Christianity, as a spiritual system, is always superior to every visible institution." Some systems and institutions may oppose greater obstacles to its progress than others; but none can become Christianity, nor can they do any thing for it except to give it free scope to do its own work upon individual character. It is not monarchy, it is not democracy, it is not Episcopacy, it is not Congregationalism; it is something which may pervade and bless society where any of these exist, and which may be withdrawn and leave either of these standing as an organization through which human passion and corruption shall work out their own unmixed and unmitigated effects. Hence, too, Christianity attacks no visible institutions as such. It goes to the slave, and tells him he is the Lord's freedman; it goes to the master, and tells him he is Christ's servant. It tells both master and slave that they are brethren. It goes to the king, and tells him he is the subject of a higher power; it goes to the subject, and tells him he may become a king and priest to God. It raises all men to the level of a common immortality; it depresses them all to the level of a common sinfulness and exposure; it subjects all to a common accountability; it offers to all a common salvation; it proposes to all a law of perfect equity and a principle of universal love; and then it leaves these principles and motives to work their own effect — assured that, in proportion as they act, they must change the nature, if not the name, of all visible institutions opposed to its spirit. It is capable of taking human organizations, as culture took the peach when it was dwarfed and its fruit was poisonous, and of causing other juices and vital fluids to circulate through the pores of those same organizations, and far other fruit to hang upon their branches. It understands perfectly that no change of form is of any permanent value without a change of spirit; and seeks (and oh that men would learn this lesson!) a change of form only through a change of spirit. Hence it works like leaven, that passes on from particle to particle, and finds no limit till the whole lump is leavened. Hence, too, I may remark here, Christianity is the most formidable of all foes to tyrants and to every form of oppression. No walls, or fortifications, or armed legions, can keep it out, and no weapon can smite it. Working silently upon the consciences of men, it is impossible to say where it is, or to what extent, and the opposer knows not where to strike. The very executioner chosen by persecution offers himself to die with the martyr; and when it is supposed that the two witnesses are dead, and there is great rejoicing, they suddenly rise and stand upon their feet.

Positive adaptations. — But the fitness of Christianity to become universal does not result from any properties merely negative, nor from the possibility of its becoming so; but from all those adaptations by which it appears that it contains the moral laws of God, and lays down the only conditions of individual and social well-being. Of some of these adaptations I have spoken; and, for my present purpose, it can not be necessary that I should speak further, because, whatever men may think of the divine origin of Christianity, — however far they may be from yielding practically to its claims, — they almost universally concede that its tendency is good, and that society is improved just so far as it prevails. This is conceded by philosophers, and politicians, and men of the world; and, with the exception of a few of the lowest and most bigoted of them, by infidels themselves. They can not deny its tendency to promote industry, and honesty, and temperance, and peace, and good order. And, if this is so, then Christianity has a positive fitness to become universal in the same way that any truth or practical knowledge has; and, if there is ever to be any thing like universal order, it must take its place as a part of it.

If fitness, then tendency. — But, if there is this *fitness* in Christianity to become universal, then it must have a *tendency* to become so, or else there is neither a tendency to progress, nor a law of progress, for man. The whole of our hope here rests on the belief that there is inwrought into the constitution of things a tendency by which those things that have a fitness to promote happiness shall gradually remove obstacles, and become universal. That the Saviour intended his religion should become universal is plain, because he left it in charge to his disciples to preach it to every creature. That a real apprehension of its truths, and of their value to the race, would lead a benevolent mind to wish to communicate them, is equally plain; and hence we say that, from the command of Christ, and from the very nature of Christian truth and of Christian motives, Christians themselves can never rest till they have carried this gospel over the earth. But we say, further than this, that Christianity has the same tendency to prevail that reason has to prevail over brute force, or that virtue has to prevail over vice, or truth over error, — the same tendency that correct doctrines respecting peace, or justice, or political economy, have to prevail over those that are false. Man is capable of scientific insight, and he seeks to be happy. There are certain moral laws of God, as fixed and unchangeable as any physical laws, in accordance with which alone he can be so. Those laws, we say, are a part of Christianity, and that all true progress in society must be a progress toward the realization and establishment of those laws. We say that every step in the progress of moral and political science shows that, when these shall be complete, they will be seen to be only the scientific expression of the precepts and laws of Christianity. Hence there is the same tendency to universality in Christianity, — not as a mode of salvation, but in its earthly aspects, — that there is to any advancement and progress in morals, or in politics, or in political economy. The true laws of these, and of human happiness as depending on them, will be found to be identical with the spirit of Christianity, and they can never be practically applied except as that spirit prevails.

Conclusion. — Thus we see a preparation made, in the adaptation of Christianity to the nature and wants of man as man; in the command of Christ; in the nature of Christian love and of Christian motives; and in the identity of Christianity, in some of its aspects, with moral and political science, for that final and universal triumph predicted by the prophets and waited for by the church; and through these, in connection with that divine aid which is promised and has never been withheld, we think it rational to expect, not only that it will be perpetuated till the end of time, but that "the mountain of the Lord's house will be established in the top of the mountains, and that all nations will flow unto it."

ARGUMENT VIII.

CHRISTIANITY HAS ALWAYS BEEN IN THE WORLD.

Having thus spoken of the continuance of Christianity till the end of time, I will close this lecture by observing that, in substance, if not in form, it has continued from the beginning. That it should have been always in the world, is mentioned by Pascal as the mark of a religion from God. It is a mark which we might expect would belong to the true religion, and this mark Christianity, and that alone, has. The patriarchal, the Jewish, and the Christian dispensations, are evidently but the unfolding of one general plan. In the first we see the folded bud; in the second, the expanded leaf; in the third, the blossom and the fruit. And now, how sublime the idea of a religion thus commencing in the earliest dawn of time; holding on its way through all the revolutions of kingdoms and the vicissitudes of the race; receiving new forms, but always identical in spirit; and, finally, expanding and embracing in one great brotherhood the whole family of man! Who can doubt that such a religion was from God?

LECTURE VII.

ARGUMENT NINTH: CHRISTIANITY COULD NOT HAVE BEEN ORIGINATED BY MAN.

IF we could possibly be called on to argue the question whether the ocean was made by God, or whether it was an artificial salt lake, made by man, we should show, on the one hand, that it was worthy of God, and that it corresponded with his other works; and, on the other, that it was impossible it should have been made by man. Every fact respecting its vastness and depth would show that it was worthy of God, and every relation that could be pointed out between that and the other works of God would be an argument to show that they were fashioned by the same hand. Probably no one could see the sun evaporating its waters, the atmosphere bearing them up in clouds, the clouds pouring them down upon the waiting tribes of vegetation, the springs welling them up for the service of animals and of man, without being convinced that He who made the sun, and the air, and the grass, and the animals, and man, made also the ocean. Such relations of mutual dependence could exist only in the different departments of the works of one Being.

Method of the argument. — Hitherto, I have endeavored to show that Christianity was worthy of God, and that it so corresponds with his other works, that He who made nature, and the mind, must have been the author of Christianity. I now proceed to show that it could not have been produced by man. It may, perhaps, amount to the same thing, whether I attempt to show that Christianity must have come from God, or could not have come from man; but as the terms of comparison are different, it will lead to a presentation of the subject in an entirely different point of view.

Reason for continuing it. — I continue to pursue this method of proof, bringing Christianity, in different relations, alongside of the human mind, because it is perfectly within the reach of every person of good sense, whether learned or unlearned. We know the capacities of the human mind, and we are capable of forming, within certain limits, a judgment, respecting what it can or can not do, upon which we may rely. The powers of the mind are limited no less than those of the body; and as we can judge what man can do, in given circumstances, by his physical strength, and, in some cases, be sure we are right, so we can judge what he can do intellectually and morally, in given circumstances, and, in some cases, be sure we are right. The question, then, is, whether it is possible that the human mind should have originated the Christian system, under the circumstances in which it was placed. Had unassisted man the capacity to originate such a system? Was there any motive to lead him to labor for its establishment? Upon this point I have already incidentally touched, but it requires further attention.

Christianity to be accounted for. — And here I observe, that the question concerning the origin of Christianity can not be disposed of by a general reference to the facility with which mankind are deluded, and the frequency of impostures in the world. This may do when speaking of the origin of local and temporary movements, but not when we approach the deepest and mightiest movement that has appeared on the earth. It is admitted that delusions are not uncommon; that fanaticism, and enthusiasm, and interest, and fraud, and, possibly, all these combined, may go a great way; but is it possible that any thing thus originated should overturn systems the most deeply seated, and receive the homage of the highest intellect and of the most extensive learning the world has ever seen, and gain vigor by opposition, and survive, for eighteen hundred years, every change in the forms of society, and, at the end of that time, stand at the head of those influences which are leading mankind on to a higher destiny? For such a religion, or delusion, or movement, to arise, is not an every-day occurrence. It is altogether unprecedented in the history of the race; and to put aside the question of its origin by telling us that mankind are easily deceived, is much the same as it would be to put aside the question about the origin of the Gulf Stream by telling us that water is an element very easily moved in different directions. Certainly, water is a fluctuating and unstable element; but to say this, is not to account for a broad current in mid ocean that has been uniform since time began; nor is it any account of a uniform current of thought and feeling, setting in one direction for eighteen hundred years, to say that the human mind is fluctuating and unstable; that man has been often deceived; and that there have been great extravagances in belief. The origin of such a movement is to be investigated, and not to be shrouded in mist. The New Testament gives a full and satisfactory account of it; and it behooves those who do not receive that account, to substitute some other that shall, at least, be plausible. This they have failed to do.

Five causes of Gibbon. — Perhaps no one was more

competent to do this, or has been more successful, than Gibbon; and yet the five causes which he assigns for the spread of Christianity — namely, "the zeal of Christians," "their doctrine of a future life," "the miraculous powers ascribed to the primitive church," "their pure and austere morals," and "their union" — are obviously effects of that very religion of which they are assigned as the cause.

Must be from God. — To me, when I look at this religion, taking its point of departure from the earliest period in the history of the race; when I see it analogous to nature; when I see it comprising all that natural religion teaches, and introducing a new system in entire harmony with it, but which could not have been deduced from it; when I see it commending itself to the conscience of man, containing a perfect code of morals, meeting all his moral wants, and imbosoming the only true principles of economical and political science; when I see in it the best possible system of excitement and restraint for all the faculties; when I see how simple it is in its principle, and yet in how many thousand ways it mingles in with human affairs, and modifies them for good, so that it is adapted to become universal; when I see it giving an account of the termination of all things, worthy of God and consistent with reason; — to me, when I look at all these things, it no more seems possible that the system of Christianity should have been originated or sustained by man, than it does that the ocean should have been made by him. These considerations, however, have been adduced to elucidate that phase of the argument by which it was intended to show that the religion must have come from God; and I shall not further apply them here except as —

Cardinal points taken for granted. — I observe, that the more we examine the state of opinions among the

Jews, or among the surrounding nations, at the time Christianity arose, the greater will be our surprise that it should be what it is, respecting almost all those cardinal points which it does not so much reveal as take for granted. Such are the unity and spirituality of God, his holy character, the spirituality of his worship, his paternal relation to us, the doctrine of a resurrection and of human accountability. The most of these doctrines are not so much systematically taught, as implied, in Christianity; and they are not only consistent with reason, but are essential as conditions to the end which Christianity proposes to itself.

End impossible to an enthusiast. — And this leads me to observe, that the end proposed by Christianity, distinctly announced from the first, and perseveringly adhered to, was one which could not have been adopted either by an enthusiast or an impostor. In the very first annunciation of the gospel, it was said by the angel, "Thou shalt call his name JESUS; for he shall save his people from their sins." Christ himself said that he came "to seek and to save that which was lost" — "that the world through him might be saved." Peter calls upon men to "repent, and be baptized in the name of Jesus Christ for the remission of sins;" and, again, to "repent and be converted, that their sins may be blotted out." Nothing can be plainer than that the great end of Christianity is to deliver men from the power and the consequences of sin under the government of God. With the light which we now have, we can see that the object of a religion from God must be to correct the state of the heart; but this object could never have been adopted by enthusiasm. It is not of a character to awaken enthusiasm, for it implies a recognition of guilt, and, moreover, it involves a clear perception of the deepest and most fundamental truth on which the reformation of the world depends. Before the miseries of the world can be removed, their cause must be known; and this shows an insight into the cause of human wretchedness such as we find nowhere else. Men are unhappy, perhaps wretched, and they impute it to fate, to others, to the want of wealth or of external advantages, or to the constitution of society; but Christianity takes it for granted that sin, moral guilt, is the true cause, the cause of all the other causes, of the unhappiness of man; and that, in saving him from this, it saves him from every thing that a rational being has to fear. And is not this so? Does not man bring upon himself, by his sins, the greater part of the evils which he suffers? Remove war, and the fear of it; remove dishonesty of every kind; remove indolence, and intemperance, and licentiousness, and envy, and detraction, and revenge, and pride, and a selfish ambition,— and let the virtues opposite to these reign; remove, also, those apprehensions and terrors of conscience, and that fear of death, which come in consequence of sin, — and this world would become comparatively a paradise. Christianity, then, strikes at the true cause of all the miseries of man. Instead of endeavoring to check or control particular streams of evil, it goes at once to the fountain whence all those streams flow, and would seal that up forever. To my mind, nothing can be clearer than that moral evil is the true cause of the miseries of the world; but can this deep, and sober, and philosophical view of the cause of human misery, and an attempt to remove it, be the product of enthusiasm? Of all feelings, a consciousness of guilt is that which most represses enthusiasm. An enthusiast, therefore, could not come to those only who would acknowledge themselves guilty, and call them to the unwelcome duty of repentance, and of renouncing cherished indulgences and habits. He could not say, "They that are whole need not a physician, but they that are sick;" "I am not come to call the righteous, but sinners, to repentance."

Or an impostor. — But if such an object could not have been selected by an enthusiast, much less could it have been by an impostor. An impostor must have a personal and selfish motive; but suppose this object gained, of what advantage would it be to him? Is it not a contradiction to suppose an impostor to call upon men to repent of all sin, when, in the very act of thus calling upon them, he is guilty of one of the blackest sins of which man is capable? And, further, an impostor estimates the chances of success. But let any man look at the state of things when Christ appeared, and see what chance there could have been, in the eye of an impostor, that such an object should succeed. The great doctrines which lie at the foundation of repentance were but very imperfectly known. Superstition and formality had almost entirely excluded the spirit of any true religion, whether natural or revealed. Sin, as such, was not disliked or deplored; and if in any case it should be, the Jews had a mode for its removal, as they supposed, divinely constituted, and with which they were satisfied; while the Gentiles were attached to their own religions, and hated and despised the Jews. Now, in such a state of things, for an *impostor* — a young man without learning, or wealth, or influential friends; a Jew, who would naturally have shared in the prejudices and national feelings of his countrymen — to arise and call upon men to repent of sin in general, and believe in him; at the same time proposing no definite scheme, either political or ecclesiastical; directing the energies of his followers to nothing that could gratify their ambition, or love of gain or pleasure, on earth; and proposing rewards, hereafter, that can be enjoyed only as men are morally good, — and yet to make such an impression upon the world as to overturn systems that had stood for ages, — does seem to me far more improbable than any miracle recorded in the Bible. The disparity between the means employed and the effect to be produced would not be greater, if a single, unaided man should attempt to unseat Mount Atlas, and lift it from its bed. In making it its object to remove guilt, and to rectify the state of the heart before God, Christianity stands alone; and we can now see that this is the only ultimate object which a religion from God could propose. To my mind, therefore, the simple choice of this object, requiring such breadth and accuracy of view, so impossible to have been chosen by enthusiasm or imposture, taken in connection with the movement produced by Christianity, is a sufficient proof that it originated with God, and was accompanied by a divine power.

No adaptation to prejudices. — But perhaps the success in carrying forward this object may be accounted for by a skillful adaptation of some features of the system to the prejudices, or wants, or habits of thought, of the age. Did Christ, then, adapt his system to the prejudices and expectations of the Jews? So far from this, nothing could have been more strongly opposed to all the habits of thought and long-cherished associations both of Jews and of Gentiles. This point has been most ably presented by Bishop Sumner, of whose labors I shall avail myself in the particulars I shall adduce respecting it.

Appealed to no sect. — The Jews were divided into three great sects — the Pharisees, the Sadducees, and Essenes. The sentiments and modes of thought of the first two are sufficiently known. The Essenes were a comparatively small sect, professing a community of goods and the most austere celibacy. Among these sects were found the great and influential men of the nation; but neither of these did Christ endeavor in the least to propitiate; he attacked them all equally. With the general tone of thought, and laxity of morals, of the Sadducees, his whole system was in direct conflict; and we all know how terrible were his denunciations of the Pharisees and scribes, as hypocrites and formalists, and as having put false glosses upon the law of God. The spirit of sect is among the most bitter and formidable that can be aroused; but, instead of taking advantage of this, or of commending himself to any party, Christ armed every influence that could be drawn from such sources against himself.

Opposed the whole Jewish system. — But, though the Jews were divided into sects, there were many points which they held in common as Jews, and which were to them the ground of a strong and exclusive national feeling. If we can suppose it possible that Christ himself should have risen superior to all the prejudices and associations of his nation, yet, if we look at him either as an enthusiast or an impostor, we can not suppose he would have gone counter to every feeling that was strongly and distinctively Jewish; much less can we suppose he would have attempted to bring to an end a system which he himself, in common with all his countrymen, acknowledged to be from God, and to the rites of which he conformed. Yet so did Christ.

Jewish notions of the Messiah. — Hence I observe, that, while Christ claimed to be the Messiah expected by the Jews, his whole appearance, and character, and object, were totally opposed to all their interpretations of prophecy, and wishes, and long-cherished anticipations. In the language of Sumner, "They looked for a conqueror, a temporal king, and had been accustomed to interpret in this sense all the prophecies which foretold his coming. The Jews were at the time suffering under a foreign yoke, which they bore with great uneasiness and impatience. And whether we suppose Jesus to have been an impostor or enthusiast, this is the character which he would naturally assume. If he were an enthusiast, his mind would have been filled with the popular belief, and his imagination fired with the national ideas of victory and glory. If he were an impostor, the general expectation would coincide with the only motive to which his conduct can be attributed — ambition and the desire of personal aggrandizement. How, then, can we explain his rejecting, from the first, and throughout his whole career, all the advantage which he might have derived from the previous expectation of the people, and even his turning it against himself and his cause? Why should he, as a Jew, have interpreted the prophetic Scriptures differently from all other Jews? Why should he, as an impostor, have deprived himself of all personal benefit from his design?" *

Set aside the ceremonial law. — Again : "No feeling could be stronger, or better founded, than the veneration of the Jews for the Mosaic law. The account of its origin which had come down to them from their ancestors; its singularity; the effect that singularity had produced in establishing a wide separation between themselves and other nations; above all, the important results which they expected from obeying it, as entitling them to the favor and protection of God; all these circumstances united to render that attachment to their national law, which is common among every people, inconceivably strong in the case of the Jews." Yet Christ said to these same Jews, "The law and the prophets *were* until John." Himself acknowledging its divine origin, he yet abrogated the ceremonial law, and put new interpretations upon the moral law. Of the distinction between these he had the most accurate

* Sumner's Evidences, chap. ii.

perception; for, while he struck down the one, declaring that the hour had come in which men need no longer worship at Jerusalem, but that every where the true worshipers should worship the Father in spirit and in truth, he yet declared that heaven and earth should pass away sooner than one jot or tittle of the moral law should fail. But though he retained the law as the moral code of the universe, he yet abrogated it so far as it applied exclusively to the Jews, and in all those respects in which it was chiefly valued by them.

Destroyed exclusiveness. — Further: " It was a favorite belief among the Jews, confirmed by the whole course of their history, that their nation enjoyed the exclusive regard and protection of the true God. But the first principle of the Christian religion tended to dislodge the Jews from these high pretensions, and to admit all other nations, indiscriminately, within the pale of God's church."

Jerusalem, the temple. — And, once more : "The city of Jerusalem was universally believed to be secure under the especial care of God, as being the seat of the only true religion, and its temple consecrated to his peculiar service by divine institution and ancient usage. Yet Christ and his disciples declared that total destruction was quickly approaching both the temple and the city."

Neither Jews nor Gentiles conciliated. — Thus Christ not only armed against himself the spirit of sect, but also that peculiar national feeling which was stronger among the Jews than among any other people. But while he did this, and while it was declared, from the first, that he should be a light to lighten the Gentiles, he himself never went among the Gentiles, but declared that he was not sent but to the lost sheep of the house of Israel. All this, we may safely say, neither an enthusiast nor an impostor could have done.

17

Essential to a universal religion. — But, while the origin of Christianity is so anomalous and inexplicable on the supposition that the agents were actuated by merely human motives, every thing becomes perfectly consistent and reasonable the moment we suppose they were the agents of God to introduce a new and universal religion. If such a religion was to be introduced, the whole Jewish economy must of necessity have been removed. But was a Jewish peasant, unlettered and untraveled, going up with his countrymen every year to Jerusalem, the person to see this? Was he to have the inconceivable arrogance to assume to himself the authority to remove that dispensation, at the same time that he admitted it to be from God?

If an impostor, Christ not the author of Christianity. — I proceed to another point: Extraordinary as was the character of Christ, and unaccountable as was his conduct while he was alive, yet, if we suppose him to have been either an enthusiast or an impostor, there must have been some one among his disciples, after his death, whose character and conduct were still more extraordinary and unaccountable; for it is to be remembered that, on this supposition, Christ can not, with any propriety, be said to be the originator of the system which bears his name. This is a point not sufficiently noticed, if indeed it has been noticed at all.

It will not be denied that the resurrection of Christ lies at the foundation of the system. It did so in the mind of Paul when he wrote to the Corinthians that, if Christ were not raised, their faith was vain; and it has been regarded as fundamental by Christians ever since. Did Christ, then, or did he not, know the place which his death, and the story of his resurrection, were to have in the Christian system? If we suppose him to have been any thing except what he claimed to be, he could not have known this. Without the gift of prophecy, he could not have known that the Roman governor would sentence him to death. Besides, it is absurd to suppose that any enthusiast or impostor could frame a scheme of which his own death on the cross, and a story of his resurrection, to be started and substantiated by others, should form a necessary part. His death must, then, on the supposition on which we are arguing, have been unexpected, both to himself and to his followers. His schemes, whatever they were, must have perished with him; for of the Christian system as contained in the New Testament, involving his own death and resurrection, he could by no possibility have had any conception. This system did not become possible till after his death. Previous to that, the very foundation of it had no existence, nor could it even have had if his death had not been public; for, otherwise, his death would not have been certain, and the story of the resurrection would have excited no attention.

Who, then, was that man, the true author of Christianity, of quick and original thought, who, in that moment when the Jews supposed they had triumphed, when the plans of Christ himself, whatever they were, had failed, saw, from the very fact of the crucifixion, that a story of a resurrection might be framed, and be so connected with the former life and instructions of Christ, and with the Jewish Scriptures, as to form the basis of a new religion? Who was this master-spirit, — for the unity of the system shows that it must have been the product of one mind, — who was so prompt in combining the fearful fact of his master's execution, and the strange story of the resurrection, with his former life and teachings, so as to make one connected whole? Who rallied the dispersed and disheartened disciples, opened to them his plan of deception, assigned to each his part, and induced them to stand firm by the cause even unto death? Certainly, if Christ was not what he claimed to be, there was some one concerned, in the origin of the Christian system, who was a greater and more extraordinary person than he, and the true author of that system is unknown.

Scheme impossible. — But here let me ask, supposing such a scheme to have been originated, whether any person of common sense could possibly have hoped for its success; whether any but madmen could have been persuaded to engage in it. For what was the scheme? It was nothing less than to persuade all mankind to receive one as a Saviour, and to believe in him as the final Judge of the world, who, they themselves acknowledged, had been put to death by crucifixion between two thieves. And, in order to realize fully what this undertaking was, we must further, first, remember how alien from all the habits of thought among the Gentiles and among most of the Jews, how utterly improbable, the story of a resurrection must have been; and, secondly, we must divest ourselves of all the associations which we have gathered around the cross, and, going back to that period, must furnish our minds with those which were then prevalent. We must remember that the cross was not only an instrument of public execution peculiarly dreadful, but also peculiarly ignominious; that it was unlawful to put a Roman citizen to death in this way; and that it was a punishment reserved only to slaves, and persons of the lowest description.

And, now, with these facts before us, I ask whether the idea of the resurrection of a person thus put to death, and of his exaltation to be the Saviour of men and the Judge of the whole earth, occurring to a person without any manifestation of miraculous power, is in accordance with the laws of human thought; whether an attempt to make mankind believe such a story, and to cause them — the very Jews who had just crucified him, the Gentiles who held all Jews in contempt, and would more especially despise and abhor a crucified Jew — whether the attempt to cause them to forsake their own religions, and to acknowledge such a Saviour and Judge, is compatible with what we know of the laws of human action. Can we conceive of any enthusiast so utterly wild, of any impostor so utterly foolish, as to suppose he could make such a story and such a proposition the basis of a religion which should overthrow all others, and become universal? Can we conceive, not only that such an attempt should be made, but that it should succeed? The man who can believe this, can believe any thing. What an astonishing contrast between such a point of departure of the Christian religion, and that moment when a Roman emperor turned his expiring eyes to heaven, and said, "O Galilean, thou hast conquered!"

And here, again, what is so entirely unaccountable if we exclude divine agency, is perfectly accounted for the moment we allow that these men were what they claimed to be, and were endowed with power from on high.

Conduct of the disciples. — I might pursue this train of thought at great length, applying it to the conduct of the disciples individually and as a body, and particularly to the conversion and subsequent course of the apostle Paul. I think it can be shown, on the supposition of imposture or enthusiasm, — and no other is possible without admitting the truth of the religion, — that the conduct of these men was as contrary to known and established laws of human action as any miracle can be to the laws of nature.

Jewish and Christian system — would not have been connected. — But I proceed to observe that no enthusiast or impostor either would or could have effected that peculiar connection, doctrinal, typical, and prophetical, which exists between the Jewish and the Christian religion. This no man *would* have done. For while, as I have just shown, they rejected so much, and such parts, of the system as would excite to the utmost the hostility of the Jews, they yet declared it to be identical in spirit with the Jewish religion, and thus presented themselves at a great disadvantage before the Gentiles. Accordingly, we find the Roman magistrates speaking in the most contemptuous manner of the whole thing, as being a question of Jewish superstition. Thus Festus, giving an account of Paul's case to Agrippa, said, "Against whom, when the accusers stood up, they brought none accusation of such things as I supposed, but had certain questions against him of their own superstition, and of one Jesus, which was dead, whom Paul affirmed to be alive." So, also, when Gallio was the deputy of Achaia, and the Jews brought Paul before him, and he was about to defend himself, Gallio said unto the Jews, "If it were a matter of wrong or wicked lewdness, O ye Jews, reason would that I should bear with you; but if it be a question of words and names, and of your law, look ye to it; for I will be no judge of such matters. And he drave them from the judgment seat. Then all the Greeks took Sosthenes, the chief ruler of the synagogue, and beat him before the judgment seat. And Gallio cared for none of those things." This feeling was perfectly natural, and the author or authors of Christianity must have known it would be excited if such a connection was retained between the new religion and that of the Jews. The course pursued, therefore, was apparently the most impolitic that could have been adopted, whether the feelings of the Jews or of the Gentiles were regarded.

Could not have been. — But this is not the point of

the greatest difficulty. No impostor, or enthusiast, *could* have adopted such a course, if he would. For, first, no human wisdom could have taken the Jewish system, complicated as it was, and have drawn the line with a judgment so unerring between those things which ought to be rejected and those which might be retained; between those things which would, and those which would not, harmonize with the new system. And, secondly, that a system depending so much upon facts over which the authors of it had no control, such as the place of Christ's birth, and the time and manner of his death — a system that had never before been thought of, or provided for — a system springing up at a particular juncture from enthusiasm or imposture, — should have so many correspondences with a system originated thousands of years before, that the attempt should be universally made to convert the Jews by reasoning out of their own Scriptures, showing that "so it was written," — and that such a book as the Epistle to the Hebrews could be written, — is, to my mind, inconceivable. Nor is it less inconceivable — what I have spoken of in a former lecture — that man should invent a system which would permit its advocates to pass from the Jewish synagogue, where their whole argument had been based on the Old Testament Scriptures, into a company of Athenian philosophers, and, with the same confidence, and freedom, and power, argue with them from the book of nature, and the moral constitution and wants of man. Nothing can be more striking than the contrast between Paul's speech on Mars Hill and that recorded in the thirteenth of Acts, in a Jewish synagogue at Antioch, or even that before Agrippa, in which he made the appeal, "King Agrippa, believest thou the prophets?"

On the whole, then, laying aside those analogies and adaptations by which it is shown that Christianity must have come from God, and taking only the particulars adduced in this lecture, have we not reason to conclude that it could not have been originated by man?

The books. — I have thus far spoken chiefly of the *system* of Christianity. I shall devote the remainder of this lecture to the consideration of some points of evidence drawn from the books in which its records and doctrines are contained — confining myself, however, to such as must be judged of in the same way as those which we have been considering. These books open to us a field of such evidence as every man of good sense and candor can judge of, scarcely less extensive and rich than the system itself; but to this my time will permit me but briefly to refer.

I observe, then, in accordance with the general scope of this lecture, that no impostor, or enthusiast, either would, or could, have written the books of the New Testament.

No motive for a forgery. — And, first, no such person would have written them; for they are of such a character that it is impossible to assign a motive for a forgery. The motive could not have been gain. For what is the relation of these books to Christianity? Plainly, they presuppose its existence. To suppose that the books themselves, coming out as a mere bald, naked fiction, could have been received by both Jews and Gentiles, and have worked a revolution in society, and that, too, in an age when printing was unknown, and the number and influence of books were comparatively small, is absurd. Christianity must, then, have sprung up, and spread more or less extensively, and then the books must have been written to give an account of its origin and progress. If, then, gain had been the object, it was necessary to write an account that could not be discredited. No forgery could have escaped both neglect and contempt.

Not fame. — Nor could the motive have been fame. No one, from reading the Gospel of Matthew, would suspect who the author was. He speaks of himself very little, and mentions that he belonged to a class who were despised and hated by the Jews. Would any man, could any man, compose the Sermon on the Mount — a production, for its beauty, and majestic simplicity, and morality, unequaled since the world stood — for fame, and then ascribe it to a fictitious person, or one whom he knew to be an impostor?

Nor power. — Nor could his motive have been power or influence. No book was ever more unskillfully constructed for such a purpose. It had no connection with politics or parties, nor does it contain any thing to give distinction or influence to its author. What, then, could have induced a man capable of surpassing, as a moralist and as a deep thinker, all the philosophers of antiquity, to conceal himself entirely behind an impostor? How could he have induced the world to mistake that impostor for himself?

The Epistles. — And what is thus true of the Gospels, and of the Acts, is equally true of the Epistles. Indeed, there are some circumstances which would seem to render a forgery of these peculiarly improbable. If I were to select the last form in which a forgery would be likely to come before the world, it would be this. These are extraordinary productions, and it is inconceivable that any man should introduce them into the world by the fiction of addressing them to a church, and should connect such admirable sentiments with the details of their peculiar difficulties, and with salutations addressed to many persons by name. Let any man read the last chapter of the Epistle to the Romans, (which is almost entirely made up of greetings and salutations,) and ask himself if it is possible that any man, writing a letter for the purpose of deception, could have written it. Observe his particularity. Not only does Paul himself salute many persons, but Timotheus, his work-fellow, is joined with him, and Lucius, and Jason, and Sosipater, his kinsman, and Tertius, who wrote the Epistle, and Gaius, his host, and Erastus, the chamberlain of the city, and Quartus, a brother.

If, however, it should be said that there were forgeries afterward, I reply, that all great originals, all genuine articles of great value, present temptations to imitation and forgery, but there is no such temptation to forge the original work. No instance of such a forgery can be adduced.

Could not have been forged. — The strong point here, however, is, that no enthusiast or impostor *could* have forged these books. This is manifest from the marks of honesty which they bear upon their face. It is with books as with men. Without stating to ourselves the ground of it, we all form a judgment of the character of men from their appearance. There is in some men an appearance of openness, and candor, and fairness, in all they do and say, which can hardly be mistaken. There is often something in the appearance and modes of statement of a witness on the stand, there are certain undefinable but very appreciable marks of honesty or of dishonesty, which will and ought to go very far, with one who has been accustomed to observe men under such circumstances, in fixing the character of his testimony. Now, this is remarkably the case with the writings of the New Testament. We can not read a chapter without feeling that we are dealing with realities. The writers show no consciousness of any possibility that their statements should be doubted. They have the air of persons who state things perfectly well known. They express no wonder; they do not seem to expect that their statements, extraordinary as they are, will excite any; they enter into no explanations, attempt to remove or evade no difficulties; they speak freely of their own faults and weaknesses; they flatter no one; they express no malice toward any. There is no ambition of fine writing, no special pleading, no attempt to conceal circumstances apparently unfavorable — as the agony of Christ in the garden, so liable to be imputed to weakness; the fact that he was forsaken of God on the cross, that Peter denied him, and that the disciples forsook him and fled. Their narratives are minute, circumstantial, graphic, giving the names of persons and the time and the place of events. At every step they lay themselves open to detection if their accounts are, I will not say fabrications, but false in any respect. Do they give us the Sermon on the Mount? They tell us that multitudes heard it. Do they give an account of the resurrection of Lazarus? They give the place and the family, and state its effects upon different classes of persons. Do they speak of the Roman governor, or of the high priest? They mention his name. There is the Sea of Galilee, and Capernaum, and Jerusalem, and the temple with its goodly stones. There are the Jewish feasts, and their sects, and traditions. Every thing is thoroughly Jewish, and still there is the publican and the Roman soldier. All these seem to stand before us with the distinctness of life — not by the force of rhetorical painting, but by the simple narration of truth.

Number of the books — discrepancies. — The chief difficulty, however, in fabricating these books, would not have been in giving them singly an air of truth, however striking and life-like, but in constructing so many of them with such numerous and incidental marks of correspondence as to negative entirely the supposition of imposture. And here it ought to be observed, that the number of books is itself a strong reason for supposing that there was no imposture. An imposture would naturally have appeared in one well-considered and well-guarded account. So have all impostures of the kind appeared. The Koran was wholly written by one man. So was the Mormon Bible. But here we have twenty-seven books, or letters, written by eight different men, each implying the truth of most of the others, and, as they stand, giving an opportunity for comparison, and for what the lawyers would call cross-questioning, which must have proved fatal to any fabrication, and to which imposture was never known to subject itself. We have four independent histories of Christ. Between these there are a few apparent discrepancies respecting minor points, such as will always occur when independent witnesses state their own impressions respecting a series of events. These lie for the most part on the surface, are such as might have been easily avoided, and such as imposture certainly would have avoided. They show that the witnesses were independent, that there was no collusion between them; while the points of agreement are so many, and of such a character, as can be accounted for only on the supposition of truth.

Conscious security of truth. — Of the advantages thus furnished, the opposers of Christianity have eagerly availed themselves; but they are careful not to state, if, indeed, they reflect, that the very fact that these advantages are thus gratuitously furnished shows the conscious security of truth, and affords the strongest possible presumption that nothing can be made of them. The discrepancies are few in number, and may be reconciled; while the coincidences, evidently undesigned, between the four Gospels, and between the Gospels and the Acts, are so numerous as to have been collected, by Mr. Blunt, into a volume.

The Acts, and the Epistles of Paul. — But, as if to furnish the best possible opportunity for this species of proof, we have the history of the apostle Paul stated fully and circumstantially in the Acts; and then we have thirteen letters of the same apostle, purporting to have been written during the period covered by the history. If, therefore, the history and the letters are both genuine, we should expect to find the same general character ascribed to the apostle in the history that is indicated by his letters; we should expect to find in the letters numerous minute and undesigned references, such as could not be counterfeited, to the facts stated in the history. And all this we do find. The character of Paul was strongly marked, and no one can doubt whether the Epistles ascribed to him were written by such a man as he is described in the history to have been. How different are the characters of Paul, of Peter, and of John! and yet how perfectly do the writings ascribed to each correspond with his character! If the history had given us an account of a person like John, and then these letters had been ascribed to him, how differently would our evidence have stood!

Horæ Paulinæ. — But the argument from the coincidences between the different Epistles, and between the Epistles and the Acts, has been presented in a full and masterly manner by Paley, in his Horæ Paulinæ, a book to which, so far as I know, infidels have judged it wise not to attempt an answer. In this argument, Paley does not notice those coincidences which are direct and striking, and which might have been fabricated; but those which are evidently undesigned, which are remote and circuitous, and so woven into the web that the supposition of art or imposture is impossible. This argument is best illustrated by examples. Thus we find, in the First Epistle to the Corinthians, the following passage : " Even unto this present hour we both

hunger and thirst, and are naked, and are buffeted, and have no certain dwelling-place; and labor, working with our own hands." We are expressly told, in the history, that at Corinth St. Paul labored with his own hands: "He found Aquila and Priscilla; and, because he was of the same craft, he abode with them, and wrought; for by their occupation they were tent-makers." But, in the text before us, he is made to say that he labored "even unto this present hour," that is, to the time of writing the Epistle, at Ephesus. Now, in the narration of St. Paul's transactions at Ephesus, delivered in the nineteenth chapter of the Acts, nothing is said of his working with his own hands; but in the twentieth chapter we read that, upon his return from Greece, he sent for the elders of the church at Ephesus to meet him at Miletus; and in the discourse which he there addressed to them we find the following : "I have coveted no man's silver, or gold, or apparel; yea, ye yourselves know, that these hands have ministered unto my necessities, and to them that were with me." That manual labor, therefore, which he had exercised at Corinth, he continued at Ephesus; and not only so, but continued it during that particular residence at Ephesus, near the conclusion of which this Epistle was written; so that he might, with the strictest truth, say, at the time of writing the Epistle, "even *unto this present hour*, we labor, working with our own hands."
"The correspondency is sufficient, then, as to the undesignedness of it. It is manifest to my judgment that, if the history in this article had been taken from the Epistle, this circumstance, if it appeared at all, would have appeared in its *place* — that is, in the direct account of St. Paul's transactions at Ephesus. Nor is it likely, on the other hand, that a circumstance which is not extant in the history of St. Paul at Ephesus should have been made the subject of a factitious

allusion in an Epistle purporting to be written by him from that place; not to mention that the allusion itself, especially as to time, is too oblique and general to answer any purpose of forgery whatever.

Again we find, in the Second Epistle to the Thessalonians, iii. 8, "Neither did we eat any man's bread for naught; but wrought with labor, night and day, that we might not be chargeable to any of you; not because we have not power, but to make ourselves an ensample unto you to follow us." Here, again, his conduct — and, what is much more precise, the end which he had in view by it — is the very same which the history attributes to him in this discourse to the elders of the church at Ephesus; for, after saying, "Yea, ye yourselves know, that these hands have ministered unto my necessities, and to them that were with me," he adds, "I have showed you all things, how that, *so laboring, ye ought to support the weak.*" "The sentiment in the Epistle and in the speech is, in both parts of it, so much alike, and yet the words which convey it show so little of imitation, or even of resemblance, that the agreement can not well be explained without supposing the speech and the letter to have really proceeded from the same person."

Do we find Paul saying abruptly, and without explanation, to Timothy, "Let not a widow be taken into the number under threescore years old"? We also find, from the Acts, that provision was made, from the first, for the indigent widows who belonged to the Christian church. Does he say to Timothy that from a child he had known the Holy Scriptures? The Acts tells us that his mother was a Jewess. Do we hear him exhorting the Corinthians not to despise Timothy? We hear him saying to Timothy himself, "Let no man despise thy youth;" and again, "Flee also youthful lusts." Does Paul, in the Epistle to Timothy, refer particularly to the afflictions which came unto him at Antioch, at Iconium, and at Lystra? We find from the history, in the most indirect way imaginable, that Timothy must have lived in one of those cities, and have been converted at the time of those persecutions. Does Paul, in the Epistle to the Romans, ask their prayers that he might be delivered from them that did not believe, in Judea? We hear him saying, in the Acts, with reference to the same journey, "And now, behold, I go bound in the spirit unto Jerusalem, not knowing the things that shall befall me there; save that the Holy Ghost witnesseth in every city, saying that bonds and afflictions abide me." Do we hear him, in the Epistle to the Romans, commending to them Phœbe, a servant of the church at Cenchrea? We find, from the history, that Paul had been at Cenchrea, only from the following passage: "Having shorn his head in Cenchrea, for he had a vow." Of such coincidences Paley has pointed out, perhaps, a hundred, and he has by no means exhausted the subject.*

And not only do we find Epistles directed to churches, —the last species of composition that an original impostor, whether we suppose that the church did or did not exist at the time, could have thought of fabricating, — but we have, in more than one instance, two letters addressed to the same church, the last having all that reference to the first that we should expect. We find it also directed that the letter to one church should be read in another; we find it implied that one of the churches had written to the apostle, and his letter is partly in reply to theirs; we find such points discussed as would naturally have arisen in societies constituted as Christian churches must then have been; and, finally, we find a strength of personal feeling, a depth of tenderness and interest, a promptness in bestowing

* Horæ Paulinæ, passim.

deserved censure, a tone of authority, and a fullness of commendation, which could have sprung only from the transactions of actual life. Am I not, then, even from this view of their internal evidence, so briefly and imperfectly presented, justified in the assertion that no impostor either would, or could, have fabricated these books?

Conclusion. — And now, whether we look at the relations which Christianity must have sustained either to the Jews or to the Gentiles; at the course pursued either by Christ himself or by the apostles; at the connection between the Christian and the Jewish system; or at the impossibility of fabricating the books of the New Testament, — I think we may reasonably conclude that this religion, and these books, did not originate with man.

LECTURE VIII.

ARGUMENT TENTH: THE CONDITION, CHARACTER, AND CLAIMS OF CHRIST.

THUS far, we have attended to the *system* of Christianity, to its marvelous adaptations, and to the impossibility that it should have come from man. We now turn from the system to its Author. Who was the author of this system? What were his condition, his claims, and his character? We have already seen that the object he proposed, and the system he taught, are worthy of God, and correspond perfectly with the nature of man. But, were his condition in life, the claims he preferred, and the character he sustained, such as we can now see ought to have belonged to one who claimed the spiritual headship of the race? Is it possible that he should have been an impostor? Do we not find, meeting in him alone, so many things that are extraordinary, as to forbid that supposition? These questions it will be the object of the present lecture to answer.

Basis of the argument. — And if there is any subject to which we can apply, not only the tests of logic, but the decisions of intuitive reason, and of all the higher instincts of our common humanity, it is the condition in life, and teachings, and proposed object, and character, of one who presents himself with the claims put forth by Jesus Christ. We have an intuitive insight into character. We have, in the history of the world, large experience of it in all its combinations. We are all capable, when our moral nature is quickened, of judging whether the character of one who claims the homage both of the understanding and of the heart is in accordance with such a claim. "I know men," said Napoleon Bonaparte, "and I tell you that Jesus Christ was not a man." We also know men, and, presented as Christ is to us by the evangelists, not by description or eulogy, but standing before us in his actions and discourses, so that he seems to live and to speak, we feel that we can judge whether he bore the true insignia of his office or the marks of an impostor. If his claim had been to any thing else, it would be different. A claim to property, or to external homage, or to belief in a particular case, may be substantiated by external testimony; but when any being claims that I should believe a thing because he says it, — when he claims an affection from me greater than that which I owe to father, or mother, or brothers, or sisters, or wife, or children, — I not only do not, but I can not, and I ought not to, yield this confidence and affection on the ground of any external testimony. There must be presented an object of moral affection which shall commend itself as worthy, to my immediate perception, before I can do this. We can not yield our affections except to perceived excellence; and, since no man becomes a Christian who does not make Christ himself an object of affection, it is plain that his character, as well as his teaching, is a point of primary importance.

Christianity unique. — Character of Christ central. — And here, again, as in every thing else, Christianity stands by itself. If other systems are, to some extent, vulnerable through the character of their authors, no other presents its very heart to be thus pierced. In an abstract system of philosophy, we do not inquire what the character of its author was. The truth of the system of Plato, or of Adam Smith, or of Jeremy Bentham, does not depend on the question whether they were good or bad men; but if it could be shown that Christ was a bad man, — nay, if we were simply to withdraw his character and acts, — the whole system would collapse at once. His character stands as the central orb of the system, and without it there would be no effectual light and no heat. This arises from two causes. The first is the very striking peculiarity, — which, in considering the evidences, has not been enough noticed, — that the Author of Christianity claims, not merely belief, but affection. What would have been thought of Socrates, or Plato, if they had not merely taught mankind, but if they and their disciples had set up a claim that they should be loved by the whole human race with an affection exceeding that of kindred? This affection Christ claimed, and his disciples claimed it for him. Paul says, "If any man love not the Lord Jesus Christ, let him be anathema, maranatha," making the mere absence of the love a crime. But if he is to be thus loved by all men, he must first place himself in the relation to them of a personal benefactor, and then, by the very laws of affection, he must present a character which ought to call forth their love. The second cause why the character of Christ is so essential is, that in the moral and spiritual world power is manifested, and movement is effected, only by action. A moral system must, indeed, like any thing else, be the object of the intellect; but no abstract system of moral truth, no precepts merely enunciated, but not embodied and manifested in actual life, could ever have been the means of moral life to the world. Men need, not only truth, but life — the truth and life embodied. They need a leader, some one to go before them as the Captain of their salvation, whose voice they can hear saying, "Follow me." While, therefore, in all other systems, the character of the founder is of little importance, it is vital here. But no one can fail to see the infinite difficulty and hazard of introducing such an element as this into any system of imposture. It opens a point of attack against which no such system could ever rear an effectual barrier.

Condition in life. — Let us, then, first, as was proposed, look at the condition in life * of the Author of Christianity, and at the suitableness of that condition to one who was to be the teacher and spiritual deliverer of man. And here I need hardly say that our Saviour was in humble circumstances, and was entirely without property. This fact we find indicated by himself in the simplest and most affecting manner. He did not speak of it in the language of repining and complaint, nor yet of stoical indifference and contempt of wealth, but in the language of kindness, and to prevent disappointment in one who proposed to follow him, without understanding the true nature of his kingdom. He had become celebrated, both as having the power to work miracles and as a great teacher. Multitudes followed him; and a certain man, no doubt with some hope of worldly gain, said unto him, "Lord, I will follow thee whithersoever thou goest. And Jesus said unto him, Foxes have holes, and birds of the air have nests; but the Son of man hath not where to lay his head." The beasts of the field and the fowls of heaven had places of rest and shelter; but the greatest benefactor of men, when he came to dwell among them, had nothing that he could call his own. He had no legal title to any thing, no control over any thing which men call

---

* The argument from this topic is so similar to what is said respecting it by the author of the "Philosophy of the Plan of Salvation," that I think it proper to say, that it was copied almost literally from an unpublished discourse, delivered before the publication of that work.

property. And not only was he poor after he commenced his ministry, but from his early days. His parents had no such wealth and consideration as would procure them a place in an inn in Bethlehem when there was a crowd, and accordingly he was cradled in a manger. He was early driven into a strange country; and when he returned, his parents, through fear, turned aside and dwelt in a place where there was neither wealth nor refinement, and which had connected with it no elevating associations. He was called a Nazarene by way of reproach, and it was asked, "Can any good thing come out of Nazareth?" So poor were Joseph and Mary, that they do not seem to have been able to give their children any particular advantages of education; for it is said that, when Christ taught, the Jews marveled, saying, "How knoweth this man letters, having never learned?" He chose for his companions poor and unlettered men; and as he went from place to place, he was supported — shall I say by charity? Yes; but there are two kinds of charity. He was not supported by that kind of charity which is drawn forth in view of distress, and accompanied with pity; but, wherever he went, there were those who received him in the spirit of his mission, to whom his words were gracious words, and who esteemed it an honor and a privilege to minister to him of their substance. Support flowing from such a source, which was but a simple reflection of the spirit which he himself manifested, he was willing to receive, and did receive, and never seems to have had any other.

Fitness of — to exclude wrong motives. — Such was the condition in life of the Author of Christianity, and it was fit and important that it should be so; first, to show that his kingdom was not of this world, and to prevent any from attaching themselves to it from worldly motives. There is a kingdom of matter, governed by gravitation and the laws of affinity; there is a kingdom of sense and of sensitive good, governed by desire and by fear; and there is a moral and spiritual kingdom. In this kingdom the government is by rational motives, by a perception of right and of wrong, and by moral love. The motives by which a man is led to become a subject of this kingdom can have nothing to do with any thing material. The moment any consideration of wealth or of power comes in, to induce any one to enter into its visible inclosure, its very nature becomes changed. It was of infinite importance that this point should be guarded; and in no way could this have been done so effectually as by the humble condition, the entire separation, on the part of the Author of Christianity, from all connection with wealth or with power. Perhaps such a separation was even required by consistency, in one who said that his kingdom was not of this world.

For personal dignity. — Secondly, such a condition was necessary to the personal dignity of Christ as the head of a spiritual kingdom, and to the highest evidence of the reality of such a kingdom. If Christ was what he claimed to be, he could not receive title-deeds from men. He came out from God on a great mission, as the embassador of an infinite and an eternal kingdom; and it would not only have interfered with that mission in its spirit, but would have debased and degraded it beyond expression, if he had shown any regard for wealth, or had had any thing to do with the petty strifes of men for temporary power. Moreover, it could not otherwise have appeared that his true kingdom could stand by itself, and that it needed none of those attractions and supports at which alone men are accustomed to look. If Christ had possessed either wealth or power, I should feel that I was conducting this argument at an immense disadvantage.

To give wealth and power their place. — Thirdly, such a condition was necessary, not only that he might show his own estimate of wealth and power, but that he might lead his followers to a right view, and a right spirit, concerning them, and concerning the distinctions which they bring. They are external to the spirit. They have nothing to do with that state of it in which character consists, and on which its true dignity and happiness must depend. Christ came to prepare men for a kingdom where neither property nor wealth exists as an element of enjoyment, but where all things will be as the air and the sunlight; and where, if intellectual and moral beings differ, it will be only as one star differs from another star in glory. It is impossible, therefore, that any one who truly sympathizes with the spirit of Christ should have that selfish and idolatrous attachment to them which has been the cause of so much disorder and unhappiness among men.

To show the dignity of man. — And, once more: this condition of Christ was requisite to show the true worth and dignity of man as man. In a world where respect for man as an immortal being, in the image of God, had so far given place to respect for wealth and rank, it was of the first importance that a spiritual teacher should himself stand in the simple grandeur of a true and perfect manhood. By doing this, Christ furnished to the poor in all ages, many of whom were to be his disciples, a model, and a ground of self-respect; and he made it impossible that there should not be, wherever the spirit of his religion prevails, a true respect for every human being. With that estimate of man, or, if you please, of men, which ministers to the pride of talent, or of wealth, or of power, he had no sympathy. He looked at man as a spirit, at all men as standing upon the same level of immortality; and his teachings, his labors, and his sufferings, were equally for all.

Who can see the humble walks of life thus trodden, and not feel that the race is one brotherhood, and not be ready to give the hand of fellowship, of sympathy, and of aid, to every one whom Christ thus represented, and for whom he thus cared?

Strange, then, and offensive as it was at the first, as it always has been to many, it must yet be admitted that, if Christ was to be a spiritual deliverer, to eradicate pride and selfishness, and to unite all men in one brotherhood, it was essential that he should appear in the very circumstances and condition of life in which he did appear.

Claims of Christ. — We next inquire what were the claims of this man, — so humble in his condition; so lowly; so destitute of learning, of wealth, of influential friends; whose public ministry but little exceeded three years, and was terminated by crucifixion. In general, he claimed to be the Messiah, the Son of God, and the Saviour of men. As I wish to avoid here all disputed points, I shall not move the great question whether he claimed to be a truly divine person, or to be "the Lamb of God, that taketh away the sins of the world," in the sense of making an atonement, but shall observe, —

1. That he claimed to be a perfect teacher;
2. To set a perfect example; to be the model man of the race;
3. To be a perfectly sinless being;
4. That all men should love and obey him;
5. To work miracles as no other man ever did;
6. That in him the prophecies of the Old Testament were fulfilled;
7. That he would himself rise from the dead;
8. To be the final judge of the world.

Such were his claims — claims till then unprecedented, unheard of, undreamed of, by the wildest and most extravagant imagination.

Character of Christ. — Let us next see, so far as we have the means of determining, how he sustained these claims. In doing this, we shall, of necessity, as was proposed, consider his character.

Nothing local or temporary. — And here, before saying any thing under the particular heads specified, I shall enrich this lecture with three general remarks from one whose eloquent voice will long echo in the public halls of this city. "We are immediately struck," says Dr. Channing, in his Dudleian lecture, "with this peculiarity in the Author of Christianity, — that whilst all other men are formed in a measure by the spirit of the age, we can discover in Jesus no impression of the period in which he lived. We know, with considerable accuracy, the state of society, the modes of thinking, the hopes and expectations of the country in which Jesus was born and grew up; and he is as free from them as if he had lived in another world, or with every sense shut on the objects around him. His character has in it nothing local or temporary. It can be explained by nothing around him. His history shows him to us a solitary being, living for purposes which none but himself comprehended, and enjoying not so much as the sympathy of a single mind. His apostles, his chosen companions, brought to him the spirit of the age; and nothing shows its strength more strikingly than the slowness with which it yielded, in these honest men, to the instructions of Jesus."

Vastness of views. — Again: "One striking peculiarity in Jesus is the extent and vastness of his views. Whilst all around him looked for a Messiah to liberate God's ancient people, — whilst, to every other Jew, Judea was the exclusive object of pride and hope, —

Jesus came, declaring himself to be the deliverer and light of the world; and in his whole teaching and life you see a consciousness, which never forsakes him, of a relation to the whole human race. This idea of blessing mankind, of spreading a universal religion, was the most magnificent which had ever entered man's mind. All previous religions had been given to particular nations. No conqueror, legislator, philosopher, in the extravagance of ambition, had ever dreamed of subjecting all nations to a common faith."

Confidence. — Once more: he says, "I can not but add another striking circumstance in Jesus; and that is, the calm confidence with which he always looked forward to the accomplishment of his design. He fully knew the strength of the passions and powers which were arrayed against him, and was perfectly aware that his life was to be shortened by violence; yet not a word escapes him implying a doubt of the ultimate triumphs of his religion. * * * This entire and patient relinquishment of immediate success, this ever-present persuasion that he was to perish before his religion would advance, and this calm, unshaken anticipation of distant and unbounded triumphs, are remarkable traits, throwing a tender and solemn grandeur over our Lord, and wholly inexplicable by human principles, or by the circumstances in which he was placed!"

Christ a perfect teacher. — *The matter of his teaching.* — I now proceed to observe, 1. That, under that general claim to which these remarks apply, Christ claimed to be a perfect teacher — to be not only *a* light, but *the* light of the world. And who can point out any defect in his teaching, either in respect to matter or to manner? As a teacher of religion, he set before us, in the matter of his teaching, the paternal and the holy character of God, and taught us to love him, and to worship him in spirit and in truth. It is evidently impossible that we should have a higher conception of God in any of his attributes, or of his worship, than he communicated. In the same character, he taught us the great doctrines of a perfect human accountability, of the immortality of the soul, of the resurrection of the dead, and of the final reward of the righteous and punishment of the wicked. As a teacher of morality, he introduced a system, the great characteristics of which are, (1.) That it establishes a perfect standard. (2.) That it takes cognizance of the heart. (3.) That it forbids all the malevolent and dissocial passions. (4.) That it forbids all merely selfish passions, as vanity and pride. (5.) That it forbids all impure passions. (6.) That it includes all its positive duties under the two great requisitions of love to God and love to man, which all moralists now agree is the sum of human duty. If we look at man as a practical being, what point is there on which Christ did not shed light enough to lead him, if he will but follow his instructions, to his true happiness, whether in this world or the world to come?

The manner. — Nor was the manner of his teaching less extraordinary. He taught them as one having authority, and not as the scribes, or as the philosophers who ran into subtile distinctions, and deduced every thing from the nature of things. In opposition to all the learning, and authority, and prejudices of his age and nation, he simply said, "Verily *I* say unto you." He spoke with the calmness, and dignity, and decision, of one who bore credentials that challenged entire deference. But, if his manner was authoritative, it was also gentle and condescending; if it was dignified, it was also kind; if it was calm, it was also earnest. While his instructions were the most elevated that were ever uttered, they were uttered with such plainness, were so clothed in parables, and illustrated by common objects, that they were also the most intelligible. Nothing can exceed, nothing ever equaled, in depth and weight, some of his discourses and parables; and yet they are simple and beautiful, "are adapted to the habits of thinking of the poor, are opened and expanded to their capacities, separated from points of difficulty and abstraction, and presented only in the aspect which regarded their duty and hopes."* The most exalted intellect can not exhaust his instructions, and yet they are adapted to the feeblest. "Never man spake like this man." No teacher ever so combined authority and condescension, dignity and gentleness, zeal and discretion, sublimity and plainness, weight of matter and a facility of comprehension by all.

Christ a perfect example and model. — 2. But if the claim to be a perfect teacher was so high, far higher was that to set a perfect example, and to stand before the world as the model man.

The need of this. — In every practical science, a perfect system of instruction must include both precept and example. If God was to institute a perfect system for the instruction and elevation of man, both as a speculative and a practical being, it was necessary that he should not only give him perfect precepts, but that he should cause a perfect example to be set before him. The constitution of man requires this. He is, and must be, more affected by example than by precept. Even in the exact sciences, when a rule is given, though it really covers every possible case, it is yet necessary to give examples to show practically its application. Much more must this be needed in the ever-varying adjustments of moral relations. A great example will speak, though silently, yet powerfully, to the sympathetic feelings, and will aid the imagination in giving direction and definiteness to its ideas of perfection.

* Wilson.

Its adaptation to man.—And here we find one great adaptation of the Christian system to the moral condition and wants of man, which is not even attempted in any other. It is one on which I did not dwell when on the subject of adaptations, because I intended to speak of it here. The Author of Christianity, in claiming to give such an example, at least showed his knowledge of what a perfect system required; and if he has done it, he has not only done what unassisted man could not do, but what I am inclined to think he could not even conceive of. It was not in the power of man to form a conception of the character of Christ before he appeared. It is one thing to recognize a perfect character as such, when it is presented, and quite another so to combine the qualities as to form such a character, and to manifest it in action. It is at this point that we find all the difference between the common power of judging of the productions of genius in the fine arts, and of producing models of excellence in those arts; and I do not hesitate to say that, as a work of art, a product of genius, simply, the exhibition in life of a perfect model of human nature would be the highest conceivable attainment. That man has genius who can embody the perfection of material forms in his imagination, and cause those forms to live before us in the marble, on the canvas, or on the printed page; and he has higher genius still who can arrange the elements of character into new yet natural combinations, and cause his personages, as organized and consistent wholes, to speak and act before us. In all these cases, when Michael Angelo produces a statue, or Allston a painting, or Milton a landscape, or Shakspeare a character, we can judge of it, though we could not have made that combination. It is, indeed, the great prerogative of genius to produce thoughts, and forms, and characters, and I will add here *actions*, of which other men recognize the excellence, but which they could not have produced. Yes, I add actions; for if the conception and delineation of an original course of action require genius, it must be equally required, and in combination, too, with high practical qualities, to realize that same conception in the bolder relief of actual life. The power to act thus does not always, perhaps not generally, involve the power of delineation, but it does involve the very highest form of genius, and something more; and it is only because there is genius, that expresses itself in great action, that that of delineation has either dignity or worth.

Its difficulty. — Now, as the highest effort of genius in statuary would be to produce a perfect human form, one of which it might be said that, though no form in nature ever equaled it, yet that every form was perfect in proportion as it approximated toward it, so it would be the highest conceivable effort of genius, involving its most complex elements, to present, as an organized and consistent whole, and to cause to speak and act before us in all the diversified relations of life, a perfect human being, — one of whom it might be said that, though no other ever manifested the same excellence, yet that all others were excellent in proportion as they approximated toward him. Philosopher, man of genius and of taste, here is a task for you. We challenge you to it. Would you, could you, not merely describe in general terms, but present in detail, the words and actions even of a consistent and perfect piety? No. You would not, and you could not. Attempts had often been made to portray a model character, but it does not appear that it was within the power of human genius; and when the majestic, the simple, the beautiful, the perfect character of Christ appeared, it was seen how poor those attempts had been. Certainly, applying the most philosophical tests, if the evangelists did invent this character, they manifested higher genius than any other men that ever lived. But if the bare representation of such a character would be so difficult, who could have thought of really being such a person, of expressing it in life and action?

Of philosophical interest. — Now, the question whether the true model of humanity has been really thus presented, is one, to my mind, not only of religious, but of the deepest philosophical interest. If mankind are ever to advance intelligently in excellence, they must have the true model before them. There can be no true progress, either of individuals or of society, without this. The greatest amount of human activity, hitherto, has had no tendency to advance the cause of humanity, and it never can have till men adopt a right model, and seek to conform themselves to that. To conform ourselves to such a model we do aspire in our better moments. Is there one here who has not felt the stirrings within him of something that would lead him to take hold on this? Wherever there is any thing truly elevated in human nature, it is this that it seeks for; it is this that, in its blindness and moral ruin, it still gropes after; it is this respecting which many, very many, when they have beheld the character of Christ, have exclaimed, with a deeper joy than that of the philosopher, " Eureka, Eureka!" — I have found it, I have found it!

Part of the system. — Yes, we do claim that this model was presented, as a part of the system of Christianity, in the character of Christ; this deep want of human nature we say that he has supplied. The more we look at the character of Christ, the more we shall be satisfied that there is there presented what we seek — the more ready shall we be to exclaim, " Who is this that cometh up . . . traveling in the greatness of his strength?" It is obviously not every part of his life that was intended to be an example to man, but only that in which he stood in the relations common to men, in which he moved and walked as one of them. And he did move and mingle freely with men of all classes and of all conditions. He was placed not only in such a condition in life, but in so many situations — he came into collision with human passion and interest in so many ways — as most fully to test his character, and make him an example to all. At this example we will briefly look.

His piety. — I observe, then, first, that his piety was most exemplary.* On all occasions he acknowledged God, and *always* did those things that pleased him. He conformed to the ceremonial law. He expounded the Scriptures, and honored them as the word of God. He attended public worship on the Sabbath. There are indications that he was in constant habits of devotion, and on all solemn occasions he prayed. "It is recorded of him on no less than six occasions, that he gave thanks to God on partaking and distributing food." When he was baptized, he prayed. Before he chose his twelve disciples, he went out into a mountain to pray. When he had wrought a great number of cures publicly for the first time, he "rose up a great while before it was day, and went into a desert place, and prayed." When many came together to hear him, and to be cured of their infirmities, he retired into desert places, and prayed. When he had fed five thousand with five loaves and two fishes, he dismissed the multitudes, and went up into a mountain apart, to pray. On one occasion, he continued all night in prayer. He prayed for Peter. He prayed, if it may be called prayer, at the grave of Lazarus. He prayed at the close of the institution of the Lord's supper. He

---

* On this whole subject, see Archbishop Newcome's "Observations on our Lord."

prayed in his agony. He prayed on the cross. He taught his disciples to pray, and gave them that form of which Paley says that, "For a succession of solemn thoughts, for fixing the attention upon a few great points, for suitableness to every condition, for sufficiency, for conciseness without obscurity, for the weight and real importance of its petitions, it is without a rival." In all things he had reference to the will of God, so that he could say that it was his meat to do his will. The doing of God's will perfectly was evidently the great element in which he lived. And this piety was a rational piety, without any tinge of mysticism, or gloom, or fanaticism, or extravagance. For, —

His benevolence. — Secondly, it was equaled only by his benevolence. Of this it can not be necessary that I should adduce particular instances. His whole history, in this respect, is comprised in five words — "He went about doing good." All his acts were entirely unselfish. He never refused to relieve the distress of any, but never used his miraculous powers for his own benefit, or to gain applause. His benevolence was universal, embracing, in direct opposition to the spirit of his age and nation, not only the Jews, but the Samaritans and the Gentiles. His benevolence rose superior to injuries. He neither reviled, nor complained, nor ceased from his labors and sufferings for the good of men, when he was the most cruelly treated.

Compassion — combination of opposite qualities. — And not only was he benevolent, but compassionate. He had compassion on the multitude when they were hungry and faint. He wept over Jerusalem. He was full of sympathy. When he saw Mary weeping, and the Jews also weeping who came with her, "Jesus wept." He was full of gentleness and condescension, taking up little children in his arms and blessing them; and yet he was fearless and terrible in his reproofs of iniquity in high places. He "came eating and drinking," and was free from all austerity; and yet he was "pure in spirit." He had great meekness and lowliness, in union with an evident consciousness of the highest dignity. He washed his disciples' feet, at the same time that he told them that he was their Lord and Master. He was not elated by popularity, nor depressed when his followers deserted him. He had a zeal which led his friends to say he was beside himself; and yet his prudence, as shown by his answers to those who would entrap him, was equal to his zeal. Nor was his zeal indiscriminate; for, while he insisted on the silent worship which is in spirit and in truth, he yet gave their proper place to external observances, even to the tithing of mint, and he rebuked zeal in his own cause, when it did not proceed from a pure motive. He was keenly sensible to suffering, and yet he bore it without murmuring. He was subject to his parents in early life, and remembered his mother on the cross. There is no virtue which he did not exemplify, and man can be placed in no situation in which his example will not be applicable.

Positions to try piety and benevolence. — But, to sum up what has been said of the example of Christ, it has often seemed to me remarkable that he should have been brought into such positions as to try, in the highest possible manner, both his piety and his benevolence, and to lead him to give of each of these the highest possible example. No doubt this was so ordered of God. The two great principles of conduct, which men need to have constantly set before them, are love and submission to God, and benevolence to men. And did not he manifest a perfect love and submission to God, who could say, in the prospect of his dreadful sufferings, and in the hour of his agony, "Not my will, but thine, be done"? Did not he love others as himself, and exemplify his own most difficult precept of forgiving injuries, who prayed for his murderers on the cross? "Behold the man!"

A perfect example, and something more. — And here I would observe, that I do not regard the setting of a perfect example, in every thing that may strictly be called a duty, as comprising every thing that should belong to a perfect humanity. A perfect humanity implies a sensibility, a refinement, a grace, a beauty of character, which can not be said to be required by duty. And all these the Saviour had in the highest degree. There was no pure and exquisite emotion of human nature to which he was not keenly alive; and it is the union, in him, of every thing that is tender and gentle with those higher and sterner qualities, which renders him a fit example, not for man only, but for woman. How just and perfect must have been his perception of the beauties of nature, who could say of the lilies of the field, that Solomon, in all his glory, was not arrayed like one of these! In all the attitudes in which Christ was placed, in all the words that he uttered, there is nothing unseemly, or offensive to a just taste. His susceptibilities to both joy and suffering were intense. He rejoiced in spirit, and his joy instantly burst forth in devout thanksgiving. He was prone to compassion, and repeatedly melted into tears. The innocence of children engaged his affection. His heart was open to impressions of friendship. "Jesus loved Martha, and her sister, and Lazarus." He had a beloved disciple. When he saw an amiable young man, he loved him. He was grieved at unbelief, and had a generous indignation against vice.

An example, and yet the Messiah. — In all these respects — in his piety, in his benevolence and other virtues, in the refinement and delicacy of his character — he is a suitable example for us. But, as difficult as it must have been to present in action this combination of human excellences, it must have been much more so to combine with them those qualities, and that deportment, which were appropriate to him as the Messiah and Saviour of the world. Is it possible that He who claimed to be greater than Solomon, to command legions of angels, to raise the dead, — who spoke of himself as the Son of God, and as the final Judge of the world, — should so move, and speak, and act, as to sustain a character compatible with these high pretensions, and yet have the condescension, and gentleness, and meekness, of Christ? And yet such is the character presented by the evangelists. There is no break, no incongruity. Like his own seamless garment, the character is one. He seems to combine, with perfect ease, these elements, apparently so incompatible. This, I confess, excites my astonishment. The presentation of a perfect manhood in a lowly station had been beyond the power of human genius; but when this is combined with the proprieties and requisitions of a public character, and an office so exalted as that of the Messiah and the Judge of the world, then I have an intuitive conviction that I stand in the presence of no human invention; then this character presents itself to me with the grandeur and wonder that belong to the great mountains and the starry heavens.

Rousseau. — Is there an infidel who hears me, and who says that these impressions are made on a mind predisposed to receive them, and that they are not those which would legitimately be made? — let him hear what one of his own prophets has said. "I confess," says Rousseau,* "that the majesty of the Scriptures astonishes me; that the sanctity of the gospel speaks to my heart. View the books of the philosophers, — with all their pomp, what a littleness have

---

* Emile, as translated by Newcome.

they when compared with this! Is it possible that a book at once so sublime and simple should be the work of men? Is it possible that he whose history it records should be himself a mere man? Is this the style of an enthusiast, or of an ambitious sectary? What sweetness, what purity, in his manners! what affecting grace in his instructions! what elevation in his maxims! what profound wisdom in his discourses! what presence of mind, what delicacy, and what justness, in his replies! what empire over his passions! Where is the man, where is the philosopher, who knows how to act, to suffer, and to die, without weakness and without ostentation?* . . . Where could Jesus have taken, among his countrymen, that elevated and pure morality of which he alone furnished both the precept and the example? The most lofty wisdom was heard from the bosom of the most furious fanaticism; and the simplicity of the most heroic virtues honored the vilest of all people. The death of Socrates, serenely philosophizing with his friends, is the most gentle that one can desire; that of Jesus, expiring in torments, injured, derided, reviled by a whole people, is the most horrible that one can fear. When Socrates takes the poisoned cup, he blesses him who presents it, and who at the same time weeps; Jesus, in the midst of a horrid punishment, prays for his enraged executioners. Yes; if the life and death of Socrates are those of a philosopher, the life and death of Jesus Christ are those of a God."

A perfect example and sinlessness. — 3. According to the idea of many, the claim to set a perfect example involves the claim to be perfectly sinless. But, in some respects, the claim to be sinless involves more

---

* Part of this passage is here omitted. I wish to add the following: "What prejudices, what blindness, must they have, who dare to draw a comparison between the son of Sophroniscus and the son of Mary! What distance is there between the one and the other!"

than the claim to *exhibit* a perfect model of humanity, since this exhibition respects an outward manifestation; and who can say that it may not be compatible with some wrong feeling or affection? And, in some respects, again, the claim to be a model man is more extensive than that to be perfectly sinless. A human being might be sinless, and be destitute of many of the perfections of the character of Christ. And then, again, these claims look in such different directions, and respect such entirely different objects, that there is a propriety in considering them apart. The claim to present a perfect manhood has respect to the wants of man; the claim to be sinless has respect to the relations of the individual to God, and to his fitness to be a Redeemer from sin. It must, I think, be conceded, that he who would deliver others from the power of sin must himself be free from its power — be entirely above and aloof from it. While, therefore, we can conceive of an *exhibition* of our nature that would appear to us faultless, while we might not be certain that it was sinless, yet we can not conceive of one, coming as a redeemer and deliverer from sin, who had himself ever swerved from moral rectitude even in thought or feeling. But since the great purpose for which Christ came was to "save his people from their sins," it became necessary that he should himself be, and claim to be, entirely free from sin.

Christ claimed to be sinless. — That Christ made this claim, and that his disciples made it for him, there can be no doubt. They made it implicitly, and they made it expressly. Christ said, "Which of you convinceth me of sin?" — that he did always those things that pleased the Father — that he was one with the Father. Peter says, expressly, that he "did no sin," that he was "the holy one and the just;" and Paul says that he was "holy, harmless, undefiled, and separate from sinners."

Bearings of this claim. — But what a claim is this! — a claim never made by any other human being. Such a claim, the most extraordinary, and the most difficult to be sustained, of any that was ever set up, while it is implied in the idea of a redeemer from sin, must have been fatal to any impostor. Is this claim admitted, or is it denied? If it is admitted, the claims of Christianity are admitted with it. If it is denied, the claims of Christianity, as a religion, are denied; for, as a mode of deliverance from sin, and of salvation, its whole value turns upon this. Men may have what knowledge they please of external evidences, and of mere facts, but this can never work a spiritual renovation. They must come to Christ, and believe in him as a sinless Redeemer, or there can no virtue go out of him for their spiritual healing.

Proof. — The proof that Christ was a sinless being will be founded, first, on the same facts that prove his perfect example. Here, too, we may properly receive his own testimony, since he could not have been deceived on this point. His perfect sinlessness is also to be inferred from the effects produced by his life upon his disciples; from its effects upon the world; and from the fact that, as the mind of any individual becomes more pure and elevated, he perceives a greater and greater purity and elevation in the character of Christ, so that, to whatever height he may attain, he still perceives the majestic form of the Redeemer moving before him. I leave the point by remarking, that if any wish to see it fully illustrated, I would refer them to an excellent essay upon it by Dr. Ullman in the "German Selections," translated by Edwards and Park.

Claims of Christ to obedience. — 4. Christ also claimed that all men should love and obey him. This — the assertion of a right to a paramount and spiritual dominion, not over one race or one age only, but over all mankind, and through all coming ages — was, as I have already said, entirely peculiar. It must imply a claim to stand in the relation of a personal benefactor to every one, and to possess such a character as ought to call forth affection. After the other claims of Christ, we need not be surprised at this. But what a glorious kingdom of affection and love does it open before us! Here is the foundation of that kingdom of love of which Napoleon spoke when he compared the kingdom of Christ with his own. "Alexander, Cæsar, Charlemagne, and myself," said he, "founded empires; but upon what foundations did we rest the creations of our genius? Upon force. Jesus Christ alone founded his empire upon love, and, at this hour, millions of men would die for him. . . . I die before my time, and my body will be given back to the earth to become the food of worms. Such is the fate of him who has been called the great Napoleon. What an abyss between my deep misery and the eternal kingdom of Christ, which is proclaimed, loved, and adored, and which is extending over the whole earth!"

To work miracles. — 5. Christ claimed to work miracles. I mention this, not because he alone has made this claim or has wrought miracles, but because, all the circumstances considered, he stands entirely by himself in this respect. I have already spoken of the character of his miracles, as sufficient of itself to confirm his divine mission. They were none of them wrought for his personal advantage, or for display, or capriciously, or to gratify curiosity. They were all benevolent and worthy of God. He was peculiar, too, in the number of his miracles. It is probable, from the accounts given, that, on a single occasion, he wrought more miracles than had been wrought by all the prophets from the beginning. He was also peculiar in his manner of working miracles. He performed them with entire simplicity and facility, and generally, so far as appears, by his own authority. "He commanded the unclean spirits, and they came out." He said to the sea, "Peace, be still." When he raised the dead, he simply said, "Young man, I say unto thee, Arise." The apostles did their miracles in the name of Christ, and the manner of the prophets was entirely different, giving no such impressions of power and majesty.

That the prophecies were fulfilled in him. — 6. Christ also claimed that in him the prophecies of the Old Testament were fulfilled. I mention this among the claims which he must be acknowledged to have made, but shall not dwell upon it here, because I intend to speak of it more fully at another time. The claim, however, is not a slight one, to stand as the subject of prophecy and the antitype of all the types in the old dispensation from the beginning, — the claim that he was a person of such importance as to have been spoken of from the first by holy men, and to appeal to the Scriptures as testifying of him.

That he would rise from the dead. — 7. Christ claimed that he would rise from the dead. What could have induced him to make so strange a claim as this? And yet, to substantiate this claim, thus put forth, we have an accumulation of evidence such as we have for scarcely any other ancient fact.

And be the Judge of the world. — 8. Of the claim of Christ to be the final Judge of the world I shall say nothing, because, from the nature of the case, I have no means of verifying it. The fact that he made this claim, however, is all that is needed for the purpose of my present argument; and I will only observe, that it is not more extraordinary than his other claims, and is in perfect keeping with them. If we admit his other claims, we shall of course admit this.

Was he deceived? — Such were the condition, the claims, and the character, of Jesus Christ. And now, is it possible that he was either deceived or a deceiver? Was he sincere in making these claims? If he was, and they are not well founded, then I ask, Could a young man, poor, unlearned, brought up in an obscure village, accustomed to a humble employment, make such claims, and not be utterly insane? Can we conceive of a wilder hallucination? Is there one of all the vagaries entertained by the tenants of our lunatic asylums that is more extravagant than these? No mere self-exaltation or enthusiasm, nothing short of insanity, can account for such claims. I mention this the rather, because I remember to have been struck by it in reading the New Testament in my early days. When I heard this man, apparently so lowly, saying that he was the light of the world, — "If any man thirst, let him come unto me and drink," — that he was one with God, that all things were delivered to him by his Father, that he that had seen him had seen the Father, that whatsoever the disciples should ask in his name he would do it, that he would rise from the dead, and come in the clouds of heaven, attended by myriads of angels, to judge the world, — I felt that I had evidence, either that those claims were well founded, or of a hopeless insanity. No wonder those who did not believe said of him, "He hath a devil, and is mad: why hear ye him?" But then, as now, there was the unanswerable reply, "These are not the words of him that hath a devil. Can a devil open the eyes of the blind?" When we look at his discourses, at their calmness, at their deep insight and profound wisdom; when we see that the discoveries of all ages have only shed luster upon their wisdom, and that the wisest and best portion of the race now sit at his feet as their instructor; when we see the more than propriety, the self-possession, the dignity of his deportment under the most trying circumstances, — we feel that not a voice from heaven could make it more certain that his was not a crazed, or a weak, or an unbalanced intellect. This fact is borne witness to by the light of its own evidence; it shines by its own brightness.

Was he a deceiver? — Did he, then, in the exercise of a sound mind, put forth those claims with the intention to deceive others? This, as I have just intimated, I hold to have been impossible. No impostor of common sense could have had the folly to prefer such claims. But, if this consideration is conclusive, how much more is that drawn from the moral character of Christ? Look at his unaffected and all-pervading piety, at his universal and self-sacrificing benevolence; look at his purity and elevation above the world; listen to his prayer for his murderers on the cross; and say, is it possible that through all this he was meditating a scheme of deception deeper, more extensive, involving greater sacrifices and sufferings, and more ultimate disappointment to human hope, than any other? Do we not *know* that this was not so? If we could believe this, would not that faith in goodness, which is the vital element in the atmosphere of our moral life, be destroyed? And what would remain to us but the stifling, and oppressive, and desolating conviction, that there could be no ground of faith in any indications of goodness? We can not believe this, we will not believe it. Take away, if you will, the vital element of the air, disrobe the sun of his beams, but remove not from me, this life of my life; leave to me the full-orbed and unshorn brightness of the character of Christ, the Sun of righteousness.

We have found the Messias. — It only remains that I should refer to what has, indeed, been implied throughout the preceding part of the lecture — that gathering about the person of Christ of so many and such extraordinary circumstances; that clustering upon him of so many wonderful and diverse characteristics and appropriate insignia of a messenger from God; that accumulation of evidences which come in, as it were, from the four winds, and become as a crown of many stars upon the head of the Redeemer. It is to be distinctly noticed, in estimating the evidence, that it is not one only of the surprising offices and characteristics which have been mentioned that he sustained so perfectly, but all of them. It is the same great Teacher around whose system natural religion, and the old dispensation, and all human science, stand up and do obeisance, as did the sheaves of Joseph's brethren around his sheaf, who also set a perfect example, and stands before us as the model man. It is the same person who "did no sin," who wrought miracles, who fulfilled the prophecies, who rose from the dead, around whom there shines, as I shall show hereafter, such an effulgence of external evidence, whose life and death have been followed by such amazing effects. If we were to estimate by the doctrine of chances the probability that so many extraordinary circumstances, each of which could be confirmed by so much evidence, should meet upon a single person, the fraction expressing that probability would be infinitely small. Had any *one* of these characteristics belonged to any other individual, it would have placed him among the most distinguished personages of history; but when we see them all clustering upon the lowly Jesus, the Crucified One, we must say, with one of old, "We have found the Messias."

LECTURE IX.

THE EXTERNAL EVIDENCE. — GENERAL GROUNDS ON WHICH THIS IS TO BE PUT. — ARGUMENT ELEVENTH: AUTHENTICITY AND INTEGRITY OF THE WRITINGS OF THE NEW TESTAMENT.

WHEN we came into life, we found Christianity existing. It was our business, as independent thinkers, to examine it in its relations to the human constitution and to human well-being. This we have done in the preceding lectures; and if the system be such as it has been represented to be, then we may well feel a deep interest in every thing relating to its origin and history — in what have been called its external evidences. To those evidences, then, we now turn.

Object of inquiry, facts. — In this department of the evidences, the object of our inquiry is, not adaptations, or doctrines, or opinions, or inferences, but simply historical facts.

To be judged of by their own evidence. — Was there such a person as Jesus Christ? Was he crucified? Did he rise from the dead? These are questions which we are to settle precisely as we would settle the questions whether there was such a man as Augustus Cæsar, and whether he became the sole ruler of the Roman empire. These are no abstract questions, and we are not to let any of the uncertainty which must often belong to the discussion of such questions connect itself with these.

There is a science of evidence; there are laws of evidence; and all we ask is, that those laws may be applied to the facts of Christianity precisely as they are to any other facts. We insist upon it that the evidence ought to be judged of by itself, simply as evidence; that no man has a right first to examine the facts, and make up an antecedent judgment that they are improbable, and then transfer this feeling of improbability over to the evidence. We hold to the principle of Butler, that, to a being like man, objections against Christianity, as distinguished from objections against its evidence, unless, indeed, it can be shown to contain something either immoral or absurd, really amount to nothing.

Facts essential. — It is, indeed, a striking peculiarity of the Christian religion, that the truth of its doctrines, and the power of its motives, are inseparably connected with the reality of certain facts which might originally be judged of by the senses, and which are now to be determined by the same historical evidence as we employ in judging of any other facts. As fully as I have entered upon the internal evidence, as satisfactory as I regard the proof it furnishes, as heartily as I should deprecate a merely historical religion, necessarily destitute of any life-giving power, I would yet say, distinctly, that I believe in no religion that is not supported by historical proof. Unless Jesus Christ lived, and wrought miracles, and was crucified, and rose from the dead, Christianity is an imposture — beautiful, indeed, and utterly unaccountable, but still an imposture.

Christianity peculiar in this. — Perhaps it is not enough considered how much Christianity is contradistinguished, in this respect, not only from other systems of religion, but from all systems and questions of philosophy. Christ said, "Though ye believe not me, believe the works." So said not Mohammed. The facts on which his system, as a *religion*, rests, depend solely on the testimony of one man. So says not any system of philosophy. It is a totally different thing for the philosopher to present certain doctrines for our reception on the ground of his reasoning, and for the witness to testify, "That which we have heard, which we have seen with our eyes, which we have looked upon, and our hands have handled, — declare we unto you." Christianity is, indeed, a spiritual religion; but it is a spirituality manifesting itself through facts, clothed in substantial forms. It says to the unbelieving, "Reach hither thy finger, and behold my hands; and reach hither thy hand, and thrust it into my side." In saying this, it offers itself to be tried by a new test — such a one as no other religion can stand. But the Christian religion shrinks from no test. We wish it to be fully tried. We know that, like the pure gold, the more it is tried, the more clearly it will be seen to be genuine. That a religion intended for the race would need the kind of evidence of which I am now to speak, is plain; but the difficulty is immeasurably increased when it is attempted to sustain an imposture by evidence of this kind, freely thrown open to all.

Ground of belief in similar facts. — As, then, our object is to ascertain the reality of certain alleged facts, it may be well to look at the grounds on which we believe other and similar facts. It has generally been said, that the sole ground on which we believe facts that we have not ourselves witnessed, is that of testimony. In some cases this is so, but in many others I should think it an inadequate account of the grounds of our belief. When a man finds an ancient mound at the west, and in it human bones and the implements of civilization, is it on the ground of testimony that he believes that this continent was once inhabited by a race now extinct? Or, again, if I were required to prove that such a man as General Washington ever existed, and performed the acts generally ascribed to him, should I rest on the ground of testimony alone? Perhaps the evidence of testimony is involved in the fact that his birthday is celebrated; but that fact is something more than mere testimony. So, when I go to the house where it is said he lived, and the tomb where it is said he is buried, when I see the sword presented to Congress which it is said he wore, I find, in the existence of the house, the tomb, the sword, an evidence distinct from that of naked testimony. So, again, when I look at the independence of this country, and at its republican institutions, and find them ascribed by universal testimony to what Washington did, and when I find existing no other account of the manner in which our independence was achieved, and our institutions established, then I find, in the fact of the independence of this country and the existence of its free institutions, an evidence distinct from that of mere testimony. Every lawyer knows the difference between naked testimony and testimony thus corroborated by circumstantial evidence.

Facts differently substantiated. — Here, then, we find the ground of a wide distinction between the different classes of facts for which we have evidence. They may be divided into those which rest on the evidence of testimony alone, and those which we receive, not merely on the direct evidence of testimony, but which produced permanent effects in the world that are now manifest, and which can be reasonably traced to no other causes than those assigned by the testimony. And of this latter kind, especially, some are so substantiated, that no miracle could be more strange, or more difficult to be believed, or more a violation of the uniform course of our experience, than that such evidence should deceive us. The existence and history of Washington, for example, are so much involved in the present state of things, the evidence for them comes from so many sources, it touches so many points, that to deny them would be a practical absurdity. We should think it no breach of charity to say to him who questioned such evidence, that he was insincere.

Those of Christianity in the strongest way. — Now, it is on this general ground that the evidence for Christianity rests; and we say that no man can pluck away the pillars on which it rests, without bringing down the whole fabric of historical evidence in ruins over his head. We say that this evidence can not be invalidated without introducing universal and absolute historical skepticism. Christianity, with all its institutions, exists. Christendom exists, and it is important to our argument that the greatness of this fact should not be overlooked. It is the great fact in the history of the world. Here is a religion, received by a large portion of the human race; by that portion, too, which takes the lead in civilization and the arts. It confessedly supplanted other religions; it produced a revolution in the opinions and habits of men, unparalleled in the history of the world. It has not merely accomplished religious and moral revolutions, but, incidentally, social and civil changes, so as completely to transform the face of society. It came to its ascendency through great opposition and persecutions, such as no other religion ever did or could withstand; and now it does not live by flattering the natural passions of men, or by letting them alone and requiring of them no sacrifices. It has not, like other religions, depended for its existence and power upon its connection with the state; for, though it has often been connected with the state, and, in some particular form, upheld by it, yet it flourishes best when left to find its own way, and to control the hearts of men by its own proper force.

The religion to be accounted for. — Now, the existence

of such a religion as this, in the world, requires to be accounted for. It would be absurd to suppose that, in a period of high intellectual cultivation, it should spring up and subvert other religions, without being challenged by mankind, and having its credentials demanded, and its history known. But if the facts on which the religion was based were once known, it would seem in the last degree improbable that the knowledge of them should perish, and the religion remain; or, what would be still more strange, not only that all knowledge, oral or written, of these facts should have perished, but that a false and most minute account should have been substituted for the true one, and received from the first.

Tradition.—Moreover, it is chiefly with facts that exert an important influence on the destiny of mankind, that tradition connects itself; and this, in connection with institutions which enter into the fabric of society, or with monuments or observances handed down by an unbroken succession of persons, who have felt a deep interest in the facts in question, can not fail to preserve the great outlines of events as long as such observances and monuments remain. If all written records were blotted out from this time, and yet the independence of this nation were to be preserved, and the fourth of July were to continue to be annually celebrated, who can suppose that, in any length of years, all trace of the true origin of the day should be lost, and another, entirely false, substituted for it? So, when we find a Christian church, that has existed as a separate independent body from the origin of the religion, celebrating an ordinance once a week, or once a month, or once in two months, in commemoration of the death of Christ, if we had no other evidence for it than that of tradition, the presumption would be very strong that, at least, such a man as Christ lived and died, and was supposed to have conferred some distinguished benefit. And in this case the evidence is peculiarly strong, because the ordinance has been so frequently repeated and so widely extended. No delusion, from national pride or local feeling, can be suspected, because we find the same tradition, and the same ordinance, in the most distant and remote countries. Millions of Christians now regard this rite as the most sacred one belonging to a religion for which they are ready to lay down their lives; they received it from those who were equally attached to it; and so it must have been up to the point — a point perfectly well defined in history — from which the tradition, and the written history, and the ordinance, started together.

If true, all natural and plain. — *The reverse.* — Here, then, we find Christendom, and the Christian church — a body of men as distinctly organized and as intimately associated as those of any state — having its institutions, its traditions, and its records, all perfectly harmonizing with each other. These records bear on the face of them the marks of veracity; there is nothing known that is contradictory to them; they contain a fair and plausible account of the origin of the church. Admit the account, and every difficulty is removed. Refuse to admit it, and you destroy the very foundations of historical proof in any fact whatever. So much, indeed, are the general facts of Christianity implied in the present state of the world, and so much has it of that conviction which springs from universal notoriety, and which we can neither doubt, nor trace to any particular source, that I do not hesitate to say, that the objections brought by Archbishop Whately against the existence and general history of Napoleon Bonaparte are quite as plausible as any that can be brought against the existence and general history of Christ.

We receive other facts. — And more especially ought we to receive facts thus substantiated, when we remember how fully we believe those which are established by testimony alone. This, as was said in a former lecture, may be the ground of a certainty as full and perfect as any of which we can conceive. Can I doubt that there is such a city as Rome, or such a person as Queen Victoria? or that there has been such a person as Napoleon Bonaparte, or George the Fourth? And yet I know these facts solely by testimony. Who doubts, or can doubt, that Augustus Cæsar was emperor of Rome? Who would fear to stake his life on the fact that such a man as Alexander the Great existed? And yet no trace of that fact remains in the present organizations or customs of society, and the written and traditionary evidence for it is as nothing compared with that of Christianity.

All testimony does not deceive. — It is not, then, true of every kind of testimony that it sometimes deceives us. There may be testimony of such a nature as never was, and never can be, false; and it was a poor fallacy of Hume to attempt to transfer over to all testimony that uncertainty which belongs to it only in some cases. We affirm that the testimony for Christianity, taken by itself, is such as could not possibly be deceptive, as was never known to be so since the world began; and we challenge infidels to point out an instance of such deception. When they do this, they may talk of the uncertainty of testimony.

Nor lose weight by age. — I may properly refer here, also, to another common fallacy respecting testimony, which is based on the same principle of transferring to the whole what belongs only to a part, and which has had some influence. It is, that testimony loses its weight by age; that every century steals something from its probability. As if testimony that was once true, would not always be true; and the question whether it shall appear more or less true to the minds of men, after longer or shorter periods have elapsed, is one that must be determined by circumstances. Nothing can be more untrue than the general assertion, as made universally; and, as applied to the evidences of Christianity, I deny it altogether. Age itself, as such, has no tendency to impair the force of testimony; and it often happens that, by the discovery of coins, or ruins, or hieroglyphics, or inscriptions, or manuscripts, testimony which had been doubted for ages is fully confirmed. It is, indeed, a fact, that, from fuller research, and from such discoveries, the historical testimony for Christianity, instead of being diminished within the last hundred years, has been greatly increased and strengthened.

No facts of history so well sustained. — But, valid as is the evidence of testimony, we do not feel that we rest upon that alone, but that the facts of Christianity are sustained by every species of evidence by which it is possible that any past event should be substantiated. The great facts in history are very few — I think of none — which are implied in the present state of the civilized world as are those of the Christian religion. It is as if the taking of Constantinople by the Turks were to be confirmed by a reference to its present state. Let us suppose, to illustrate this point more fully, that a book purporting to be a history of the Turks, and giving an account of their taking the city of Constantinople and making it their capital, were put into the hands of a man who had never heard of that people. If it bore upon its face evidence of its being a true history, he might receive it, and this would be naked testimony. But, if he should afterward travel, and find this same people making a city of that name their capital, and find still dwelling among them the remains of a subjugated people, and should find, both among Turks and others, one unvarying tradition of the same events, and should find, moreover, other and independent histories agreeing in all respects with the history he had first seen, and the original letters of the commanders of the army in those days, he would feel that all room for doubt was removed. But all this evidence, and more, would he have who should have the Gospel of Matthew and the Acts of the Apostles put into his hands, and should then be made acquainted for the first time with the present state of the world, and with the other books of the New Testament.

ARGUMENT XI.
AUTHENTICITY AND INTEGRITY OF THE CHRISTIAN FATHERS.

With this general statement of the nature of the evidence, I proceed to consider more particularly, in reference to the books of the New Testament, the two great questions of their authenticity and their credibility. The question of credibility is, of course, the great question; but, in the present case, that of authenticity is so intimately connected with this, that it can not be omitted.

Authenticity. — Let us inquire, then, what evidence we have that the books of the New Testament were written by the persons whose names they bear, and at the time they purport to have been written. The great storehouse of learning on this subject is Lardner; and to him all subsequent writers refer, doing little more than to quote and abridge him. For ordinary purposes, however, such works as those of Horne and Paley are sufficiently full.*

Books and authors. — We have the New Testament, consisting of twenty-seven separate books, written by eight different authors. Some of these books are formal

---
* It is chiefly on their authority that the quotations on the subsequent pages are made.

histories — one is a personal narrative — but the most of them are letters addressed to associated bodies of Christians. That they were written by the persons to whom they are ascribed, and at the time claimed, we believe, —

Quoted and referred to from the first. — First, because they are quoted and referred to by a series of writers in close and uninterrupted succession, from that time till the present.

Peter and Paul. — 1. We find one apostle referring to the writings of another. Peter refers to the writings of Paul, characterizing them, just as many do now, as containing some things hard to be understood; but, what is remarkable, recognizing them as of the same authority with the other Scriptures. The force of this incidental reference to the writings of Paul, by Peter, is less felt from the fact that both writings are bound up in the same volume; but it is really as great as if the Epistle of Peter were now discovered for the first time. The Epistle of James, as no student of it can doubt, refers to the perversion, by some, of Paul's doctrine on the subject of faith and works, as contained in the Epistle to the Romans. The supplementary character of John's Gospel implies the previous composition and circulation of some, at least, of the other Gospels. Jude evidently refers to and quotes the Second Epistle of Peter.

Apostolical Fathers. — 2. We have writings bearing the names of persons, who, because they were contemporary with some of the apostles, are called "apostolical" fathers. Respecting the genuineness of some of these writings, as those ascribed to Barnabas and Hermas, there has been much controversy. I shall refer only to those universally admitted, and of which there can be no reasonable doubt. We have no need of inferior kinds of evidence.

Clement. — The Epistle ascribed to Clement is an epistle from "the church of God sojourning at Rome, to the Church of God sojourning at Corinth." It does not contain his name, but is spoken of by the ancients as acknowledged by all to be his. Irenæus says it was written by Clement, "who had seen the blessed apostles, and conversed with them, who had the preaching of the apostles still sounding in his ears, and their traditions before his eyes." And Dionysius, bishop of Corinth, about the year 170, — that is, eighty or ninety years after the Epistle was written, — bears witness that it had been read in that church from ancient times. In it there are quotations from, or evident allusions to, eight of the books of the New Testament. He expressly names only Paul's First Epistle to the Corinthians, but of the origin of the passages there can be no doubt. Thus, "Especially," says Clement, "remembering the words of the Lord Jesus, which he spoke, teaching gentleness and long-suffering; for thus he said: 'Be ye merciful, that ye may obtain mercy; forgive, that it may be forgiven unto you; as you do, so shall it be done unto you; as ye judge, so shall ye be judged; as ye show kindness, so shall kindness be shown unto you; with what measure ye mete, with the same it shall be measured to you.' By this command, and by these rules, let us establish ourselves, that we may always walk obediently to his holy words." Can any one doubt where Clement found these words, or the following? "Remember the words of the Lord Jesus; for he said, 'Woe to that man by whom offenses come: it were better for him that a millstone should be tied about his neck, and that he should be drowned in the sea, than that he should offend one of these little ones.'"[*] That such passages are not referred to the evangelists by name, — for all the apostolical fathers

---

[*] Epistle of Clement, in "Apostolical Fathers."

quote in this way, — is so far from making, as has been objected, against our argument, that it is one of its strong confirmations. It is just thus, and only thus, that we now always quote and refer to works that are the most perfectly familiar, both to ourselves and to our readers or hearers. It implies for the New Testament Scriptures, and as nothing else could, precisely the place that we claim for them.

As this Epistle of Clement was written in the name of the church at Rome, and addressed to the church at Corinth, it must be regarded as expressing the judgment of those churches.

Ignatius. — Ignatius, bishop at Antioch, suffered martyrdom about the year 107. The authority of his name led to its use for several interpolated or spurious writings. In the few short Epistles generally acknowledged as genuine, there are quotations from two of the Gospels and four of the Epistles. He expressly names that to the Ephesians.

Polycarp. — Polycarp, a companion of Ignatius, was a bishop at Smyrna. Irenæus, who in his youth had seen him, says, "I can tell the place in which the blessed Polycarp sat and taught, and his going out and coming in, and the manner of his life, and the form of his person, and the discourses he made to the people, and how he related his conversation with John and others who had seen the Lord, both concerning his miracles and his doctrine, as he had received them from the eye-witnesses of the Word of life; all which Polycarp related *agreeably to the Scriptures*." Of Polycarp we have one Epistle, concerning which there is no reasonable doubt. In this, though short, there are clear allusions to fourteen of the books of the New Testament. He expressly names the Epistle to the Philippians.

Papias. — Papias was a companion of Polycarp. Of

his we have nothing remaining; but Eusebius quotes from a work of his, in which he ascribes their respective Gospels to Matthew and Mark.

We have thus, from persons contemporary with some of the apostles, numerous quotations or plain allusions to most of the books of the New Testament; and they uniformly treat them with the reverence belonging to inspired books.

And here I will make a remark that needs to be borne in mind in all our use of dates, in speaking of the early history of Christianity. It is, that the century commences with the birth of Christ, whereas the history of the religion does not commence till thirty-three years afterward, — so that the end of the first century was only sixty-seven years from the first attempt by the apostles to establish the new religion. And when it is remembered that the first three Gospels were published, probably as soon as the year 60, or certainly before the destruction of Jerusalem, and that John lived till nearly the close of this century, it will be seen that the means of verifying every thing were very abundant.

Justin Martyr. — Twenty-five or thirty years after Polycarp follows Justin Martyr, universally known in the ancient church. He was a convert from heathenism after he had arrived at mature age, and was distinguished as a philosopher, a Christian, and a writer. Of his writings we have remaining only — two Apologies for the Christians, one addressed to the Emperor Titus Antoninus Pius, and the other to the Emperor Marcus Antoninus, and the senate and people of Rome; and his Dialogue with Trypho the Jew. We find, however, in these, thirty-five plain quotations from the Gospel of Matthew alone, and, in one case, a considerable part of the Sermon on the Mount, in the very words of Matthew. He either quotes, or clearly refers to, the

Acts of the Apostles, and nearly all the Epistles, and says expressly that the Revelation was written by John. He calls the books from which he quotes, "Memoirs composed by the Apostles," "Memoirs composed by the Apostles and their Companions,"—which description, the latter especially, exactly agrees with the titles which the Gospels and the Acts of the Apostles now bear. This manner of reference " shows that the books were perfectly notorious, and that there were no other accounts of Christ then extant so received and credited as to make it necessary to distinguish these from the rest." Justin also tells us, in his first Apology, that the memoirs of the apostles, and the writings of the prophets, were read and expounded in the Christian assemblies for worship, which shows that the Gospels were at that time well known in the world. To this testimony of Justin, who sealed his belief in the Christian religion with his blood, there is no objection, except that he does not quote the different writers by name; but skepticism itself can not suppose that books were read and expounded in the Christian churches so generally that he should mention it in an apology to the emperor, and yet that all trace and record of those books should have been lost, and that others should have been fabricated, and substituted in their place. We find in this author almost a complete history of Christ; and yet he mentions only two circumstances which are not contained in our Gospels.

Tatian. — After Justin Martyr follows Tatian, a disciple of his. About the year 170, he composed a harmony of the Gospels, which he called "Diatessaron," — that is, of the four, — showing that there were then four, and only four, Gospels.

Pothinus. — About this time, the churches of Vienne and Lyons, in France, sent a relation of the sufferings of their martyrs to the churches of Asia and Phrygia, and the epistle is preserved by Eusebius. Among the victims was the aged bishop of Lyons, Pothinus. He was ninety years old, so that his testimony would join on to that of the apostles. In this we find the following: "Then was fulfilled that which was spoken by the Lord, that whosoever killeth you will think that he doeth God service;" with similar references to Luke and to the Acts.

Irenæus. — To Pothinus, as bishop of Lyons, succeeded Irenæus, who was, in his youth, a disciple of Polycarp. He wrote many works, but his five books against heresies are all that remain. In these he has shown a full acquaintance with the Scriptures both of the Old and New Testament. Being only a century distant from the time of the publication of the Gospels, and only one step removed from the apostles, he speaks of himself and his contemporaries as being able to reckon up, in all the principal churches, the succession of bishops from the first. He mentions the code of the New Testament, as well as the Old, and calls the one, as well as the other, the Oracles of God. His testimony is full and explicit to all the books of the New Testament, except the Epistle to Philemon, the Third of John, and the Epistle of Jude. And here we find, for the first time, what we might now expect to find — an appeal to the books as the ground of the Christian faith. "We have not received," says Irenæus, "the knowledge of the way of our salvation by any other than those by whom the gospel has been brought to us; which gospel they first preached, and afterward, by the will of God, committed to writing, that it might be for time to come the foundation and pillar of our faith. For, after our Lord rose from the dead, and they were endued from above with the power of the Holy Ghost coming down upon them, they received a perfect knowledge of all things. They then went forth to all the ends of the earth, declaring to men the blessing of heavenly peace, having all of them, and every one alike, the gospel of God. Matthew, then, among the Jews, wrote a Gospel in their own language, while Peter and Paul were preaching the gospel at Rome, and founding a church there. And, after their exit, Mark, also the disciple and interpreter of Peter, delivered to us in writing the things that had been preached by Peter; and Luke, the companion of Paul, put down in a book the gospel preached by him. Afterward, John, the disciple of the Lord, who also leaned upon his breast, he likewise published a Gospel while he dwelt at Ephesus, in Asia." We could certainly wish nothing more explicit than this; and there are other passages not less so.

Clement. — After Irenæus, we come to Athenagoras, about the year 180, and to Theophilus, bishop at Antioch, and to Clement of Alexandria, (A. D. 150–220,) an author of note, who quotes from almost all the writers of the New Testament so largely, that the citations would fill a considerable volume. He gives us an account of the order in which the Gospels were written, and then says that he received the account from presbyters of more ancient times.

Tertullian. — About the same time with Clement lived Tertullian, a presbyter of the church of Carthage, whose testimony is very full and explicit. After enumerating the apostolical churches he says, "I say, then, that with them, but not with them only, which are apostolical, but with all who have fellowship with them in the same faith, is that Gospel of Luke received, from its first publication, which we so zealously maintain." He adds, "The same authority of the apostolical churches will support the other Gospels which we have from them, — I mean John's and Matthew's, — although that likewise which Mark published may be said to be Peter's, whose interpreter Mark was." In another place,

Tertullian says that the three other Gospels were in the hands of the churches from the beginning.

With Tertullian I close my citations from the authors of the second century, of whom it has been said with truth, so numerous are their quotations from the New Testament, that, if that book had been lost, it might be almost compiled anew from these citations.

Extent of assent. — And here we may remark, with Paley, "the wide extent through which the reputation of the Gospels and the Acts of the Apostles had spread, and the perfect consent, on this point, of distant and independent societies. It is now only about one hundred and fifty years since Christ was crucified; and within this period, to say nothing of the apostolical fathers, we have Justin Martyr of Neapolis, Theophilus at Antioch, Irenæus in France, Clement in Alexandria, and Tertullian at Carthage, quoting the same books of historical Scriptures, and, I may say, quoting them alone." These men, too, — which is an important point, — being bishops and presbyters, their testimony involves that of large bodies of men. It gives us the authority of common consent. And certainly such an authority and assent, extending over thousands of miles, could never have been gained to books esteemed as these were, except on the best grounds. There are no other books of antiquity that can be placed at all in competition with them in this respect.

It has been usual to continue citations down as far as the fourth century; but can this be necessary? I think not, especially as they now multiply upon us on every side. It has also been usual, and is, perhaps, more strictly logical, to trace the testimony upward; but, in the present state of this argument, that can not be important.

Peculiar titles. — But I observe, secondly, not only were these writings thus quoted, but, when they were, it was with peculiar titles and marks of respect. Thus Theophilus, bishop of Antioch, who flourished a little more than a century after the books were written, says, "These things the Holy Scriptures teach us, and all who were moved by the Holy Spirit, among whom John says, 'In the beginning was the Word.'" Origen (A. D. 185–254) says, "That our religion teaches us to seek after wisdom, shall be shown both out of the ancient Jewish Scriptures, which we also use, and out of those written since Jesus, which are believed in the churches to be divine."

Read in public assemblies.—These writings, moreover, as has already been stated, were early read in the public assemblies of Christians. Justin Martyr, who wrote only about one hundred years after the crucifixion, giving an account of Christian worship, has this remarkable passage: "The memoirs of the apostles, or the writings of the prophets, are read according as the time allows, and, when the reader has ended, the president makes a discourse." This passage is of great weight, because Justin speaks here of the general usage of the Christian church, and because he speaks of it as a long-established custom. That by "memoirs of the apostles" he means our Gospels, is evident, because he tells us, in another place, that they are what are called "Gospels," and because he has made numerous quotations from them, and from no others.

Collected into a volume.—At what time the books of the New Testament were collected into a distinct volume, and became known to the churches in that collected form, is not certainly known; but there is no doubt it was very early, and that this volume was ranked from the first with the Scriptures of the Old Testament. Polycarp says, "I trust ye are well exercised in the Holy Scriptures, as in these Scriptures it is said, 'Be ye angry and sin not.'" This passage, thus quoted by

Polycarp, shows that in his time there were Christian writings distinguished as the "Holy Scriptures." This is in perfect accordance with what we should expect after the recognition, by Peter, of the writings of Paul as a part of the Scriptures. Justin Martyr, also, in the "Apology" of which I have already spoken, (which was written about thirty years after the Epistle of Polycarp,) says, "For the apostles, in the memoirs composed by them, which are called 'Gospels,' have thus delivered it, that Jesus commanded them to take bread and give thanks."

Completion of the canon. — I speak of this subject because it has been said that no such book as the New Testament existed before the fourth century, and because our evidence on this point stands just as we could wish — that is, it stands just as we should suppose it would from the nature of the case. Here are twenty-seven separate pieces written within the space of sixty years. It is not to be supposed that all these pieces should be possessed at once by all the churches, or that there should be at once a perfect agreement in regard to them all. We should expect that copies would be taken, and collections made, of those writings concerning which there was no question, and that these would be quoted and incidentally referred to, precisely as our books are, till some question was raised about the introduction of another book, or about the authority or authenticity of any part of it. Then we should expect to find the grounds stated on which the books were received, and formal catalogues made out of such as were received. If, then, by saying that there was no such book as the New Testament before the fourth century, it is meant that the canon, as it is called, was not formally settled by a council till that time, it is true; but if it be meant, as is insinuated, that the writings were then first published, no man can make such an assertion, except from the grossest ignorance, or as a willful falsehood.

The truth is, that we have in the first century, that is, within less than seventy years after the death of Christ, numerous quotations, and allusions to our sacred books, in which we have an incidental and unintentional testimony, more satisfactory than any formal testimony could be; and, in these quotations and allusions, nineteen or twenty of our present books are recognized. In the second century, we find the testimony more express and full, and the quotations so numerous, that a large part of the New Testament might be collected from them. Of this age there are thirty-six writers of whose works some part has come down to us. In the third and fourth centuries, we have more than a hundred authors whose works testify to the authenticity of these books. During these two centuries, catalogues of the authentic works were expressly drawn up, harmonies were formed, versions were made into many languages, and the canon was fully settled.

Eusebius. — In settling the canon, we find, from Eusebius, writing about the year 315, that there were seven books concerning which there was some hesitation, and the grounds of the doubts are fully given.* Eusebius begins his enumeration of Scriptures universally acknowledged in the following manner: "In the first place are to be ranked the sacred four Gospels; then the book of the Acts of the Apostles; after that are to be reckoned the Epistles of Paul; in the next place, that called the First Epistle of John, and the Epistle of Peter, are to be esteemed authentic; after this is to be placed the Revelation of John, about which we shall observe the different opinions at proper seasons. Of the controverted, yet well known, or approved by

---

* He has preserved a catalogue by Origen, probably of the year 210, which is substantially the same as his own.

the most, are that called the Epistle of James, and that of Jude, and the Second of Peter, and the Second and Third of John, whether written by the evangelist or by another of the same name." Concerning these last, however, all doubt was gradually removed, so that, by the time of Jerome and Augustine, A. D. 342–430, many catalogues are given, including all our present books, and none other.

While, therefore, it appears that many of the writings of the New Testament were collected while some of the apostles were yet living, or immediately afterward, and known under the name of the Gospels and the Apostles; while the references to this volume, during the second century, are almost numberless; while no doubt ever arose respecting the mass of them, — still the book which we now receive was not, in all its parts, formally agreed upon, in consequence of a careful examination of ancient testimony, till between three and four hundred years after the birth of Christ. It will be remembered, however, that if every part of the New Testament, concerning which there had been dispute, or doubt, were blotted out, the argument for the truth of Christianity would not be in the least invalidated. There is, therefore, direct evidence, as perfect as the nature of the case admits, that those writings on which we depend for the truth of the Christian religion have existed, and were received without doubt from the very first.

Rival parties. — So full and unexceptionable is the testimony thus given by early writers, that it would seem, in the absence of any thing to contradict it, or to throw over it the slightest discredit, that further evidence could not be needed. Indeed, if we were to stop here, we should have a body of evidence for the authenticity of these writings such as can be adduced in favor of no others of equal antiquity. The writings of Cicero are quoted by Quintilian, which shows that they were then extant and ascribed to him. But the works of Cicero excited no controversy, they gave rise to no general opposition, they created no sects; hence we have no means of knowing how those works were regarded by enemies, or by rival parties, appealing to their authority. This, when it can be obtained, is the very highest kind of evidence, and, in respect to the Christian Scriptures, it is most full and satisfactory. The heretical writers do, indeed, sometimes deny that the apostle or writer is an infallible authority; but they never deny that the books were written by those to whom they were ascribed. Thus the Cerinthians and the Ebionites, who sprang up while St. John was yet living, wished to retain the Mosaic law, and hence rejected the Epistles of Paul, while they retained the Gospel of Matthew. And Marcion, A. D. 130, who rejected the Old Testament, and was excommunicated, though greatly incensed, and though he speaks disparagingly of several of the books, yet nowhere intimates that they were forgeries. The same may be said of all the ancient sects.

Enemies. — We have, also, the indirect testimony of the enemies of Christianity — as Celsus, Porphyry, and Julian. Of these, Celsus flourished only about a hundred years after the Gospels were published, and was an acute and bitter adversary; and it seems quite impossible that any one of them, much more the whole, should have been forged, and yet he not know or suspect it. He attacks the books, he speaks of contradictions and difficulties in them, but he hints no suspicion that they were forged. Indeed, he claims the writings, for he says, "These things, then, we have alleged to you out of your own writings, not needing any other weapons." In Porphyry, born A. D. 233, (the most sensible and severe adversary of Christianity that antiquity can produce,) we find no trace of any suspicion that the Christian writings were not authentic, though he pronounces the prophecy of Daniel a forgery. Porphyry did not even deny the truth of the Gospel history. He admitted that the miracles were performed by Christ, but imputed them to magic, which he said he learned in Egypt. Julian, commonly called the Apostate, flourished from A. D. 331 to 363. He quotes the four Gospels and the Acts, and nowhere gives any intimation that he suspected the whole, or any part of them, to be forgeries.

Ancient versions and manuscripts. — Another source of evidence is to be found in ancient versions and manuscripts. The Syriac version was probably made early in the second century, and the first Latin versions almost as early. Of course the New Testament must have existed, and been received as the standard of Christian truth, before those versions were made. Of ancient manuscripts, containing the New Testament or parts thereof, there are several thousands. About five hundred of the most important have been collated with great care. Many of them are of great antiquity. The Codex Vaticanus is believed, on very satisfactory evidence, to be of the fourth century, and the Codex Alexandrinus, of the fifth, — perhaps both much earlier. Thus these manuscripts connect with manuscripts compared by Jerome and Eusebius, A. D. 315–420, who prepared critical editions of the New Testament from manuscripts then ancient. The prodigious number of these manuscripts, the distant countries whence they were collected, and the identity of their contents with the quotations of the fathers of different ages, place the New Testament incomparably above all other ancient works in point of authenticity.

Is there, then, we are ready to ask, any kind of external evidence conceivable, which is wanting to our sacred books?

Internal evidence. — But, strong as is the external proof, it hardly equals that which is to be derived from the circumstances of the case, and from internal evidence.

We are little apt to consider how difficult the thing to be done was. It was to make an addition, and under peculiar circumstances, to the number of books then held sacred. These books were not confined to one spot, and guarded by one set of men, and shrouded in mystery. Moses and the prophets were "read in the synagogues every Sabbath day." From the synagogue the early church was an outgrowth, as Christianity from Judaism; and it was composed of Jews nurtured to a high reverence for their sacred books, and to great scrupulousness in guarding them. For the first fifteen years at least, the Old Testament Scriptures, and those only, were read in the assemblies of Christians. And now consider what it was for such men to receive, individually, and in numerous, and large, and independent bodies, other writings, and to put them on an equality with those so venerable, and held so sacred. And yet, within sixty years this was done in respect to more than twenty separate productions, and with almost entire unanimity. It was a marvel, especially looking at the origin and position in society of the early Christians, that they should originate productions which the instinctive judgments of men could tolerate by the side of those, so wonderful, of the old seers, and bards, and prophet-kings, even if they had not been regarded as inspired; it was, perhaps, a greater marvel that they should incorporate them at once with those productions, as a part of their sacred books. According to every law of human thought or action, this could not have been done without the most searching scrutiny. The world has nothing to show like it. It was as if some man, or body of men, should attempt to add a book to our Bible, that should be universally received.

Could not be forged. — For, if these writings are not authentic, they must be forgeries; and they are of such a character, and purport to have been written under such circumstances, as to render a forgery of them impossible. Here, for example, are no fewer than nine letters which claim to have been written to numerous bodies of men, and received by them; and can any man believe that such letters, often containing severe reproof, could have been received and read, as we know these were, by the early Christians, if they were forgeries? "Come now," says Tertullian, — born only sixty years after the death of St. John, — "come now, thou who wilt exercise thy curiosity more profitably in the business of thy salvation, run through the apostolical churches in which the very chairs of the apostles still preside, in which their authentic letters are recited, sounding forth the voice and representing the countenance of each." Can any man suppose that letters thus spoken of at that early day could be forged? Besides, when could they have been forged? Not, certainly, during the lives of the apostles, for then they would have confuted them; and, after their death, it is morally impossible such letters should have been received as from them by any body of Christians.

Opposed by both heathen and Jews. — It is to be added, also, that Christianity sprang up in the midst of opposition, keen-sighted and relentless. It was opposed by Heathenism and by Judaism, and, moreover, there were always in its own bosom some who were false-hearted and ready to betray it. During almost three hundred years it was often the subject of violent and bloody persecutions; and, in such circumstances, it is morally impossible that twenty-seven books should be forged, and imposed as authentic upon both friends and foes, and no one, for the first four hundred years, hint a suspicion of the authenticity of the most of the books. When Celsus reproached the Christians with dissensions, in the second century, Origen admits the truth of the accusation, but says, nevertheless, that the four Gospels were received by the whole church of God under heaven.

Language and style. — Again: the authenticity of the New Testament is confirmed by the language and style in which it is written. It could have been written only by men who were born Jews, and who lived before the destruction of Jerusalem. Every where their Jewish prejudices and habits of thought appear, and the references to Jerusalem and the temple, as then standing, are so blended with the whole narrative, that we feel it impossible it should not have been written at that time. This, however, is still more obvious from the peculiar language in which the New Testament is written. Greek was then a kind of universal language; but the Greek spoken in Palestine was not the Greek of Attica. It was Hebraic Greek — that is, Greek mixed with the peculiar dialect of Hebrew then in use in Palestine; and in such Greek are the Gospels written. After the destruction of Jerusalem, this peculiar dialect ceased. Probably there was not a man living, after the death of the apostle John, who could have blended the peculiar elements of language which we find in the New Testament. But, if these books were written before the destruction of Jerusalem, they must be authentic, because no books could have been forged in the names of the apostles, while they were yet living, and have been undetected.

Judgment by separate churches. — It is to be remarked, too, that the books of the New Testament were received and judged of by the churches separately. The Gospel of Matthew was received by the churches on its own merits, and the question of its reception was not embarrassed by that of any other book. So the

Epistle of Paul to the church at Rome was judged of as authentic by that church, without any reference to the Epistle to the Ephesians. If, therefore, the New Testament is a forgery, it is not an instance of a single successful forgery, but of twenty-seven separate ones, imposed upon intelligent men whose interests were all involved in detecting the fraud. If, now, we consider how seldom literary forgeries are undertaken — that they are, in fact, nearly or quite unprecedented, unless they come out under the shadow of some great name — that no possible motive can be assigned for the forgery of *such* books; — if we consider the difficulty of it in any case, and the moral impossibility of it in reference to books of such pretensions, and that have, in fact, commanded the reverence of the civilized world, — I think we shall feel that twenty-seven successful forgeries, within the space of sixty years, is a supposition not to be entertained for a moment.

Not one mark of spuriousness. — Once more: the reasons which render the authenticity of a work suspicious are thus laid down by Michaelis: 1. When doubts have been entertained, from its first appearance, whether it was the work of its reputed author. 2. When the immediate friends of the author have denied it to be his. 3. When a long series of years has elapsed, after his death, in which the book was unknown, and in which it must have been mentioned or quoted, had it been in existence. 4. When the style is different from his other writings, or, in case no others remain, from what might be reasonably expected. 5. When events are recorded which happened later than the time of the pretended author. 6. When opinions are advanced contradictory to those which he is known to have advanced in other writings. Of these marks of spuriousness, not one can be attached to a single book of the New Testament.

Contrasted with other books. — I observe, finally, that this evidence is, if possible, heightened by the contrast in all respects between our books and those which have been regarded as spurious. The fact that such books existed is sometimes made use of to create the impression that they were once of nearly equal authority with ours, and that there was difficulty and uncertainty in making the distinction. Nothing can be farther from the truth. For, 1. There is no evidence that those spurious or apocryphal books existed during the first century; indeed, they all were manifestly forgeries of a later age. 2. No Christian history, besides our Gospels and the Acts, is quoted by any writer now known within three hundred years after the birth of Christ. 3. None of these apocryphal writings were read in the churches. 4. None of them were ever admitted to the volume of the New Testament. 5. Nor do they appear in any catalogue. 6. Nor were they alleged by different parties, in their controversies, as of authority. 7. Nor were they the subjects of commentaries, or versions, or expositions. 8. Nor were they ever received by Christians of after ages, but were almost universally reprobated by them.

And, now, is not this point proved? Is it not fully established that these books were written by the men whose names they bear, and at the time when they purport to have been written?

Integrity. — I close by a very brief reference to a single point more, which properly belongs here. How do we know that the integrity of the books of the New Testament has been preserved? I answer, first, we know it from the nature of the case. Augustine, in the fourth century, reasoning with a heretic, puts this well. "If any one," says he, "should charge you with having interpolated some texts alleged by you, would you not immediately answer, that it is impossible for you to do such a thing in books read by all Christians — and that, if any such attempt had been made by you, it would have been presently discerned and defeated, by comparing the ancient copies? Well, then, for the same reason that the Scriptures can not be corrupted by you, they can not be corrupted by any other people." We know the same thing, secondly, from the agreement of our books with the quotations in the works of the early Christian fathers. These quotations are so abundant that almost the whole of the New Testament might be gathered from them; and yet, except in six or seven verses, there is an agreement in all material respects between those quotations and the corresponding parts of our books. We know it, thirdly, from the entire agreement of our books with ancient versions. The old Syriac version, called Peshito, was certainly in use before the close of the second century. This was not known in Europe before the close of the sixteenth century. It came down by a line perfectly independent of that by which our Greek Testament was received; yet, when the two came to be compared, the difference was altogether unimportant. Is it possible that evidence should be more satisfactory?

Various readings. — The subject of various readings was at one time so presented as to alarm and disquiet those not acquainted with the facts. When a person hears it stated that, in the collation of the manuscripts for Griesbach's edition of the New Testament, as many as one hundred and fifty thousand various readings were discovered, he is ready to suppose that every thing must be in a state of uncertainty. A statement of the facts relieves every difficulty. The truth is, that not one in a thousand makes any perceptible, or at least important variation in the meaning; that they consist almost entirely of the small and obvious mistakes of transcribers, such as the omission or transposition of letters, errors in grammar, in the use of one word for another of a similar meaning, and in changing the position of words in a sentence. But, by all the omissions, and all the additions, contained in all the manuscripts, no fact, no doctrine, no duty prescribed, in our authorized version, is rendered either obscure or doubtful.

There was a time when the rubbish of antiquity did gather around these pillars of our evidence. The keen eye of the infidel saw it, and he hoped to show that they rested upon rubbish alone. But, like every similar attempt, at whatever point directed, a full examination has served only to show how firm is the rock upon which that church rests which is "the pillar and ground of the truth."

LECTURE X.

ARGUMENT TWELFTH; CREDIBILITY OF THE BOOKS OF THE NEW TESTAMENT.

OUR next subject, as will have been anticipated, is the credibility of the books of the New Testament; and I proceed directly to the discussion. This question is purely one of historical evidence; and if there is left for me very little that is new, either in the matter or in the manner of presenting it, I shall yet hope for attention, from the important place which this point holds, and always must, in the Christian argument.

Authenticity. — And the first consideration which I adduce in favor of the credibility of these books is their authenticity. It was because I regarded every testimony adduced, in the last lecture, to prove the authenticity of the gospel histories as also a testimony to their truth, that I dwelt so fully on that subject. The fathers did not quote so largely from those books because they were written by apostolical men, but because they regarded them as true, and as having an authority paramount to all others. The testimony of antiquity, therefore, thus given to the authenticity of these books, is equivalent to its testimony to the reality of the facts which they contain.

Moreover, when men publish an account of facts under their own names, especially of facts that are within the immediate knowledge of the most of their readers, and facts, too, that have excited great attention, they must either publish what is substantially true, or willfully, and without motive, sacrifice both character and reputation. There is no instance on record of the publication by any one, under his own name, of an account purporting to be of facts that were public, and recent, and concerning which a deep interest was felt by the community, which was not mainly true. But here are four men who claim to have been witnesses of most of the events which they relate, or, if not, to have had a perfect knowledge of them. These events must have been known, at the time the books were published, to thousands of others, both friends and foes, as well as to them. Nothing could have prevented the instant detection of any falsehood; and yet these men published their histories at the time, in the face of the world, and on the spot where the transactions took place. This consideration alone ought to be decisive, and in any other case it would be.

Means of knowing the facts. — But, secondly, these books are credible because the authors of them had the best possible means of knowing the facts which they state. For the most part, they had a personal knowledge of them. Compare our evidence, in this respect, with that for other ancient events. The main facts were not such as were concealed in cabinets, or in the intrigues of a court, but were few, and such as all might know. But of the events of the life of Alexander, we have no contemporary historian, and yet they are not doubted. Of how few of the events in the histories of Livy, or of Tacitus, had they personal knowledge! With how few of the men, whose lives he wrote, had Plutarch personal acquaintance! In some cases, indeed, — as in the account of the Retreat of the Ten Thousand, or the Commentaries of Cæsar, — we have the story of a person who was present, and saw what he narrates;

and no one can fail to feel that the credibility of those accounts is greatly increased by that circumstance. In these cases, however, we have but a single witness, and the writers are the heroes of their own story; and still these writings are received with entire confidence. And this leads me to observe, —

The number of witnesses. — Thirdly, that the events recorded in our books are worthy of credit from the number of witnesses. To put this in its true light, let us suppose that there should now be discovered, among the ruins of Herculaneum, the writings of an officer and companion of Cæsar, giving an account of the same campaigns and battles. Let us suppose that there was a substantial agreement, but such incidental differences as to show that the writings were entirely independent of each other; then, if we had before been inclined to call the whole a fiction, or to attribute any thing to the ignorance, or the prejudices, or the vanity of Cæsar, we should feel all our doubts removed on those points in which the accounts agreed. And if, after this, we should still find another independent manuscript, and still another, differing entirely in style and general manner, and yet agreeing in regard to the facts, — if, moreover, there should be found letters written in that day incidentally confirming these accounts by many allusions and undesigned coincidences, — we should feel that historical evidence could not go farther, and that skepticism would be preposterous. If events thus attested are not to be believed, it will not be for want of evidence. If they are not to be believed, no ancient history can be; for there is no one for which we have any thing like this amount of evidence. But all this evidence we have for the facts of the gospel. The fact, that the four Gospels and the Acts were bound up together, is not to be permitted to weaken their force as separate testimonies. This is as far as historical testimony can go with respect to ordinary events; but the facts of Christianity are of such a character that even this may, and does, receive additional confirmation. If Cæsar's wars had given rise to parties, and these different parties had all appealed to these writings as of undoubted authority, and if, moreover, we had, at no distant day, the distinct admission of the enemies of Cæsar that these books were trustworthy as to matters of fact, then I think that we can conceive of nothing that could be added; and all this we have in favor of the facts of the New Testament. If we lay aside all consideration of the nature of the events, and look at the evidence alone, we shall see that it has all the force of which historical evidence, as such, is capable.

Difficulties and discrepancies. — It is true, as was mentioned in a former lecture, that there are difficulties and apparent discrepancies in these accounts. They relate chiefly to the two genealogies; to the time of the taxing mentioned by Luke; to the two versions of the Sermon on the Mount. to the time of the last supper, and to the accounts of the crucifixion, and of the resurrection.

Require minute criticism. — The explanation of this class of difficulties would require a minute criticism, not here in place. For this; reference may be made to the Commentaries and Harmonies. It may, however, be said of them in general, —

Do not affect the main features. — 1. That there are none which affect the great features of the narrative.

Are mostly negative. — 2. That many of them are based on mere omissions. It is said, for example, that there is a discrepancy between the account by Matthew and Mark of the demoniacs. Matthew says there were two, while Mark mentions but one. He does not say there was not another; but one may have been less prominent and fierce, and so not have been mentioned by him. In the same way it is objected that John speaks of the presence of Nicodemus at the burial of Christ, while nothing is said of it by the other evangelists; and this is called a discrepancy.

May be explained. — 3. Of the above-mentioned difficulties, those connected with the accounts of the resurrection seem the most considerable; and we may apply to all of them, in substance, what is said of those in particular, in a recent excellent work: "This examination of the several narratives shows us how many of the data are wanting which are necessary to enable us to form a regular, harmonious, and complete history of this eventful morning. Each of the evangelists gives us some particulars which the others omit, but no one of them aims to give us a full and connected account; and for us to supply the missing links in the chain, is impossible. To a superficial examination there seem many discrepancies, not to say contradictions; but a thorough investigation shows that the points of real difference are very few, and that in several ways even these differences may be removed. Whilst thus we can not say of any order that we can frame that it is certain, we can say of several that they are probable; and if they can not be proved, neither can they be disproved. This is sufficient for him who finds in the moral character of the Gospels the highest vouchers for their historic truth." *

Peculiar testimony. — But I observe, fourthly, that this evidence is powerfully confirmed by the peculiar testimony which was given by their authors to the truth of these books. To state one of the fundamental propositions of Paley: "There is satisfactory evidence that many, professing to be original witnesses of the Christian miracles, passed their lives in labors, dangers, and sufferings, voluntarily undergone in attestation of the accounts which they delivered, and solely in conse-

* The Life of our Lord. By Samuel J. Andrews.

quence of their belief of those accounts; and that they also submitted, from the same motives, to new rules of conduct." Into the proof that they did thus labor and suffer Paley enters at large. But it is so obvious that men who, in that day, should attempt to propagate an exclusive religion, that was entirely opposed both to Judaism and heathenism, and also to the natural passions and inclinations of men, would be obliged to undergo labor and suffering in proportion to their sincerity and earnestness, that it seems to me scarcely to need proof. Then the idea of this is so much implied in the whole narrative, and regarded as a matter of course, — it is so much taken for granted in the exhortations, and promises, and consolations, given to the disciples by Christ himself, and in the letters of the apostles, and it is so fully testified to by heathen writers, — that I can not think it necessary to dwell upon it. If, then, these men did labor, and suffer, and finally die, in attestation of the truth of their accounts, then are our books confirmed in the highest possible manner, and as no other historical books ever have been.

Testimony of others than the writers. — It was not, however, — and here we come to one of the strongest points of the Christian testimony, — it was not simply those who compiled the accounts who thus gave their testimony, but thousands of others; and, though their testimony is unwritten, yet it is so involved in the circumstances of the case, that it comes to us with no less force than if they had certified, under their own hands and seals, the truth of our accounts. Every Christian who, in that early age, abandoned the prejudices of education, and friends, and property, to become a Christian, especially every one who was persecuted and suffered death for the cause, gave his testimony, in the most emphatic manner possible, for the truth of the facts of the Gospels. Every member of a church which received an Epistle of Paul, and to which it was read, was a witness of its authenticity, and of the truth of the facts of Christianity, which is implied in all his Epistles. The great force of this unwritten testimony is fully set forth by Chalmers, as also the fallacy by which we are so often led to feel that heathen testimony is superior in point of force to that of Christians, as if the very strength of conviction which would lead a man to become a Christian should not also furnish the best evidence of his sincerity. It would be inconsistent that a heathen should testify to the truth of the religion without becoming a Christian, and it is surely unreasonable to make the very act by which he testified, in the highest possible manner, his sincerity and consistency, a reason for not receiving his testimony. This testimony meets a positive cavil. It may be said that the eight writers of the New Testament were actuated, in their labors and sufferings, by a desire to be of reputation, to be the founders of sects, or to preserve their consistency. But no such motives can be imputed to the mass of Christians in that day, each of whom did as really and as impressively testify to his belief in the facts of the New Testament as if he had written a book. Men may have motives for being impostors, but they can have none for being imposed upon, especially when the imposition costs them all that men usually hold dear. When, therefore, I see the apostles and their associates, and especially when I see vast numbers of persons, in the ordinary walks of life, preferring to relinquish any thing, and to undergo any thing, rather than to deny the truth of these facts; when I see them led, one by one, or, perhaps, numbers together, to scourging and torture; when I see them standing as martyrs, and, in that act, as it were lifting up their dying hand to heaven, and taking an oath of their sincerity, — then I know that they believed the facts for which they died; then I think I have found the case of which Hume speaks, when he says, "We can not make use of a more convincing argument" (in proof of honesty) "than to prove that the actions ascribed to any persons are contrary to the course of human nature, and that no human motives, in such circumstances, could ever induce them to such a conduct."

Authors neither deceivers nor deceived. — I observe, fifthly, that our books are worthy of credit, because it can be shown that their authors were neither deceivers nor deceived; and this is the only alternative possible unless the religion is true. The alternative that, unless Christ and his apostles were what they claimed to be, they were either impostors or dupes, was first presented by Pascal; and since his time this whole question has often been argued under it. The same thing, in fact, is sometimes argued under a positive form, when it is shown that the primitive witnesses were both competent and honest. The only questions that can be asked respecting a witness are, Is he competent — that is, is he well informed? and, Is he honest? Does he know the truth, and will he tell it? and it obviously makes no difference whether we show that the apostles were well informed and honest, or whether we show that they were not either deceivers or deceived. In either case, the truth of the religion is established.

Not deceivers. — To one branch of this alternative — that which supposes the apostles to have been deceivers — all that was said, under the last head, of their labors and sufferings, will apply. It is not in human nature, there is no example of it, for even one man to persevere, through a long life, in undergoing labors and sufferings, and finally to die, in attestation of what he knew to be false; much less can we suppose that twelve men, yea, that hundreds and thousands, can have done this. The character of Christ and of his apostles in other respects, and the nature of the religion which he taught, forbid the supposition that they were deceivers. To suppose that men, teaching a morality more perfect than any other ever known, and exemplifying it in their conduct, living lives of great simplicity, and self-denial, and benevolence, enforcing truth and honesty by the most tremendous sanctions of a future life, should, without any possible advantage to themselves, die as martyrs in attestation of what they knew to be false, is practically absurd.

If so, by conspiracy. — Moreover, if they were deceivers, they were so by combination and conspiracy. From the nature of the case this must have been so, and the number acquainted with the secret could not have been small. But it is morally impossible, under the temptations which we know assailed them from without, and in the dissensions which, by their own confession, sprang up among themselves, that such a combination of falsehood should have held together. A readiness to deceive always implies selfishness; and, in such a company of deceivers, there would have been some one to expose any iniquity if there had been any to expose. I omit here, what I have very briefly noticed in another lecture — the general air of truth and sincerity in these narratives, their simplicity, their candor, their particularity, their minute and life-like touches. But I do say that, in the midst of all the varieties of human conduct, there are some principles as settled as the laws of physical nature; and that for men to combine to propagate such a story as this, and to devote their lives to this object, and to die solely in attestation of it, when they knew it to be false, is as contrary to a fixed and uniform experience as any miracle can be. These men, then, could not have been deceivers.

Not deceived. — But neither, on the other hand, could they have been deceived. This is evident from the nature of the facts, and from their character as indicated by their writings. And here we are to keep in mind the distinction between testimony to facts, and inferences, or doctrines, or opinions. The apostles certainly knew whether there was, or was not, such a person as Jesus Christ; whether he called them to be his disciples; whether he spoke the discourses they have recorded; whether multitudes followed him; whether he was crucified. Nor, if we consider the number and character of his miracles, and the manner in which they were performed, is it more possible they should have been deceived respecting them. We read of their bringing to him great multitudes of "sick folk," with every variety of disease, and of his healing them all, of his giving sight to the blind, to those born blind; of his raising the dead. And all this he did openly, before friends and enemies. Now, that men could be deceived respecting acts of this kind, repeated for years, under all varieties of circumstances, capable of being tested by all the senses, — that they could, for example, have failed to know that Lazarus was dead when they had the evidence of it given at his tomb, or that he was alive when they conversed and ate with him, — is impossible. Here is nothing that can be resolved into any false perception, no mere momentary effect; nor can there be any doubt whether the events, if they took place, were miraculous. But not only did Christ himself work miracles, — he communicated to his disciples that power. They retained it long after his ascension, and they could not have been deceived in supposing they wrought the cures related, if they did not. Either we must abandon our faith in the testimony of the senses, or we must admit that events thus tested really took place. No stretch of enthusiasm could have led them to believe that they saw such things if they did not see them. No enthusiasm is sufficient to account for the belief of so many, that they saw the Saviour after his resurrection, and conversed and ate with him, and, like Thomas, could touch his hands and his side. If Christ did not rise, it is equally impossible to account, on the supposition that they were deceived, for their belief that he did rise, and for the fact that the body was not produced by the Jews.

Not enthusiastic or superstitious. — But if we look into the writings of these men, we see no signs of superstitious weakness, or of enthusiastic fervors. There is nothing in their character, aside from their relation of miraculous events, and their maintaining their testimony at all hazards, that bears any marks of enthusiasm. On the contrary, their writings are marked with great good sense and sobriety. There are no extravagant expressions, no indications of excessive emotion, no high-wrought description, no praise, and no censure. There is a simple statement of the facts of the life of Christ, and a record of his discourses. Such men could not have been deceived for so long a time respecting *such* facts.

But, if they were neither deceivers nor deceived, then the facts took place, and the religion is true.

Leslie's "Short Method." — We now come to an argument for the credibility of the facts contained in our books, which never has been answered, and never can be. Infidels have repeatedly been challenged to answer it, but they have never made the attempt. It is the argument of Leslie in his "Short Method with the Deists." This argument rests solely upon the peculiarity of Christian evidence, already mentioned, by which the truth of the religion is indissolubly connected with certain matters of fact which could originally be judged of by the senses, and also upon the fact that there exist in the church certain ordinances commemorative of those facts. Thus the truth of our religion seems to be embodied in institutions that now exist, and in observances that pass before our eyes. The object of Leslie is to show, from the nature of the case, — for here we make very little reference to written testimony, — that the matters of fact stated could not have been received at the time unless they were true, and that the observances could never have originated except in connection with the facts. In showing this, he lays down four rules, and asserts that any matter of fact in which these four rules meet must be true, and challenges the world to show any instance of any supposed matter of fact, thus authenticated, that has ever been shown to be false.

Four rules. — His four rules are these : 1. "That the matter of fact be such that men's outward senses, their eyes and ears, may be judges of it." 2. "That it be done publicly, in the face of the world." 3. "That not only public monuments be kept up in memory of it, but some outward actions be performed." 4. "That such monuments, and such actions, or observances, be instituted, and do commence from the time that the matter of fact was done."

The first two rules. — "The first two rules make it impossible for any such matter of fact to be imposed upon men at *the time*, because every man's eyes, and ears, and senses, would contradict it." For example, if any man should affirm that all the inhabitants of this city yesterday, or last year, walked to Governor's Island and returned on dry ground, while the water was divided and stood in heaps on each side of them, it would be impossible that he should be believed, because every man, woman, and child would know better. It would be one of those things respecting which the unlearned and the young could judge as well as the learned and the more experienced. Equally impossible is it that the children of Israel, of *that generation*, should have believed that they passed through the Red Sea, or went out and gathered manna every morning, or drank water from the rock, or that the law was given with the terror and solemnity described in the Bible, if these things did not happen. Not less impossible is it that the five thousand should have believed they were fed by Christ; or that the relatives of Lazarus, and the Jews who knew him, should have believed that he was raised from the dead, or the parents and friends of the man born blind, that he was made to see; or that the multitudes before whom he healed the lame, and the sick of every description, should have believed that these events took place, if they did not. These miracles are of such a nature, that, unless they were really wrought, it is impossible they should have been believed at the time.

"Therefore it only remains that such matter of fact might be invented some time after, when the men of that generation wherein the thing was said to be done are all past and gone; and the credulity of after ages might be imposed upon to believe that things were done in former ages which were not.

The last two rules. — "And for this the last two rules secure us as much as the first two rules in the former case; for, whenever such a matter of fact came to be invented, if not only monuments were said to remain of it, but likewise that public actions and observances were constantly used ever since the matter of fact was said to be done, the deceit must be detected by no such monuments appearing, and by the experience of every man, woman, and child, who must know that no such actions or observances were ever used by them." "For example," continues Leslie, "suppose I should now invent a story of such a thing done a thousand years ago; I might perhaps get some to believe it; but if I say that not only such a thing was done, but that, from that day to this, every man, at the age of twelve years, had a joint of his little finger cut off; and that every man in the nation did want a joint of such a finger; and that this institution was said to be part of the matter of fact done so many years ago, and vouched as a proof and confirmation of it, and as having descended without interruption, and been constantly practiced, in memory of such matter of fact, all along from the time that such matter of fact was done; — I say it is impossible I should be believed in such a case, because every one could contradict me as to the mark of cutting off the joint of the finger; and that, being a part of my original matter of fact, must demonstrate the whole to be false."

Application to books of Moses. — The case here put is not stronger than that either of the books of Moses, or of the New Testament. For, at whatever time it might have been attempted to impose the books of Moses upon a subsequent age, it would have been impossible, because they contain the laws and civil and ecclesiastical regulations of the Jews, which the books affirm were adopted at the time of Moses, and were constantly in force from that time; and because they contain an account of the institution of the passover, which they assert to have been observed in consequence of a particular fact. If, then, a book had been put forth at a particular time, stating that the Jews had obeyed certain very peculiar laws, and had a certain priesthood, and had observed the passover from the time of Moses, while they had never heard of these laws, or of this priesthood, or of a passover, it is impossible the book should have been received. Nothing could have saved such a book from scorn or utter neglect.

To the New Testament. — But what the Levitical law, and the priesthood, and the passover, were to the Jews, baptism, and the Christian ministry, and the Lord's supper, are to Christians. It is a part of the records of the Gospels that these were instituted by Christ; that they were commanded by him to be continued till the end of time, and were actually continued and observed at the time when the Gospels purport to have been written — that is, before the destruction of Jerusalem. But if these books were fictions invented after the time of Christ, there would have been at that time no Christian baptism, nor order of Christian ministers, nor sacrament of the supper, thus derived from his appointment; and that, alone, would have demonstrated the whole to be false. Our books suppose these institutions to exist; they give an account of them; and it is impossible they should have been received where they did not exist. It is, therefore, impossible that these books should have been received at the time the facts are said to have taken place, or at any subsequent time, unless those facts really did take place. We now regard the sacrament of the supper as an essential part of the religion; it was so regarded by our fathers; nor can we conceive that it should have been otherwise up to the very time when the religion was founded. Thus we have a visible sign and pledge of the truth of our religion, handed down, independently of written testimony, from age to age; and the force of which, age has no tendency to diminish.

Strength of the evidences. — Perhaps we do not sufficiently dwell on the great strength which the Christian evidences derive from this proof, or notice the contrast it makes between the evidence for the facts of Christianity and those of ordinary history. Not only is it impossible to point out any statement of fact, substantiated by these four marks, that can be shown to be false, but none of the best authenticated facts of ancient history have them all. The fourth of July, as observed by us, may illustrate the effects of such commemorative ordinances as guarding against false historical accounts. For any man to have invented the New Testament after the time of Christ, and to have attempted to cause it to be received, would have been as if a man had written an account of the Revolution, and of the celebration of this day from the first, when no revolution was ever heard of, and no one had ever celebrated the fourth of July. Nor, when such a festival was once established, would it be possible to introduce any account of its origin essentially different from the true one. But the case of the Christian religion is much stronger; because we have several different institutions which must have sprung up at its origin; because baptism and the Lord's supper have occurred so much more frequently; and because the latter has always been considered the chief rite of a religion to which men have been more attached than to liberty or to life.

Two great arguments. — Thus I have brought into close juxtaposition these two great arguments. We have seen that it was impossible that the apostles should have been either deceivers or deceived; and that the books could not have been received, either at the time they purport to have been written, or at any subsequent time, if the facts recorded had not taken place.

Credible because no others. — But again: our books are credible because there are no others. That such a movement as Christianity must have been, involving the origin of so many new institutions, and such ecclesiastical and social changes, should have originated at such a time, and in such a place, and that no written documents should have been drawn forth by it, is incredible. And that the true account should have perished, leaving not a vestige behind it, and that false ones, and such as these, should have been substituted, is impossible. Of the origin of such institutions we should expect some account. That of our books is adequate and satisfactory. There is nothing contradictory to it, for even spurious writings confirm the truth of our books, and there is no vestige of any other.

Because of the character of the miracles. — I will only add, in this general department of evidence, that our books are credible because they contain accounts of *such* miracles. In the second lecture, I spoke of miracles as the proper and .only adequate seal of a message from God, and also noticed the peculiar import of those words of Nicodemus, "We know that no man can do *these miracles that thou doest* except God be with him," in which it seems to be implied that the character of the miracle, as well as the mere fact that a miracle was wrought, may have something to do with the weight and bearing of its evidence. I have recently met with a passage, in "The Process of Historical Proof," by Isaac Taylor, in which, from a comparison of the Christian miracles with the prodigies to which impostors have made pretension, he asserts that they so bear the stamp of divinity upon them as to stand in no need of external proof. Perhaps this is too strongly stated, but the thought is one deserving of attention. "Whoever," says he, "is duly informed of the state of mankind in ancient times, and is aware of the invariable character of the preternatural events or prodigies which were talked of among the Greeks, Romans, and Asiatics, (the Jews excepted, whose notions were derived from another source,) must allow that the miracles recorded to have been performed by Christ and his apostles differ totally from all such portents and prodigies. The beneficent restorations which followed the word or the touch of Him who came, not to destroy life, but to save, were, if the expression may be allowed, perfectly in the style of the Creator; they held forth such exhibitions of an absolute control over the material world as were most significant of the power of the doctrine to restore health to the soul. If the idea of the morality taught by Christ was absolutely new, so likewise was the idea of the miracles performed by him to enforce it." . . .

"Were there room to doubt what is the character of the native imagination of enthusiasts — of fanatics — of interested priests — when they have devised the means of giving credit to their fraudulent usurpations over the consciences of their fellows, we might read the history of superstition in ancient Egypt, India, or Greece; or, if that were not enough, we might turn to the history of those 'lying wonders,' upon which the ministers of the Romish religion in modern times have rested their pretensions." A missionary from India informs me, that the traditionary miracles of that country, at the present time, are generally connected with stories the most whimsical and absurd; that they were wrought to establish no principle, and not unfrequently for the purposes of cruelty and lust.

"The gospel miracles stand out, therefore, from the uniform history of false religions, just as the gospel morality stands out from the history of all other ethical systems. They alone are worthy of the Creator, — and that alone is worthy of the Supreme Lawgiver. Instead, then, of admitting that stronger evidence is necessary, to attest the extraordinary facts recorded in the New Testament, than is deemed sufficient in the common path of history, we assert their *intrinsic independence of external proof;* and we affirm that no sound and well-informed mind could fail to attribute them to the Divine Agent, even though all historical evidence were absent. Nothing is so reasonable as to believe that the miracles and discourses of Jesus were from God, — nothing so absurd as to suppose them to have been of men."

Summary. — Here, then, we have five authentic histories — four, of the same events — written by four different persons, who were themselves eye-witnesses, or had the best means of knowing what they relate. We have original letters, written at the time, both to bodies of men and to individuals, containing a great variety of indirect, and therefore of the very strongest, testimony. We find the books bearing every mark of honesty. We find the facts of such a nature that the witnesses could not have been deceived, and we find them laying down their lives to testify that they did not deceive others. We find institutions now existing, and rites observed, which hold such a relation to the facts of Christianity, as given in the books, that the books must be true. We find, moreover, no other account, nor the vestige of any, of the greatest revolution the world has ever known, while our accounts are in all respects simple, and natural, and perfectly satisfactory, assigning only adequate causes for effects which we know were produced; and, finally, we find in these books the only account of miracles that are worthy of God. Can any man then refuse to believe facts thus substantiated, and yet receive evidence for any past event? Can he do it, and pretend he is not governed by other considerations than those of evidence?

Heathen writers. — And here I might pause; but I am to present the evidence, and there is still another department on which I have not touched. All the evidence hitherto adduced has been drawn from our own books, or from the nature of the case. Let us now turn to that which we may derive from heathen writers, and from other sources. This evidence must be noticed, because there are those who attach to it a peculiar value. There are those who give a weight to the testimony of Tacitus the heathen, which they would not have given to that of Tacitus the Christian. This is unreasonable; because, if Tacitus had become a Christian, it would, under the circumstances, have implied both sincerity and more accurate knowledge. The very fact of becoming a Christian would have been, on his part, as it was on the part of every converted heathen, the most striking testimony he could have given of his belief in the facts of Christianity. Still, there are those who will not detach the idea of partisanship from the belief and maintenance of any great truth, and who look upon Christian testimony, as such, with suspicion. While, therefore, we say that they suffer the very circumstance, that ought to give this evidence weight, to impair its force, yet, for their sakes, as well as for its intrinsic value, the evidence from other sources must be given.

Time and place of origin. — And here, again, as at other points, the evidence of Christianity shines with a peculiar lustre. It may, indeed, almost be said that our books are credible from the very time and place of their origin. "Few persons," says the forcible writer whom I last quoted, "few persons, perhaps, give due attention to the relative position of the Christian history, which stands upon the very point of intersection where three distinct lines of history meet — namely, the Jewish, the Grecian, and the Roman. These three bodies of ancient literature, alone, have descended, by an uninterrupted channel of transmission, to modern times; and these three, by a most extraordinary combination of circumstances, were brought together to elucidate the origination of Christianity. If upon the broad field of history there rests the common light of day, upon that spot where a new religion was given to man there shines the intensity of a concentrated brightness." The Jews had their own literature; they had been formerly conquered by the Greeks, and the Greek language was in common use; they were also a Roman province, and "during more than a century, in the centre of which stands the ministry of Christ, the affairs of Syria attracted the peculiar attention of the Roman government." "No other people of antiquity can be named, upon whose history and sentiments there falls this *triple* flood of historic light; and upon no period in the history of this one people do these triple rays so precisely meet as upon the moment when the voice of one was heard in the wilderness of Jordan, saying, 'Prepare ye the way of the Lord.'"* Well, then, might an apostle say, "These things were not done in a corner." The time is not run back, like that of Indian legends, to obscure and fabulous ages; nor is it in what are called the dark ages of more modern times. It was a civilized and an enlightened age — a classic age — an age of poets, philosophers, and historians. Nor was it in Mecca — a city little known or visited by the civilized world, and where the people and language were homogeneous — that Christ arose. It was in Jerusalem, in Western Asia, — the theatre of history from the first, — and from the bosom of a people with all whose rites and usages we are perfectly acquainted. It was, perhaps, the only place on earth in which a Roman governor would have called the three languages which contain the literature of ancient civilization into requisition, to proclaim at once the accusation and the true character of Christ. "And Pilate wrote a title, and put it on the cross. And the writing was — JESUS OF NAZARETH, THE KING OF THE JEWS. And it was written *in Hebrew, and Greek, and Latin.*"

Here, then, was a mixed population, with different prejudices and interests, speaking different languages,

* Process of Historical Proof.

for that day a reading population, in a city to which not only the Jews dwelling in Palestine, but those from distant countries, and proselytes, came up yearly, as the centre and seat of the only pure worship of God on earth. And was this the place to select for the production of forged writings? or for an imposture of any kind to gather a force that should carry it over the earth?

I have already spoken of the opportunity furnished by the number and variety of the Christian witnesses for a most searching cross-examination, and we have seen how triumphantly they come out from such an ordeal. And here again they are brought to a test scarcely less trying. The contemporary writers, Jewish and heathen, in the three languages mentioned, are numerous; and whatever, in any of them, throws light on the manners, or habits, or sects, or forms of government, or general condition of the inhabitants of Palestine and the surrounding countries, will enable us to put to a most decisive test those who describe with any minuteness important events passing upon such a scene.

The Talmud. — Of Hebrew literature, then, we have the Talmud, a collection of Jewish traditions, the compilation of which was commenced as early as the second century. This speaks of Christ, and of several of the disciples, by name. It speaks also of his crucifixion. It admits, also, that he performed many and great miracles, but imputes his power to his having learned the right pronunciation of the ineffable name of God, which, it says, he stole out of the Temple, or to the magic arts which he learned in Egypt. These writings are specific in their statements respecting the destruction of Jerusalem, and throw much light on the sects and customs of the Jews.*

Greek writers — Josephus. — Of Greek writers, we

---

* See Horne.

cite first Josephus, who, though he was a Jew by birth, and a Roman by association and habits, yet wrote in Greek. Josephus lived at the time many of these events are said to have happened, and was present at the destruction of Jerusalem. In him, therefore, we have the most ample means of ascertaining every thing relating to Jewish sects, and customs, and opinions, and of testing the accuracy of our books respecting many dates and names of persons and places.

And, on all hands, it is agreed that, so far as Josephus goes, he confirms the accuracy of our books. Every thing said in relation to the sects of the Jews, and the Herods, and Pilate, and the division of provinces, and Felix, and Drusilla, and Bernice, has just that agreement with our accounts which we should expect in independent historians. The account given by Josephus of the death of Herod is strikingly similar to that of Luke. The account by Luke you will remember. Josephus says that Herod came into the theatre early in the morning, dressed in a robe or garment made wholly of silver, and that the reflection of the rays of the rising sun from the silver gave him a majestic and awful appearance, and that in a short time his flatterers exclaimed, one from one place and another from another, though not for his good, that he was a god, and they entreated him to be propitious to them. He then adds, "Immediately after, he was seized with pain in his bowels, extremely violent, and was carried to the palace." Luke gives the cause of the pain, saying he was eaten of worms. Do we find in the New Testament the Jews calling upon Pilate to crucify Jesus, and saying, We have no power to put any man to death? Josephus says that they had the free exercise of their religion, and the power of accusing and prosecuting, but not of putting any man to death. Do we find the Roman captain, when Paul was arrested, asking, "Art not thou that Egyptian, which before these days madest an uproar, and leddest out into the wilderness four thousand men that were murderers?" We find in Josephus a full account of the transaction, which happened under the government of Felix, and, what is remarkable, Josephus does not mention his name, but every where calls him "the Egyptian," and "the Egyptian false prophet." Do our books speak of Pharisees, and Sadducees, and Herodians? Josephus confirms all that is said of these in the minutest particulars. Does Luke speak of soldiers who went to John the Baptist, using a word ($στρατευομενοι$) which indicates that they were then under arms and marching to battle? Josephus tells us that Herod was then at war with Aretas, his father-in-law, and that a body of soldiers was at that very time marching through the region where John was. Does Luke speak of Herod as reproved by John for Herodias, his brother Philip's wife? Josephus tells us it was on her account that Herod had sent back his wife, and that the war was undertaken. Does Paul say of Ananias, when reproached for reviling God's high priest, "I wist not, brethren, that he was the high priest"? We find, from Josephus, that Ananias had been deposed, and his successor murdered, and that in the interim, when there really was no high priest, Ananias had usurped the place. Does Luke speak of a body of soldiers stationed at Cæsarea, called the Augustan band? Josephus says, that though that garrison was chiefly composed of Syrian soldiers, yet that there was a small body of Roman soldiers stationed there, called by this title, and he applies to them the very Greek term used by Luke. So minute and perfect are these coincidences, that no one can resist the conviction that the writers of our books lived and acted in the scenes which they relate.

But it is said that Josephus is silent respecting Christ

and Christianity. This is not true, if we admit as authentic either of two passages which are found in all the manuscripts, and which have strong external testimony. The first passage is this: "Now there was, about this time, Jesus, a wise man, if it be lawful to call him a man; for he performed many wonderful works. He was a teacher of such men as received the truth with pleasure. He drew over to him many of the Jews, and also of the Gentiles. This was the Christ. And when Pilate, at the instigation of the principal men among us, had condemned him to the cross, those who had loved him from the first did not cease to adhere to him. For he appeared to them alive again on the third day; the divine prophets having foretold these and ten thousand other wonderful things concerning him. And the tribe of Christians, so named from him, subsists to this time." * Subsequently we find the following: "Ananias assembled the Jewish Sanhedrim, and brought before it James, the brother of Jesus, who is called Christ, with some others, whom he delivered over to be stoned as infractors of the law." We also find a passage speaking of John the Baptist, in exact accordance with our Gospels. The authenticity of all these passages has been controverted, and there is so much reason for doubt, that I do not quote them as authoritative. If they are interpolations, then Josephus is silent on the whole subject. But that silence is not from ignorance. We know from Tacitus that before Josephus wrote, the Roman people, for whom he wrote, had seen the tortures of Christian martyrs suffering for their faith in Jesus Christ, whom they regarded as a Jew, and continuing himself to be a Jew, his silence becomes an indirect but very strong testimony. As a Jew, he could not confess the truth of the facts asserted by

---

* For a vindication of the genuineness of this passage, see the recent edition of Horne.

Christians; but as an historian, he did not venture to contradict them, and, as has been seen, in all collateral matters he confirms them. But, if we suppose Josephus silent, then it is certain, from Tacitus, that his silence was not from ignorance, and, inasmuch as he continued a Jew, it thus becomes an indirect testimony. He could not say any thing to contradict our books; he says nothing different from them; he confirms them in all incidental points.

Demosthenes. — But, again: does Luke speak of the Athenians as spending their time in hearing and telling some new thing? We find Demosthenes, long before, inquiring of them whether it was their sole ambition to wander through the public places, each inquiring of the other, "What news?" Does Paul speak of the Cretans as liars? We find that to "Cretize" was a proverbial expression, among the ancients, for lying.

Testimony of Pilate. — Before citing two Latin authors, I will say a word of what may be called "official" testimony to the facts of Christianity. Its early defenders, as Justin Martyr, in his first Apology, addressed to "the emperor and senate of Rome," and Tertullian, addressing the Roman governor of his province, appeal to the official communications of Pilate to the emperor Tiberius, as confirming their statements concerning Christ. The confidence with which they invite an examination of the public records, and of the other sources of information, — and this at a time when such an examination would certainly disclose the facts, — shows their unhesitating faith, not only as to the truth of the Christian history, but also as to the abundant evidence then existing and accessible, by which it was supported. If no such documents had existed, it would have been mere foolhardiness thus to refer to them; if they did exist, how perfect the evidence! *

---

* Horne, to whom, and Paley, I have chiefly referred in this part of the lecture.

Tacitus. — But I pass to Tacitus, whose testimony even Gibbon admits must be received. In connection with an account of the burning of Rome, in the tenth year of Nero, A. D. 64, which was imputed by Nero to the Christians, he tells us that Christ was put to death by Pontius Pilate, who was the procurator under Tiberius, as a malefactor; that the people called Christians derived their name from him; that this superstition arose in Judea, and spread to Rome, where at that time, only about thirty years after the death of Christ, the Christians were very numerous. The words of Tacitus, in speaking of them, are, "*ingens multitudo*," a great multitude. It is obvious, also, from the account of Tacitus, that the Christians were subjected to contempt and the most dreadful sufferings. "Their executions," says he, "were so contrived as to expose them to derision and contempt. Some were covered over with the skins of wild beasts, that they might be torn to pieces by dogs; some were crucified; while others, being daubed over with combustible materials, were set up as lights in the night-time, and were thus burnt to death." This account is confirmed by Suetonius, and by Martial and Juvenal. In his first satire, Juvenal has the following allusion, which I give as translated by Mr. Gifford: —

"Now dare
To glance at Tigellinus, and you glare
In that pitched shirt in which such crowds expire,
Chained to the bloody stake, and wrapped in fire."

This testimony of Tacitus, confirmed as it is, is perfectly conclusive respecting the time and the main facts of the origin of Christianity.

Pliny. — It would here be in place to quote the whole of the celebrated letter of Pliny to Trajan, and the reply; but as these are so well known, I will simply give two brief passages, one respecting the character, and the other the numbers, of the Christians. Pliny was propraetor of Pontus and Bithynia, a part of Asia remote from Judea, and the letter was written but a little more than seventy years after the death of Christ. Many were brought before him for their faith in Christ. If they remained steadfast in it, refusing to offer incense to the idols, he condemned them to death for their "inflexible obstinacy." Under this fear numbers consented to deny Christ. Of those accused, many said that they had once been Christians, "but had abandoned that religion, some of them three years before, some of them longer, and some even twenty years before." "They affirmed," says he, — that is, those who said they had once been Christians, but were not then, — "that the whole of their fault, or error, lay in this, that they were wont to meet together on a stated day before it was light, and sing among themselves, alternately, a hymn to Christ, as God, and bind themselves, by an oath, not to the commission of any wickedness, but not to be guilty of theft, or robbery, or adultery, never to falsify their word, nor to deny a pledge committed to them when called upon to return it. When these things were performed, it was their custom to separate, and then to come together again to a meal, which they ate in common without any disorder." This account seemed so extraordinary to Pliny, that he applied torture to two women, but discovered nothing more.

The passage in regard to numbers is — "Suspending, therefore, all judicial proceedings, I have recourse to you for advice; for it has appeared to me a matter highly deserving consideration, especially on account of the great number of persons who are in danger of suffering; for many of all ages and every rank, of both sexes likewise, are accused, and will be accused. Nor has the contagion of this superstition seized cities only, but the lesser towns also, and the open country." Here we find the testimony given in our books of the progress of the religion fully confirmed. Pontus and Bithynia were remote provinces, and it does not appear that the Christian religion had spread more rapidly there than elsewhere. How strong must have been that primitive evidence for Christianity which could induce these persons, persons of good sense, in every walk of life, to abandon the religion of their ancestors, and thus, in the face of imperial power, to persist in their adherence to one who had suffered the death of a slave!

Other writers. — We might also refer to Celsus, and Lucian, and Epictetus, and the Emperor Marcus Antoninus, and Porphyry, — who all throw light on the early history of Christianity, and all confirm, so far as they go, the accounts of our books.

Coins, medals, inscriptions. — There is a single species of evidence more, that I will just mention — that which is derived from ancient coins, medals, and inscriptions. The most striking of these relate to the credibility of the Old Testament; still, valuable confirmation to the New is not wanting, and I mention it because it shows how every possible line of evidence converges on this point.

Luke gives to Sergius Paulus a title belonging only to a man of proconsular dignity, and it had been doubted whether the governor of Cyprus had that dignity. A coin, however, has been found struck in the reign of Claudius Cæsar, (the very reign in which Paul visited Cyprus,) and under Proclus, who succeeded Sergius Paulus, on which the very title applied by Luke is given to Proclus. Luke speaks of Philippi as a colony, and the word implies that it was a Roman colony. It was mentioned as such by no other historian, and hence the authority of Luke was questioned. But a medal has been discovered which shows that this dignity was conferred upon that city by Julius Cæsar. It is implied, in the nineteenth of Acts, that there was great zeal at Ephesus for the worship of Diana; and a long inscription has been found there, by which it appears that, at one time, a whole month was set apart to games and festivals in honor of her.

There have also been found, in the catacombs at Rome, inscriptions which show, in a touching manner, in opposition to the insinuations of Gibbon and of some later writers, the cruelty of the early persecutions, and the number of those who suffered martyrdom.* Much evidence of this kind might be added.

Weak and obstinate skepticism. — Thus have we every conceivable species of historical proof, both external and internal. Thus do the very stones cry out. And, my hearers, if there may be such a thing as a weak and obstinate credulity, may there not also be such a thing as a skepticism equally weak and obstinate?

* Wiseman's Lectures.

LECTURE XI.

ARGUMENT THIRTEENTH :— PROPHECY.— NATURE OF THIS EVIDENCE.— THE GENERAL OBJECT OF PROPHECY.— THE FULFILLMENT OF PROPHECY.

THE subject of prophecy, upon which we now enter, is a great subject. It involves many questions of difficulty, and of deep and increasing interest; and I find myself embarrassed in the attempt to say any thing respecting it in a single lecture.

Force of the evidence. — The term 'prophet' meant, originally, one who spoke the words of God, not necessarily implying that he foretold future events; but, when I speak of prophecy as an evidence of revealed religion, I mean by it a foretelling of future events so contingent that they could not be foreseen by human sagacity, and so numerous and particular that they could not be produced by chance. To foretell such events, and bring them to pass, is among the most striking of all possible manifestations of the omniscience and omnipotence of God. "To declare a thing shall come to be, long before it is in being," says Justin Martyr, "and then to bring about that very thing according to the same declaration — this, or nothing, is the work of God." Hume was fully aware of the force of this kind of evidence, and justly, though for an obvious reason, classed prophecies with miracles, as furnishing proof of a revelation from God. Indeed, a prophecy fulfilled before our eyes is a standing miracle. Let it once be made out that a religion is sustained by genuine prophecies, and I see not how it is possible that evidence should be more complete or satisfactory.

Peculiar to Christianity. — In claiming prophecy as a ground of evidence, Christianity again stands entirely by itself. Miracles and prophecy — those two grand pillars of Christian evidence — are neither of them even claimed by Mohammedanism, and are neither of them the ground on which it has been attempted to introduce any other religion. Impostors have pretended, and still do, to work miracles in support of systems of paganism and of superstition already established; and, in the same way, juggling oracles have been uttered, which seem to have resembled modern fortune-telling far more than Scripture prophecy. Indeed, the contrast is not greater between the Christian miracles and the ridiculous prodigies of paganism, than it is between the prophecies of the Scriptures and the heathen oracles. Those oracles were given for purposes of gain, on special application, to gratify curiosity, or to subserve the purposes of ambition, political or military; all the circumstances under which they were given favored imposture, and the responses were generally so ambiguous, that they would apply to either alternative. "Thus, when Crœsus consulted the oracle at Delphi, relative to his intended war against the Persians, he was told that he would destroy a great empire. This he naturally interpreted of his overcoming the Persians, though the oracle was so framed as to admit of an opposite meaning. Crœsus made war against the Persians, and was ruined, and the oracle continued to maintain its credit." * But the prophecies of the Scriptures were generally uttered on no solicitation, and never for a

* Horne.

selfish end. They relate sometimes to individuals and sometimes to nations, and present us with a comprehensive view of the kingdom of God in its rise and progress, and of those events most intimately associated with it till the end of time. They are one great and harmonious system, not one of which can be shown to have failed, commencing in the garden of Eden, uttered by persons of the greatest variety of character, and extending over the space of four thousand years. A system of deception like this could have been undertaken from no conceivable motive, and could have been executed by no human power.

Gives grandeur. — This is a species of evidence which invests the Christian religion, and especially the coming of Christ, with a peculiar grandeur. As his coming is the great event to which the Christian world must always look back, so prophecy makes it the great event to which the ancient church constantly looked forward. It makes him the centre of the system, the great orb of moral day; and prophets and holy men of old it makes but as the stars and constellations that preceded and heralded the brightness of his coming.

Constantly growing. — The evidence of prophecy is also constantly growing. This results, not from the nature of prophecy, in itself considered, but from the number and nature of those unfulfilled prophecies of which there are so many, both in the Old and in the New Testament. If prophecy has laid down a map of time till the end, then the evidences from it must be more full as the scroll of Divine Providence is unrolled, and is found to correspond with this map. It has even been said that this increasing evidence of prophecy was intended to act as a compensation for the decreasing evidence of miracles; but I admit of no such decrease in the evidence for miracles. We may be as certain that miracles were wrought as those were who saw them;

just as we may be as certain that Jerusalem was besieged and taken as those were who saw it; but, in both cases, according to a common law in respect to distance in space and time, the *impression upon our minds* will be less lively than if it had been produced by the evidence of the senses, or from a near proximity in time or space. We might be as certain of the fact, if there had been an earthquake in China, as if one had swallowed up New Orleans or New York; but how much less lively would be our impressions in one case than in the other! It was a doctrine of Hume, that belief consists in liveliness of ideas, and this doctrine of a decreasing evidence for miracles seems to have resulted from confounding these two.

Specially adapted to some minds. — The evidence from prophecy, being thus conclusive, peculiar, grand, and growing, can not be omitted; though if we look at Christianity as merely requiring a logical proof, it is not needed. But the minds of men are differently constituted. Some are more struck with one species of evidence, and some with another; and it seems to have been the intention of God that his revelation should not be without any kind of proof that could be reasonably demanded, nor without proof adapted to every mind. To my mind, the argument from the internal evidence is conclusive; so is that from testimony; and here is another, perhaps not less so even now, and which is destined to become overwhelming. These are independent of each other. They are like separate nets, which God has commanded those who would be "fishers of men" to stretch across the stream — that stream which leads to the Dead Sea of infidelity — so that if any evade the first, they may be taken by the second; or, if they can possibly pass the second, that they may not escape the third.

Evidence not the sole or great object. — This evidence,

so striking and peculiar, it has generally been supposed it was the object of prophecy to give. That this was one object I can not doubt. It may even have been the sole object of some particular prophecies, as when Christ said to his disciples, respecting the treachery of Judas, "Now I have told you before it come to pass, that when it is come to pass, ye might believe." But, important as this object is, it seems to me to be only incidental. Prophecy seems, like the sinlessness of Christ, to enter necessarily into the system — to be a part, not only of the evidence of the system, but of the system itself. I speak not now of this or that particular prophecy; but I say that the prophetic element causes the whole system to have a different relation to the human mind, and makes it quite another thing as a means of moral culture and discipline. It is one thing for the soldier to march without any knowledge of the places through which he is to pass, or of that to which he is going, or of the object of the campaign; and it is quite another for him to have, not a map, perhaps, but a sketch of the intended route, with the principal cities through which he is to pass dotted down, and to know what is intended to be the termination and the final object of the campaign. It is evident that in the one case a vastly wider range of sympathies will be called into action than in the other. In the latter case, the soldiers can coöperate far more intelligently with their commander-in-chief; they will feel very differently as they arrive at designated points, and far higher will be their enthusiasm as they approach the end of their march, and the hour of the final conflict draws on. And this is the relation in which God has placed us, by the prophetic element in revelation, to his great plans and purposes. He has provided that there shall be put into the hands of every soldier a sketch of the route which the church militant is to pursue in following the

Captain of her salvation; and this sketch is continued all the way, till we see the bannered host passing through those triumphal arches where the everlasting doors have been lifted up for their entrance into the Jerusalem above. This is not merely to gratify curiosity; it is not merely to give an evidence which becomes completed only when it is no longer needed; but it is to furnish objects to faith and affection, and motives to effort, and to put the mind of man in that relation to the great plan of God which properly belongs to those whom he calls his children and his friends.

Obscurity. — Objection has been made to the obscurity of the prophecies. This objection can not lie against them as indicating the general course of events, and thus accomplishing the great end for which I suppose they were given. Nor can it lie against some of the particular prophecies, for nothing can be more direct and explicit. Others, however, are obscure. The revelations were made by symbols which are subject to their own laws of interpretation, and the meaning of which the prophets themselves did not always understand. But it is through this very obscurity, in the exact degree in which it exists, that many of these prophecies furnish the highest possible evidence of their genuineness. If the object had been to furnish the very best evidence that certain prophecies were inspired, it could have been done only by investing them with such a degree of obscurity that the events could not have been certainly recognized before their fulfillment, and yet by making them so clear that they could not be mistaken afterward. And this is precisely the principle on which many of the prophecies are constructed. Looked at in this point of view, they show a divine skill. If a prophecy had the plainness of a narration, it might be plausibly said that it was the cause of its own fulfillment. Individuals wishing it to be fulfilled might accommodate themselves to the prophecy, or, as has been done in one famous instance,* they might endeavor to prevent the fulfillment. How eagerly this objection would have been seized on may be seen from the fact that Bolingbroke says, even now, that Christ did bring on his own death willfully, that his disciples might boast that the prophecies were fulfilled in him. But when prophecy, while it spans, as with a luminous arch, the whole canopy of time, and reveals some events with perfect distinctness, yet so far shrouds others as to show only their general form, while it so far reveals them that they can not be mistaken when they stand in the light of actual fulfillment, then we see the certain signature of a divine hand; we have the very best evidence that the prophecy is from God.

Connection of the Old and the New Testaments. — Perhaps I ought to say a word on another point. Much has been said of the connection between the Old and the New Testaments. To some it has seemed that the Old Testament was only a dead weight, and that Christianity would move on triumphantly if it were once fairly cut loose from this. Its morality has seemed to them barbarous, and its narrations improbable. They would not, perhaps, say positively that those events never did take place, but they greatly doubt whether they did, and they talk of "those old *myths.*" But I have no fears that the Old Testament will drag down the New. I have no wish to cut Christianity loose from any connection with it, but would rather draw that connection closer. To me the morality of the Old Testament is the morality of the ten commandments. I find nothing sanctioned there which these would not allow, and I wish for nothing better. To me its narratives are facts; and I remember that the Saviour said of these books that they were they which testified of Him.

* That of Julian.

Four points to be established. — With these views, while I allow that there are difficulties connected with the proper interpretation of some of the prophecies, and in a few cases with the manner in which they are referred to by the New Testament writers, I yet feel that there is overwhelming evidence, 1. Of the fulfillment of those prophecies which related to events that occurred before the time of Christ. 2. That Christ and his apostles did claim that many of the Old Testament prophecies were fulfilled in him. 3. That those prophecies were thus fulfilled. And, 4. That not only the prophets of old, but Christ and his apostles, uttered prophecies which have been fulfilled since his time, and which are in the process of fulfillment now.

Prophecies relating to events before Christ. — Let us, then, look at the fulfillment of those prophecies which related to events that occurred before the time of Christ. Of these the number is very great, relating to the Jews, and to those nations with whom they were connected. Of those respecting the Jews, I shall adduce only such as relate to their Babylonish captivity and return; and of these I can give but single specimens out of large classes of passages. Jeremiah says, (xxxii. 28,) "Therefore thus saith the Lord, Behold, I will give this city into the hand of the Chaldeans, and into the hand of Nebuchadnezzar king of Babylon, and he shall take it." This is sufficiently explicit with respect to the taking of the city. He says again, (xxix. 10,) "For thus saith the Lord, that after *seventy years* be accomplished at Babylon I will visit you, and perform my good word toward you, in causing you to return to this place." Hear, now, Isaiah, a hundred and sixty years before these events, calling by name and pointing out the work of one who was not yet. Isa. xliv. 28. "That saith of Cyrus, He is my shepherd, and shall perform all my pleasure: even saying to Jerusalem,

Thou shalt be built; and to the Temple, Thy foundation shall be laid." Now let us hear the decree of this same Cyrus, made at the expiration of the seventy years. Ezra i. 2, 3. "Thus saith Cyrus, king of Persia, The Lord God of heaven hath given me all the kingdoms of the earth; and he hath charged me to build him a house in Jerusalem which is in Judah. Who is there among you of all his people? his God be with him, and let him go up to Jerusalem, which is in Judah, and build the house of the Lord God of Israel, (he is the God,) which is in Jerusalem." History itself could not be more plain or specific, and such events were plainly beyond the reach of human sagacity.

The nations chiefly connected with the Jews were the Ninevites, the Moabites, the Ammonites, the Philistines, the Edomites, the Egyptians, the Tyrians, and the Babylonians; and concerning each of these there are numerous and specific prophecies.

Of Nineveh, that exceeding great city of three days journey, the prophet says, (Nahum i. 9,) "What do ye imagine against the Lord? He will make an utter end: affliction shall not rise up the second time." And says another prophet, (Zeph. ii. 13, 15,) "He will make Nineveh a desolation, and dry like a wilderness. This is the rejoicing city that dwelt carelessly, that said in her heart, I am, and there is none beside me: how is she become a desolation!" Of the Moabites, and the Ammonites, the prophet said, (Zeph. ii. 8, 9,) "I have heard the reproach of Moab, and the revilings of the children of Ammon, whereby they have reproached my people, and magnified themselves against their border. Therefore, as I live, saith the Lord of hosts, the God of Israel, surely Moab shall be as Sodom, and the children of Ammon as Gomorrah, even the breeding of nettles, and salt pits, and a perpetual desolation." "Moab," says another prophet, (Jer. xlviii. 42,) "shall be destroyed from being a people." All this respecting Nineveh, and Moab, and Ammon, has been literally accomplished. Of the Philistines the prophet says, (Zeph. ii. 4,) "Gaza shall be forsaken, and Ashkelon a desolation: they shall drive out Ashdod at the noonday, and Ekron shall be rooted up." Of Edom the prophecies are the more remarkable, because commentators on the Bible were long troubled to know how to dispose of them, and because their literal and exact fulfillment has been known only a few years. This country was once a great thoroughfare, and a mart for commerce, and remained so long after the prophecies were uttered. Here was Petra, that city the ruins of which have recently become so celebrated. When this was discovered in the midst of such utter desolation, then, and not till then, was the meaning of such passages as the following made known. Jer. xlix. 16–18. "Thy terribleness hath deceived thee, and the pride of thine heart, O thou that dwellest in the clefts of the rock, that holdest the height of the hill. Also Edom shall be a desolation: every one that goeth by it shall be astonished, and shall hiss at all the plagues thereof. As in the overthrow of Sodom and Gomorrah, and the neighbor cities thereof, saith the Lord, no man shall abide there, neither shall a son of man dwell in it." The discovery of this country and its ruins, which no traveler seems to have visited for a thousand years, was like the resurrection of one from the dead to bear witness to the literal truth of the prophecies of God. Concerning Egypt, once so mighty, it was said, (Ezek. xxix. 15; xxx. 13,) "It shall be the basest of the kingdoms; neither shall it exalt itself any more above the nations: for I will diminish them, that they shall no more rule over the nations. And there shall be no more a prince of the land of Egypt." Upon this passage the whole history of Egypt is but one commentary.

The prophecies concerning Tyre and Babylon are well known. Of Tyre it was said, (Ezek. xxvi. 4, 5,) "And they shall destroy the walls of Tyrus, and break down her towers; I will also scrape her dust from her, and make her like the top of a rock. It shall be a place for the spreading of nets in the midst of the sea." Alexander scraped the ruins from the site of the old city for the purpose of filling up a passage to the new, and the infidel Volney tells us that it is now a place where the fishermen spread their nets. Of "Babylon, the glory of kingdoms," it was said, (Isa. xiii. 20, 21,) "It shall never be inhabited, neither shall it be dwelt in from generation to generation: neither shall the Arabian pitch tent there; neither shall the shepherds make their fold there. But wild beasts of the desert shall lie there; and their houses shall be full of doleful creatures; and owls shall dwell there, and satyrs shall dance there." No better description of the fate and condition of Babylon could be written now. These prophecies were literal, and they have been literally fulfilled. At the time they were uttered there was nothing to indicate the probability of such events. The world had then had no experience of the transfer of the seats of power and civilization. How strange that all these cities and nations should have perished! Why should not the Moabites, or the Ammonites, have remained a separate people, as well as the Jews or the Ishmaelites? The prophets of God no longer wander over those regions, but he has not left himself without a witness. No voice could be more eloquent than that of those ruined cities and desolate kingdoms, testifying how fearful a thing it is to fall under the displeasure of God, and how certainly he will execute all his threatenings.

Claim of Christ and his apostles. — I now proceed

to show that Christ and his apostles did claim that many of the Old Testament prophecies were fulfilled in him. This claim, it seems to me, if it could have been made by language, was made. I shall cite a few passages, and leave you to judge. Christ says, (John v. 39,) "Search the Scriptures, for they are they which testify of me." John v. 46. "For had ye believed Moses, ye would have believed me; for he wrote of me." "The Son of man," said he, (Matt. xxvi. 24,) "goeth, as it is written of him." Mark ix. 12. "It is written of the Son of man, that he must suffer many things." Luke xviii. 31. "All things written by the prophets concerning the Son of man shall be accomplished." Luke xxiv. 25–27. "Then he said unto them, O fools, and slow of heart to believe all that the prophets have spoken! Ought not Christ to have suffered these things, and to enter into his glory? And beginning at Moses, and all the prophets, he expounded unto them in *all* the Scriptures the things concerning himself." And it was when he thus opened to them the Scriptures, that their hearts burned within them. Again, he said, (verses 44–46,) "All things must be fulfilled which were written in the law of Moses, and the prophets, and in the Psalms, concerning me. Then opened he their understanding, that they might understand the Scriptures, and said unto them, Thus it is written, and thus it behooved Christ to suffer, and to rise from the dead." Could Christ have claimed that he was the subject of prophecy, not only in one portion of Scripture, but in all the Scriptures, more plainly than he did claim it? It is obvious, from the narrative, that the effect was scarcely greater of seeing him alive, than was that produced by his opening to them the Scriptures.

But what say the apostles? "Paul went in unto the Jews," (Acts xvii. 2, 3,) "and three Sabbath days reasoned with them out of the Scriptures, opening and alleging that Christ must needs have suffered, and risen again from the dead." And the noble Bereans "searched the *Scriptures* daily, whether those things were so." Again, (Acts xxviii. 23,) Paul "expounded and testified the kingdom of God, persuading them concerning Jesus, both out of the law of Moses and out of the prophets." Paul declared before Agrippa (Acts xxvi. 22) that he said "*none other* things than those which the prophets and Moses did say should come." Apollos (Acts xviii. 28) "mightily convinced the Jews, publicly showing, by the Scriptures, that Jesus was Christ." Peter, even in his first discourse to the Gentiles, said, (Acts x. 43,) "To him give all the prophets witness." And again, (Acts iii. 18,) "Those things which God before had showed by the mouth of *all his prophets*, that Christ should suffer, he hath so fulfilled." Again, (verse 24,) he says, "Yea, and *all* the prophets from Samuel, and those that follow after, as many as have spoken, have likewise foretold of these days." And Peter says expressly (1 Pet. i. 10, 11) that "the prophets have inquired and searched diligently, searching what or what manner of time the Spirit of Christ which was in them did signify, when it testified beforehand the sufferings of Christ, and the glory that should follow."

To me it seems that these passages show, if any thing can show it, not only that Christ and his apostles claimed that the Old Testament Scriptures were fulfilled in him, but that the great question, when they attempted to convert the Jews, was, whether they had been thus fulfilled.

Prophecies fulfilled in Christ. — Our next inquiry is, whether there are prophecies in the Old Testament which were thus fulfilled in Christ.

And here I hardly know what course to take. I might propound a theory, or make general assertions, and perhaps, as has too often been done, mystify the subject; but this would not be proof. Proof must be drawn from a comparison of scripture with scripture. Hence only can conviction arise. Will the audience then permit me to present briefly, letting the Scriptures speak for themselves, some corresponding passages of the Old and of the New Testament on this subject? It will be my intention to produce no passage which is not applicable; but, if I should, it would not invalidate the general argument. The question here is not one of small criticism. It is as when we stand in the light of open day. We should not deny, perhaps, that there might be found dark corners into which a man could run and see nothing; nor that so small an object as his hand even might conceal from him the whole horizon. So here, the question is not whether a man may not find some dark points, or some small objection which he may hold in such a position as to eclipse the glory of the whole prophetic heavens; but whether there is not, for the candid mind, one broad flood of light pouring out from the prophecies of the Old Testament, the rays of which converge, as in a halo of glory, around the head of the Redeemer. We contend that there is, and that this light began to shine even before our first parents were expelled from Eden.

To bruise the head of the serpent. — The first intimation we have of a Messiah was in the promise that the seed of the woman should bruise the head of the serpent. Gen. iii. 15. In the New Testament it is said, " God sent forth his Son, made of a woman." Gal. iv. 4. And again: He became a partaker of flesh and blood, that " through death he might destroy him that had the power of death, that is, the devil." Heb. ii. 14.

To be of the seed of Abraham. — The next general intimation was given to Abraham, and his family was predicted. "And in thy seed shall all the nations of the earth be blessed." Gen. xxii. 18. "Now, to Abraham," says Paul, "and his seed, were the promises made. He saith not, And to seeds, as of many; but as of one, And to thy *seed*, which is Christ." Gal. iii. 16. "For verily he took not on him the nature of angels, but he took on him the seed of Abraham." Heb. ii. 16.

Of the tribe of Judah. — He was to be of the tribe of Judah. "The sceptre shall not depart from Judah, nor a lawgiver from between his feet, until Shiloh come: and unto him shall the gathering of the people be." Gen. xlix. 10. "For it is evident," says Paul, "that our Lord sprang out of Judah; of which tribe Moses spake nothing concerning priesthood." Heb. vii. 14.

Of the house of David. — He was to be of the house of David. "And in that day there shall be a root of Jesse, which shall stand for an ensign of the people; to it shall the Gentiles seek: and his rest shall be glorious." Isa. xi. 10. "Behold, the days come, saith the Lord, that I will raise unto *David* a righteous Branch, and a King shall reign and prosper, and shall execute judgment and justice; and this is his name whereby he shall be called, THE LORD OUR RIGHTEOUSNESS." Jer. xxiii. 5, 6. Paul says, "Concerning his Son Jesus Christ our Lord, which was made of the seed of David according to the flesh." Rom. i. 3.

Place of birth designated. — The place of his birth was designated. "But thou, Bethlehem Ephratah, though thou be little among the thousands of Judah, yet out of thee shall he come forth unto me that is to be Ruler in Israel; whose goings forth have been from of old, from everlasting." Micah v. 2. "Now," says

Matthew, "when Jesus was born in Bethlehem of Judea." Matt. ii. 1.

The time of birth.—The time was designated. It was not only to be before the sceptre departed from Judah, but while the second Temple was standing. "And I will shake all nations," says God by Haggai, "and the Desire of all nations shall come: and the glory of this latter house shall be greater than of the former, saith the Lord of Hosts." Hag. ii. 7, 9. Daniel also said, "Seventy weeks are determined upon thy people and upon the holy city, to finish the transgression, and to make an end of sins, and to make reconciliation for iniquity, and to bring in everlasting righteousness, and to seal up the vision and prophecy, and to anoint the Most Holy." Dan. ix. 24. Accordingly we find, not only from Jewish writers, but from the most explicit passages in Tacitus and Suetonius, that there was a general expectation that an extraordinary person would arise in Judea about that time. So strong was this expectation among the Jews as to encourage numerous false Christs to appear, and to enable them to gain followers; and so certain were they that the Temple could not be destroyed before the coming of the Messiah, that they refused all terms from Titus, and fought with desperation till the last.

Elias to come first.—He was to be preceded by a remarkable person resembling Elijah. "Behold, I will send my messenger, and he shall prepare the way before me." Mal. iii. 1. "Behold, I will send you Elijah the prophet before the coming of the great and dreadful day of the Lord." Mal. iv. 5. "The voice of him that crieth in the wilderness, Prepare ye the way of the Lord, make straight in the desert a highway for our God." Isa. xl. 3. "In those days came John the Baptist, preaching in the wilderness of Judea, and saying,

Repent ye; for the kingdom of heaven is at hand."
Matt. iii. 1, 2.

Was to work miracles. — He was to work miracles. "Then the eyes of the blind shall be opened, and the ears of the deaf shall be unstopped. Then shall the lame man leap as a hart, and the tongue of the dumb sing." Isa. xxxv. 5, 6. These are precisely the miracles recorded as wrought by Christ in instances too numerous to mention.

His public entry into Jerusalem. — He was to make a public entry into Jerusalem, riding upon a colt the foal of an ass. "Rejoice greatly, O daughter of Zion; shout, O daughter of Jerusalem: behold, thy King cometh unto thee: he is just, and having salvation; lowly, and riding upon an ass, and upon a colt the foal of an ass." Zech. ix. 9. An account of the exact fulfillment of this prophecy will be found in the twenty-first chapter of Matthew.

To be rejected by the Jews. — He was to be rejected of his own countrymen. "And he shall be for a sanctuary; but for a stone of stumbling and for a rock of offense to both the houses of Israel." Isa. viii. 14. "He hath no form nor comeliness; and when we shall see him, there is no beauty that we should desire him. He is despised and rejected of men; a man of sorrows, and acquainted with grief: and we hid as it were our faces from him; he was despised, and we esteemed him not." Isa. liii. 2, 3. "He came unto his own," says John, "and his own received him not." John i. 11. And again: "Though he had done so many miracles before them, yet they believed not on him: that the saying of Esaias the prophet might be fulfilled, which he spake, Lord, who hath believed our report?" — quoting the first verse of the fifty-third of Isaiah, and thus claiming it as spoken of the Messiah. And after quoting another prophecy, the apostle says, "These things said Esaias, when he saw his glory, and spake of him." John xii. 37, 38, 41.

To be scourged and mocked. — He was to be scourged, mocked, and spit upon. "I gave my back to the smiters, and my cheeks to them that plucked off the hair: I hid not my face from shame and spitting." Isa. l. 6. "And when he had *scourged* Jesus, he delivered him to be crucified." Matt. xxvii. 26. "Then did they spit in his face, and buffeted him; and others smote him with the palms of their hands." Matt. xxvi. 67.

His hands and feet to be pierced. — His hands and his feet were to be pierced. "The assembly of the wicked have inclosed me; they pierced my hands and my feet." Ps. xxii. 16. This is remarkable, because the punishment of crucifixion was not known among the Jews.

To be numbered with transgressors. — He was to be numbered with the transgressors. "And he was numbered with the transgressors; and he bare the sin of many, and made intercession for the transgressors." Isa. liii. 12.

To be reviled on the cross. — He was to be mocked and reviled on the cross. "All they that see me laugh me to scorn; they shoot out the lip, they shake the head, saying, He trusted on the Lord that he would deliver him: let him deliver him, seeing he delighted in him." Ps. xxii. 7, 8. "Likewise also the chief priests, mocking him, with the scribes and elders, said, He saved others; himself he can not save. — *He trusted in God; let him deliver him now, if he will have him:* for he said, I am the Son of God." Matt. xxvii. 41–43.

To have gall and vinegar to drink. — He was to have gall and vinegar to drink. "They gave me also gall for my meat; and in my thirst, they gave me vinegar to drink." Ps. lxix. 21. "And when they were come unto a place called Golgotha, that is to say, A place of a skull, *they gave him vinegar to drink, mingled with gall.*" Matt. xxvii. 33, 34.

His garments to be parted. — His garments were to be parted, and upon his vesture lots were to be cast. "They part my garments among them, and cast lots upon my vesture." Ps. xxii. 18. "Then the soldiers, when they had crucified Jesus, took his garments, and made four parts, to every soldier a part; and also his coat; now the coat was without seam, woven from the top throughout. They said therefore among themselves, Let us not rend it, but cast lots for it, whose it shall be: that the Scripture might be fulfilled." John xix. 23, 24.

His death to be violent. — He was to be cut off by a violent death. "For he was cut out of the land of the living." Isa liii. 8. "And after threescore and two weeks shall Messiah be cut off, but not for himself." Dan. ix. 26.

Was to be pierced. — He was to be pierced. "And I will pour upon the house of David, and upon the inhabitants of Jerusalem, the spirit of grace and of supplications: and they shall look upon me whom they have pierced." Zech. xii. 10. "But one of the soldiers with a spear pierced his side, and forthwith came thereout blood and water." John xix. 34.

To make his grave with the rich. — He was to make his grave with the rich. "And he made his grave with the wicked, and with the rich in his death." Isa. liii. 9. "When the even was come, there came a rich man of Arimathea, named Joseph, who also himself was Jesus' disciple. He went to Pilate, and begged the body of Jesus, and laid it in his own new tomb, which he had hewn out in the rock." Matt. xxvii. 57, 58, 60.

Was not to see corruption. — He was not to see corruption. "For thou wilt not leave my soul in hell; neither wilt thou suffer thine Holy One to see corruption." Ps. xvi. 10. "Men and brethren," says Peter, after citing this passage, "let me freely speak unto you of the patriarch David, that he is both dead and buried, and his sepulchre is with us unto this day. Therefore, being a prophet, and knowing that God had sworn with an oath to him, that of the fruit of his loins, according to the flesh, he would raise up Christ to sit on his throne, he, seeing this before, spake of *the resurrection of Christ*, that his soul was not left in hell, neither his flesh did see corruption." Acts ii. 29–31.

And yet there are some who say that these prophecies are no prophecies, and were never claimed to be. But I think it evident that Peter did not belong, as an interpreter of prophecy, to the schools of German neology.

Convergence of the passages. — These passages are far from being all that might be adduced. Respecting some of them as they stand, a person without previous knowledge would be led to ask the question of the Ethiopian eunuch, "I pray thee, of whom speaketh the prophet this? of himself, or of some other man?" But when we see these passages brought together; when we see their wonderful convergence, so that the history of Christ, from his miraculous birth — of the foretelling of which I have not spoken — to his death, was only their counterpart; when we find that the Jews themselves referred most of them to the Messiah, and that they are expressly claimed by Christ and his apostles, the general argument becomes exceedingly strong. How strong it is may be seen by any one who will attempt to apply one tenth part of these passages to any other person that ever lived. Let him attempt to apply them to Titus, of whom Josephus says that he was the extraordinary person foretold, and see how he will succeed. If we admit that these prophecies were extant before the coming of Christ, — and of this we have the best possible evidence, because, as was said by an ancient father, the Jews, the enemies of Christianity, were the librarians of Christians, — and if we estimate mathematically, by the doctrine of chances, the probability that these circumstances would meet in one person, it would, as is said by Dr. Gregory, surpass the powers of numbers to express the immense improbability of its taking place.

Offices of Christ foretold. — But, striking as are these passages in their application to Christ, while many of them, if not applied to him, would seem to mean nothing, they are yet far from giving the whole weight of the argument; for not only were the circumstances of his life and death minutely pointed out, but his offices were also described.

Was to be a prophet. — He was to be a prophet, like unto Moses. "I will raise them up a Prophet from among their brethren, like unto thee, and will put my words in his mouth; and he shall speak unto them all that I shall command him." Deut. xviii. 18. This is expressly quoted by Peter, in the Acts, (iii. 22,) as fulfilled by Christ.

A priest. — He was to be a priest. "The Lord hath sworn, and will not repent, Thou art a priest forever after the order of Melchisedek." Ps. cx. 4. "Called of God," says Paul, "a high priest after the order of Melchisedek." Heb. v. 10.

A king. — He was to be a king. "Yet have I set my King upon my holy hill of Zion." Ps. ii. 6. "Thy people shall be willing in the day of thy power." Ps. cx. 3. "All power," says Christ, "is given unto me in heaven and in earth." Matt. xxviii. 18. "For he must reign," says Paul, "till he hath put all enemies under his feet." 1 Cor. xv. 25.

Kingdom of peace. — His kingdom was to be one of peace. "For unto us a child is born, unto us a son is given: and the government shall be upon his shoulder: and his name shall be called Wonderful, Counselor, The mighty God, The everlasting Father, the *Prince of*

Peace. Of the increase of his government and *peace* there shall be no end, upon the throne of David, and upon his kingdom, to order it, and to establish it with judgment and with justice from henceforth, even forever." Isa. ix. 6, 7. "And they shall beat their swords into plowshares, and their spears into pruning-hooks; nation shall not lift up a sword against nation, neither shall they learn war any more." Micah iv. 3. "They shall not hurt nor destroy in all my holy mountain." Isa. xi. 9.

To include the Gentiles. — His kingdom was also to include the Gentiles. "And he said, It is a light thing that thou shouldest be my servant to raise up the tribes of Jacob, and to restore the preserved of Israel: I will also give thee for a light to the Gentiles, that thou mayest be my salvation unto the end of the earth." Isa. xlix. 6. "And the Gentiles shall come to thy light, and kings to the brightness of thy rising. The abundance of the sea shall be converted unto thee, the forces of the Gentiles shall come unto thee." Isa. lx. 3, 5. This is especially remarkable, because there was nothing in the feeling of the Israelites, or in their relations to the nations around them, in the time of Isaiah, to indicate the possibility of a spiritual and universal kingdom, in which the Gentiles should become fellow-citizens, and have equal privileges with the Jews.

Here, then, we have the three great offices of prophet, priest, and king, united by prophecy in one person; we have a kingdom of peace, and that kingdom one which was to include all nations. How perfectly all this is fulfilled in the person and kingdom of Christ I need not say; nor how entirely impossible it would be to make these passages apply to any other person or kingdom.

Prophecies seemingly incompatible. — And not only were these three great offices united in one person, but the prophecies respecting him were so apparently incompatible and contradictory that it must have seemed beforehand impossible they should be fulfilled, and they must have caused great perplexity in the minds of those who were unwilling to receive the word of God and rest on it by simple faith. Now, he was represented as a triumphant conqueror, as a king sitting upon the throne of David, and ruling all nations, and now he was spoken of as "despised and rejected of men," as "oppressed and afflicted." It was said of the Messiah, "I have set my King upon my holy hill of Zion," and that "of the increase of his government and peace there shall be no end." It was also said of him, "After threescore and two weeks shall Messiah be cut off." What contradictions, might a Jew have said, have we here! A King who is to have perpetual dominion, and is to reign till he has put all enemies under his feet, and yet is to be despised, and rejected, and oppressed! A Messiah who is to be slain, and yet is to reign forever! These assertions might, indeed, have been received separately, by faith, as the word of God; a reasonable Jew would have so received them; but, before the event, he could not have understood and reconciled them with each other; and yet the demand made by each of these aspects of the prophecy is fully met in Christ.

Fulfilled by enemies. — How, then, can the conclusion be avoided, that these prophecies were given by inspiration of God? Not by the supposition that they were fulfilled by human contrivance, for the enemies of Christ, far more than his friends, contributed to that fulfillment. As was said by Paul, (Acts xiii. 27,) "They that dwell at Jerusalem, and their rulers, because they knew him not, nor yet the voices of the prophets which are read every Sabbath day, they have fulfilled them in condemning him." It was they that smote him, and hung him on a tree, and parted his garments among them, and cast lots, and pierced his side. It was they who paid the thirty pieces of silver, the goodly price at which they valued him, and who bought, with the price of blood, the potter's field. Nor can this conclusion be avoided on the supposition of chance; for, as has already been said, it would surpass the power of numbers to express the extreme improbability of the fulfillment of such prophecies.

Types prophetic. — Nor is this all; for it would be easy to show that the whole of the Old Testament dispensation, the ark of the covenant, with all its arrangements, the passover, the sacrifices, the ceremonies, the priesthood, were all typical, and therefore prophetic; and that the true import and substance of all these is to be found in the Christian dispensation. This, however, is a great subject, and I can not enter upon it.

Prophecies by Christ and the apostles. — We now come to the fourth point mentioned — namely, that Christ and his apostles uttered prophecies which have been fulfilled since their time, and which are in the process of fulfillment now. Fully to illustrate this position, would require a lecture. I can only glance at it.

The destruction of Jerusalem. — As the prophecy of Christ respecting the destruction of Jerusalem had for one of its objects to warn his followers to escape from that city, it was delivered in the most direct and explicit terms. Before the time of Christ, and during his life, no false Christ arose; there was no war, and no prospect of one; and the Temple, and Jerusalem, were standing in all their strength. But he foretold that false Christs should arise, and should deceive many; that there should be earthquakes and famine, and fearful sights in heaven, and wars and rumors of wars, and great tribulation, such as was not since the beginning of the world, nor ever should be; and that Jerusalem should be compassed with armies; and that a trench should be cast round about it; and that one stone of the Temple should not be left upon another; and that the Jews should be carried captive among all nations. Paul also prophesied of the great apostasy, and the coming of the man of sin; and John, in the Revelation, has spoken of the course of events till the end of time.

Josephus. — To verify the prophecies of Christ respecting the destruction of Jerusalem, and the events preceding it, we have a history of those times, written by Josephus, an eye witness and a Jew; and nothing can be more striking than a comparison of the history and the prophecy. Josephus gives particular accounts of the false Christs and false prophets, and of their deceiving many. He speaks of the distracted state of those countries, corresponding to the prophecy; of wars and rumors of wars; and says that the "disorders of all Syria were terrible. For every city was divided into parties armed against each other, and the safety of one depended on the destruction of the other; the days were spent in slaughter, and the nights in terrors." He speaks also of famines, and pestilences, and earthquakes, and especially of "fearful sights, and great signs from heaven." He tells us that just before the war, a star, resembling a sword, stood over the city, and a comet that continued a whole year; that "before sunsetting, chariots, and troops of soldiers in their armor, were seen running about among the clouds, and surrounding cities." He says, also, "At the feast of Pentecost, as the priests were going by night into the inner court of the Temple, they felt a quaking, and heard a great noise, and, after that, they heard the sound as of a multitude, saying, 'Let us depart hence!'"

Tacitus. — Nor is Josephus alone in giving these accounts. Tacitus, also, says, "There were many prodigies presignifying their ruin, which was not averted by all the sacrifices and vows of that people. Armies were seen fighting in the air with brandished weapons. A fire fell upon the Temple from the clouds. The doors of the Temple were suddenly opened. At the same time there was a loud voice declaring that the gods were removing, which was accompanied with a sound as of a multitude going out. All which things were supposed, by some, to portend great calamities." He speaks, also, of the fact that Jerusalem was compassed by an army at the beginning of the war, and that, owing to the state of parties, many of the principal men were about to open the gates; but says that the Roman general recalled the soldiers from the place without having received any defeat, and retired from the city, without any reason in the world. He then mentions that, when the Roman armies approached again, a great multitude fled to the mountains. Thus a way was made for the disciples of Christ to escape, and it is not known that a single one of them perished in that destruction. It really seems to have prefigured the final destruction of the wicked, when the righteous shall all have been gathered from among them.

Josephus also speaks particularly of the trench and wall which were made about Jerusalem by Titus. This was done with great difficulty, and, except for the purpose of a little more speedy reduction of the city, without necessity, and was contrary to the advice of the chief men of Titus. But so it was written. In respect to the tribulation of those days, of which our Saviour speaks so strongly, if the purpose of Josephus had been to confirm the words of the prophecy, he could have said nothing more to the point. "No other city," says he, "ever suffered such miseries; nor was there ever a generation more fruitful in wickedness from the beginning of the world." Again: "It appears to me that the misfortunes of all men, from the beginning of the world, if they be compared to those of the Jews, are not so considerable. For in reality it was God who condemned the whole nation, and turned every course that was taken for their preservation to their destruction." And again: "The multitude of those who perished exceeded all the destructions that man or God ever brought upon the world." The great mass of the nation was gathered within the city. They were divided into contending factions, who fought with the fury of fiends against each other. Famine did its slow but fearful work, so that women were known to eat their own children. And while those within were thus the prey of famine and of each other, those who attempted to escape were taken by the Roman soldiers and nailed on crosses, some one way, some another, as it were in jest, around the outside of the walls, till so great was the number, that room was wanting for crosses, and crosses for bodies. As Titus beheld the dead bodies that had been thrown from the walls into the valleys, "he lifted up his hands to heaven, and called God to witness that this was not his doing." These were "the days of vengeance;" and it is computed by Josephus that upward of one million three hundred thousand persons perished in the siege of Jerusalem alone. And not only so, but, when the city was taken, it was, contrary to the wish of Titus, devoted to utter destruction; and the prophecy of Christ, that not one stone of the Temple should be left upon another, was literally fulfilled.

Other prophecies. — Of the other prophecies I have not time to speak; but the Jews were carried into captivity among all nations, and their condition from that time till now has been a standing and wonderful attestation of the truth of the prophetic record, while their present condition is an evident preparation for the fulfillment of those still more wonderful prophecies which now stand like the bow of promise overarching the future. According to that expression of the prophet, so wonderfully accurate, they have been *sifted* among all nations; yet have they, of all ancient people similarly situated, alone preserved their identity, and now seem to be preparing for that restoration which shall not only be to them the fulfillment of the prophecies, but shall be as life from the dead to the Gentile nations.

Summary. — Thus, whether we look at the prophecies that related to events before the time of Christ, or to those relating to him, or to those which he uttered, or to the present state of the Jews, and indeed of the world, as indicating a complete fulfillment of the prophecies, we shall see the fullest reason to believe that "the prophecy came not in old time by the will of man, but that holy men of God spake as they were moved by the Holy Ghost."

Prophecy and Christianity as counterparts. — I will only add, as a beautiful instance of the consistency of all Scripture, that the magnificent pictures of the prophets, respecting a state of future blessedness on earth, are just such as would be realized by the entire prevalence of Christianity, and by nothing else. These pictures are not drawn at random, or in general terms. They are precise and definite. They represent a state of peace, and purity, and love — of high social enjoyment, and of universal prosperity. And it is only by the prevalence of Christianity that such a state of things can be realized. Let this become universally prevalent, not in its form only, but in its spirit, and then nation would no more lift up sword against nation, neither would they learn war any more; then the wolf also would dwell with the lamb, and the leopard lie down with the kid; then would the wilderness and solitary place be glad for them, and the desert rejoice; then, instead of the thorn would come up the fir-tree, and instead of the brier would come up the myrtle-tree; then would the inhabitants of the rock sing, and shout from the top of the mountains; the people would be all righteous, and inherit the land forever.

LECTURE XII.

OBJECTIONS. — ARGUMENT FOURTEENTH: THE PROPAGATION OF CHRISTIANITY. — ARGUMENT FIFTEENTH: ITS EFFECTS AND TENDENCIES. — SUMMARY AND CONCLUSION.

Objections. — It has been my wish to present, in this course of lectures, as I was able, the positive argument for Christianity. I commenced the course with an invitation to you to go with me round about our Zion, and tell the towers thereof. Those towers are not yet all told. To some of the most common and effective topics of argument I have yet scarcely referred, and I ought, in logical order, to proceed at once to the consideration of them. This I have thought of doing, and of omitting to say any thing upon the objections against Christianity. To the consideration of these I should be pleased to devote at least a lecture; for, while there are objections which are unworthy of an answer, — while there are persons, who make them, who would be no nearer becoming Christians if their objections were all removed, — there are objections, the force of which I think may be removed, that weigh heavily upon some who are sincerely inquiring for the truth. To every such individual I would give my hand. I would make any effort to relieve him. I know what it is to wade in the deep waters of doubt, and the blessedness of finding what seems to me to be the rock. For the sake of such I would gladly dwell upon this point at length; but as that is now out of the question, I will make a few observations on the subject of objections generally, and then go on with the argument.

Willingness to wait. — And here, if I may be permitted to drop a word in a more familiar way in the ear of the candid and practical inquirer, referring to my own experience, I would say, that I have found great benefit in being willing — a lesson which we are all slow to learn — to *wait*. It has not unfrequently occurred that I have stood in such an attitude (perhaps for months or years together) to a certain objection as to see no way of evading it, till, at length, light would break in, and I could see with perfect distinctness that there was nothing in it. Are there not many here who have unexpectedly met with something which has removed, in a moment, objections which have lain with weight upon their minds for years? I well remember when it seemed to me that there was a direct contradiction between Paul and James, on the subject of faith and works. It seemed so to Luther, and, because he could not reconcile them, and was unwilling to wait, he rejected the Epistle of James, calling it a strawy Epistle. I can now see that Paul and James, not only do not contradict each other, but harmonize perfectly. I have sometimes compared the path of a sincere inquirer to a road that winds among the hills. Who has not seen the hills, perhaps the high mountains, closing down upon such a road so as to render it apparently impossible he should proceed; and who has not been surprised, when he reached the proper point to see it, to find the road taking an unexpected turn, and holding on its own level way. And to such a point I think every sincere inquirer will come, who is willing to follow the right path so far as he can find it, and to wait, putting up the petition, and adopting the resolution, of Elihu, "That which I see not, teach thou me; if I have done iniquity, I will do no more." I have the fullest conviction, not only of the truth, but of the philosophical profoundness, of that saying of our Saviour, "If any man will do his will, he shall know of the doctrine, whether it be of God, or whether I speak of myself."

No objection that objections can be made. — But, leaving this, I observe, in the first place, that we are not to have our confidence in the Christian religion shaken, from the mere fact that objections can be made against it. There are those who seem to think that, if an objection can be made, some degree of uncertainty is introduced at once, and that there comes to be a balance of probabilities. But this is not so. When once a thing is fairly proved, all objections must go for nothing. Very plausible objections may be made to many things which we yet know to be true. Thus objections have been made to the existence of matter, and to the truth of the evidence of the senses, which a plain man would find it difficult to answer, and which yet would have no weight with him whatever. We all believe there is such a thing as motion, and yet there may be some here who would find it difficult to answer the common logical objection against it. Let me put that objection. You will, I suppose, all agree that, if any thing moves, it must move either where it is, or where it is not. But certainly nothing can move where it is, for that would not be moving at all; and it would seem quite as certain that nothing could move where it is not; and hence there is no such thing as motion. "There are objections," says Dr. Johnson, "to a *vacuum*, and there are objections to a *plenum;* but one of these must be true." But to any one who has been turned aside, and is eddying round among these shoals of doubt, I would recommend that masterly pamphlet, by Whately, the "Historic Doubts respecting the Existence and Acts of Napoleon Bonaparte." I think it would lead him to see that there may be plausible objections against that concerning which there can not be the least doubt.

General objections not valid. — I observe, secondly, that, if we would consider the objections against Christianity fairly, we must distinguish those which lie against Christianity, as such, from those which may be made equally against any religion or scheme of belief whatever. This world is in a strange state. There is a condition of things very different from what we should suppose, beforehand, there would be, under the government of a God of infinite power, and wisdom, and goodness; and it is not uncommon for men to burden Christianity with all the difficulties that are connected with the origin of evil, or the doctrine of the foreknowledge of God as connected with human freedom. But these are questions that belong to the race, and have equally exercised the mind of the Grecian philosopher, of the Persian sage, and of the Christian divine. You, as a man, may be as properly called on to solve any difficulties arising out of such questions, as I can as a teacher of Christianity. Christianity had nothing to do with the origin of evil. It takes for granted, what we must all admit, that it exists; it does not attempt to account for its origin, but it proposes a remedy. If, then, men object to Christianity, let them object to it as what it claims to be. Let them show that, when fairly received and fully practiced by all men, it would not be the remedy which it claims to be, and their objections will be valid. It is of no avail for infidels and deists to shoot arrows against Christianity which may be picked up and shot back with equal force against their own systems; and yet a much larger portion of the objections against Christianity than is commonly supposed is of this character.

Distinction of Butler. — I observe, thirdly, that we are to keep in mind the distinction of Butler, already referred to, between objections against Christianity and objections against its evidence. Of the evidence for Christianity we are capable of judging. I insist upon it that there are laws of evidence, which any man of good sense can understand, according to which we judge and act in other cases; and I only ask that these same laws may be applied to Christianity, as a matter of fact and a ground of action, just as they would be to any thing else. But of Christianity itself, as a part of an infinite scheme of moral government, having relation to the eternity that is past and to that which is to come, and perhaps to other worlds and to other orders of being, we ought as much to expect that we should find in it things beyond our reach, and which would seem to us strange and objectionable, as that there would be such things in nature. And if, as Butler has most fully shown, the objections which are made against Christianity are of the same kind with those which may be made against nature, then those very objections are turned into arguments in its favor, as they show the probability that Christianity and nature came from the same hand. Here is one principal source of the power of Butler's great work. It shows that all the chief objections which are urged against Christianity may be urged equally against the constitution and course of nature, and would equally show that that was not from God. If Christianity itself can be shown to be either immoral or absurd, we will reject it; but, with these exceptions, objections to Christianity on the part of such a being as man, as distinguished from objections against its evidence, are, in the language of Butler, "frivolous." Nor, in saying this, do we undervalue reason, or refuse to give it its true place. To quote Butler again : "Let reason be kept to; and if any part of the Scripture account of the redemption of the world by Christ can be shown to be really contrary to it, let the Scripture, in the name of God, be given up; but let not such poor creatures as we go on objecting, against an infinite scheme, that we do not see the necessity and usefulness of all its parts, and call this reasoning."

Objections to every scheme. — Character of infidelity. — But, fourthly, we are to observe that Christianity is not the only scheme against which objections can be made. From its position, its success, its uncompromising claims, Christianity has been met from the first by every objection that ingenuity, quickened by a love of pleasure and hatred of restraint, could invent; and, from the constancy with which these have been plied, it has been felt by many that Christianity was especially liable to objections. It has hence been the habit of many Christians to stand on the defensive, and infidels have felt that it was their place to attack. In proportion as any scheme has about it more that is positive, it of course presents a larger surface for objections; but as far as other schemes have any thing positive about them, they are equally liable to objections with Christianity, and have none of its evidence. And the only reason that these schemes have not been as much objected against is, that men do not care enough about them. If an infidel has nothing positive in his belief, then, of course, nothing can be objected to it. But if it were possible, as it is not, for any man to take such a position, we should object to that. We say that it is a state of mind from which no good can possibly come, either to the individual or the community. It is a poor, cold, heartless state, furnishing no ground for hope, no elevation to character, no motive to effort, that has no adaptation to the wants of man even in prosperity, and that must utterly fail him in those trying hours when he

needs such supports as religion only can give. It can
be made to appear, from the very laws of mind, that
great achievements, powerful exertions, self-denying
labors and sacrifices, must spring from a vigorous faith;
and that, in proportion as a belief, or a religion, becomes one of negations, it must lower the pulse of
intellectual, and especially of moral life. Let a man,
however, have any thing positive in his belief, — let him
bring forward his own solution of the great problems
which must be connected in the mind of every thinking
man with human life and destiny, — and it would be no
difficult matter — a very child could do it — to start objections against that solution, whatever it might be,
which it would trouble the wisest infidel to meet. Hence
I have sometimes been amused at the effect, upon a noisy
and boastful objector, of a quiet question or two in regard
to his own belief. I have seen those to whom it never
seemed to have occurred that we were thrown into this
world together with certain great common difficulties,
and that other people could ask questions as well as
they. Whenever, indeed, infidelity has thus assumed
a positive form, it has been met and fairly driven from
the field; and now, it is difficult to say what the prevalent form of it is. It has always been Ishmaelitish in
its habits, pitching its tent now here and now there,
and constantly varying its mode of attack. The infidelity of one age is not that of another, while Christianity remains ever the same. And so we are to
expect it will be while the human heart remains what it
is. Infidelity will exist. There is at present more of
it than appears. Not being reputable in its own form,
it conceals itself under various disguises. But the
infidelity that springs from the heart is not to be
reached by a course of lectures on the evidences of
Christianity. As I have already said, argument did

not cause, and argument will not remove it. For that, we look to a higher power.

ARGUMENT XIV.

THE PROPAGATION OF CHRISTIANITY.

I now proceed with the evidence. As yet I have said nothing of the argument to be derived from the mode and circumstances of the propagation of Christianity, and have only incidentally alluded to its effects and tendencies. Each of these is a standing topic of argument on this subject, and, when properly presented, sufficient of itself to prove the truth of the Christian religion. But I shall now be able to do little more than to indicate the place which these arguments hold, without giving them their proper expansion and force. These topics of argument are entirely distinct in their nature, but are so connected at certain points that it is difficult to treat of one, without involving considerations which belong also to the other.

Propagation.—First, then, of the propagation of Christianity: And in speaking of this subject, I will notice, 1, the facts; 2, the difficulties; and, 3, the instrumentality. This subject has been ably treated by Bishop M'Ilvaine, in his excellent lectures on the evidences, and I shall avail myself of his labors in presenting it.*

It would appear, then, that on the fiftieth day after the death of Christ the apostles commenced their labors. "Beginning in Jerusalem, the very furnace of persecution, they first set up their banner in the midst of those who had been first in the crucifixion of Jesus, and were all elate with the triumph of that tragedy. No assemblage could have been more possessed of dispositions perfectly at war with their message than that to which they made their first address." And what was the tenor

---

* Lecture IX.

of the address? "Jesus of Nazareth," said Peter, "being delivered by the determinate counsel and foreknowledge of God, ye have taken, and by wicked hands have crucified and slain; whom God hath raised up. — Therefore let all the house of Israel know assuredly, that God hath made that same Jesus, whom ye have crucified, both Lord and Christ." One would have supposed that the same hands that had rioted in the blood of his Master would now have wreaked their enmity in that of this daring, and, to all human view, most impolitic apostle. But what ensued? Three thousand souls were that day added to the infant church. In a few days, the number was increased to five thousand; and in the space of about a year and a half, though the gospel was preached only in Jerusalem and its vicinity, multitudes, both of men and women, and a great company of the priests, were obedient to the faith. Now, the converts, being driven by a fierce persecution from Jerusalem, went every where preaching the word, and in less than three years churches were gathered throughout all Judea, Galilee, and Samaria, and were multiplied.

About two years after this, or seven from the beginning of the work, the gospel was first preached to the Gentiles; and such was the success, that, before thirty years had elapsed from the death of Christ, his church had spread from Palestine throughout Syria; through almost all the numerous districts of Lesser Asia; through Greece, and the islands of the Ægean Sea, the sea-coast of Africa, and even into Italy and Rome. The number of converts in the several cities respectively is described by the expressions, "a great number," "great multitudes," "much people." What an extensive impression had been made is obvious from the outcry of the opposers at Thessalonica. "These that have turned the world upside-down are come hither also." Demetrius, an enemy, complained of Paul, "that not alone at Ephesus, but almost throughout all Asia," he had persuaded and turned away much people. In the mean while, Jerusalem, the chief seat of Jewish rancor, continued the metropolis of the gospel, having in it many tens of thousands of believers. These accounts are taken from the book of the Acts of the Apostles; but as this book is almost confined to the labors of Paul and his immediate companions, saying very little of the other apostles, it is very certain that the view we have given of the propagation of the gospel during the first thirty years is very incomplete.

In the thirtieth year after the beginning of the work, the terrible persecution under Nero kindled its fires; then Christians had become so numerous at Rome, that, by the testimony of Tacitus, a "great multitude" were seized. In forty years more, we are told, in a celebrated letter from Pliny, the Roman governor of Pontus and Bythinia, Christianity had long subsisted in these provinces, though so remote from Judea. Many of all ages and of every rank, of both sexes likewise, were accused to Pliny of being Christians. What he calls the contagion of this superstition (thus forcibly describing the irresistible and rapid progress of Christianity) had seized not cities only, but the less towns also, and the open country, so that the heathen temples "were almost forsaken;" few victims were purchased for sacrifice, and a long intermission of the sacred solemnities had taken place.

Justin Martyr, who wrote about thirty years after Pliny, and one hundred after the gospel was first preached to the Gentiles, thus describes the extent of Christianity in his time: "There is not a nation, either Greek or barbarian, or of any other name, even those who wander in tribes and live in tents, among whom prayers and thanksgivings are not offered to the

Father and Creator of the universe by the name of the crucified Jesus."

Clemens Alexandrinus, a few years after, thus writes: "The philosophers were confined to Greece, and to their particular retainers; but the doctrine of the Master of Christianity did not remain in Judea, but is spread throughout the whole world, in every nation, and village, and city, converting both whole houses and separate individuals, having already brought over to the truth not a few of the philosophers themselves. If the Greek philosophy be prohibited, it immediately vanishes; whereas, from the first preaching of our doctrine, kings and tyrants, governors and presidents, with their whole train, and with the populace on their side, have endeavored with their whole might to exterminate it, yet doth it flourish more and more."

Nothing can so well represent the mode in which this extension took place as the comparison, by our Saviour, of Christianity to leaven. It had an affinity for the human mind, by which it passed from individual to individual, as the leavening process passes from particle to particle, and no human power could arrest its progress. Since the world stood, no change like it has taken place, nor has any power existed that could have produced such a change.

The difficulties. — 2. In estimating the obstacles to this progress, we are to observe that the enterprise of propagating a religion, as such, and especially an exclusive religion, was then entirely new. The Jewish system was not adapted to universal diffusion, and the zeal of the Jews was directed rather to keep other nations at a distance than to bring them to an equal participation of their privileges. The Gentiles knew nothing of an exclusive religion, nor of a benevolent religion — exclusive because it was benevolent. Heathenism, being without a creed and without principle, "had nothing to contend for but the privilege of assuming any form, worshiping any idol, practicing any ritual, and pursuing any absurdity, which the craft of the priesthood, or the superstitions and vices of the people, might select. It never was imagined, by any description of pagans, that all other forms of religion were not as good for the people observing them, as theirs was for them; or that any dictate of kindness, or common sense, should lead them to attempt the subversion of the gods of their neighbors, for the sake of establishing their own in their stead." This is the species of charity and the ground of harmony — arising from a want of the knowledge of the true religion, and of its unspeakable value — which is so highly praised by Gibbon and Voltaire.

But, in such a state of things, "nothing could have been more perfectly new, surprising, or offensive to the whole Gentile world, than the duty laid upon the first advocates of Christianity to go into all nations asserting the exclusive claims of the gospel, denouncing the validity of all other religions, and laboring to bring every creature to the single faith of Christ." And then, how different the religion of the gospel, not only in its relation to other religions, but in itself, from any of which they had any conception! "Religion, among the Gentiles, was a creature of the state. It consisted exclusively in the outward circumstances of temples, and altars, and images, and priests, and sacrifices, and festivals, and lustrations. It multiplied its objects of worship at the pleasure of the civil authorities; taught no system of doctrine; recognized no system of morality; required nothing of the heart; committed the life of man to unlimited discretion; and allowed any one to stand perfectly well with the gods, (on the trifling condition of a little show of respect for their worship,) to whatever extent he indulged in the worst passions and lowest propensities of his nature. Nothing could have been more foreign to every habit of thought, in the mind of a native of Greece or Rome, than the Scripture doctrines of the nature and guilt of sin, of repentance, conversion, faith, love, meekness, and purity of heart."

Both Jews and heathen opposed. — The priests. — In the nature of the case, such a religion "must have arrayed against it all the influence of every priesthood both among Jews and heathens." With the power of the priests among the Jews, and their bitterness against Christianity, we are sufficiently acquainted, but are less familiar with the superstitious dread in which they were held, and with their power among other nations. "The religion of the nations," says Gibbon, "was not merely a speculative doctrine professed in the schools or taught in the temples. The innumerable duties and rites of polytheism were closely interwoven with every circumstance of business or of pleasure, of public or of private life; and it seemed impossible to escape the observance of them without at the same time renouncing the commerce of mankind. The important transactions of peace and war were prepared and concluded by solemn sacrifices, in which the magistrate, the senator, and the soldier, were obliged to participate."

Speaking of the priests, the same author says, "Their robes of purple, chariots of state, and sumptuous entertainments, attracted the admiration of the people; and they received from the consecrated lands and public revenue an ample stipend, which liberally supported the splendor of the priesthood, and all the expenses of the religion of the state." It is stated, as an evidence of the extent and power of the organizations with which this priesthood was connected, that, sixty years after Christianity had been the established religion of the Roman empire, there were four hundred and twenty-four temples and chapels, at Rome, in which their worship was celebrated. "In connection with all this organization and deep-rooted power of heathenism, consider its various tribes of subordinate agents and interested allies, — the diviners, augurs, and managers of oracles, with all the attendants and assistants belonging to the temples of a countless variety of idols; the trades whose craft was sustained by the patronage of image-worship, such as statuary, shrine-mongers, sacrifice-sellers, incense-merchants; consider the great festivals and games by which heathenism flattered the dispositions of the people, and enlisted all classes and all countries in its support, — and say, what must have been the immense force in which the several priesthoods of all heathen nations were capable of uniting among themselves, and with the priests of the Jews, in the common cause of crushing a religion by whose doctrines none of them could be tolerated. That with all their various contingents they did unite, consenting in this one object, if in little else, of smothering Christianity in her cradle, or of drowning her in the blood of her disciples, all history assures us."

The magistrates. — And with the influence of the priests was associated the power of the magistrate. The true principle of toleration was entirely unknown among heathen nations, and is to this day. Toleration, in its true sense, — as distinguished from indifference on the one hand, and from zeal, manifesting itself through a wrong spirit and in a wrong direction, on the other, — is not natural to man. It is a Christian virtue. The heathen were ready to tolerate any thing which did not interfere with the established worship of the state; but the moment a religion arose which forbade its followers to unite in that, the fires of a relentless persecution were every where kindled, and the whole force of the civil arm was brought to bear upon it.

The populace. — With this position of the priesthood and of the magistracy toward Christianity, we should naturally expect the tumults and outbreaks of popular passion which we find were generally excited when it was first preached. Vicious, unprincipled, accustomed, in many instances, to gladiatorial shows and sights of blood, — it was from the populace that the more immediate danger to the preachers of Christianity often arose.

The philosophers. — Nor was Christianity less opposed to the philosophers, or less opposed by them, than by other classes of the community. " Their sects, though numerous, and exceedingly various, were all agreed in proudly trusting in themselves that they were wise, and despising others. Their published opinions, their private speculations, their personal immorality, made them irreconcilable adversaries of Christianity. It went up into their schools, and called their wisdom foolishness, and rebuked their self-conceit. ' What will this babbler say? He seemeth to be a setter forth of strange gods,' were the taunting words of certain of the Epicureans and Stoics when they encountered St. Paul. Mockery was the natural expression of their minds when they heard of the resurrection of the dead. The apostles, therefore, in attempting to propagate the gospel among the Gentiles, were opposed by all the wit, and learning, and sophistry, — all the pride, and jealousy, and malice, — of every sect of philosophers."

General state of the world. — These remarks will enable us to judge whether the state of the world was at that time favorable to the propagation of Christianity; for on this point very different views seem to be entertained by different persons. Of those who think the state of the world was thus favorable, there are two classes. Some have thought they could see the hand of Divine Providence in the arrangements and preparations which they think were made for its introduction; while others evidently speak of it in this way for the purpose of diminishing the force of the argument usually drawn from the propagation of Christianity. To the most, however, it has seemed that the state of the world never opposed greater obstacles to the propagation of such a religion. On the one hand, it is said that the world was at peace, and was united under one government, and that it was easy to pass from place to place, and to affect a large mass, and that the force of the old superstitions was expended, and that the minds of the people were prepared for a new religion. On the other hand, it is said that if it was an age of peace, that only gave opportunity to examine the claims of the new religion with the more care; that it was an enlightened age, an age of literature and refinement, of vice, of a general prevalence of the Epicurean philosophy, and of skepticism; and that it was the very last period in the history of the world in which any thing false or feeble would have been likely to succeed. This is my impression.

For the extension of such a religion as Christianity, with its indubitable evidence and mighty motives, there were certainly many things most favorable; but if Christianity had not been what it claimed to be, certainly the most enlightened, and civilized, and skeptical age which the world had ever seen would have been the most unfavorable period for its propagation. What would the infidel have said, if, instead of springing up in this age of light and refinement, Christianity had first been spread among an ignorant and barbarous people? But, however this point may be decided, if any man thinks it could be an easy thing, under any circumstances, to cause such a religion as Christianity to take the place of any thing, or of nothing, in the mind of any human being, so that that person, too, should become a centre of influence to extend the religion to others, he has only to try the experiment any where, and under the most favorable circumstances. Let him take the first unconverted man he meets in the streets, and try to make him an active Christian, — such as tens of thousands and millions must have become on the first preaching of Christianity, — and he will have some conception of the difficulty of working a change in the wills, and habits of thought, and object of pursuit, and whole mode of life, of people of different nations, of the most various belief, of every age and condition. But this did the apostles.

The instrumentality. — 3. And now, by what instrumentality did they accomplish this? On this I need not dwell. Eleven men, — for it was not till after the death of Christ that the great enterprise of converting the world was commenced, — eleven men, without learning, or wealth, or rank, or power, from the humble walks of life, among a despised people, never resorting to force, and having no connection with politics, by a simple statement of facts, by preaching Christ and him crucified, subverted the divinely-appointed institutions of Judaism, and overturned the superstitions of ages throughout the known world. The history of the race has nothing to show that can for a moment compare with this. If Mohammedanism may be compared with Christianity in respect to the rapidity of its extension, it is yet in entire contrast with it in all the circumstances in which it arose, and in all the means adopted for its diffusion. While it confined itself to persuasion, it accomplished nothing worthy of notice; and it never has been extended at all in the only method by which it can be clearly shown that a true religion must be extended. Its sway is perpetuated only as it holds its sabre over the neck of its followers, and threatens them with instant death if they turn to any other religion.

Whether, then, we examine the nature of the case, or look at it in the light of history, we must feel that the propagation of such a religion, in opposition to such obstacles, with such rapidity, and by such means, is a moral miracle, and can be reasonably imputed only to the power of truth and of God. How will the infidel account for it? Does he believe that these men were weak and deluded? Then he believes that weak and deluded men could accomplish a work requiring greater moral power than any other. Does he believe they were deceivers? Then he believes that these men labored, and suffered, and died, to cause others to believe that which they did not believe themselves

ARGUMENT XV.

EFFECTS AND TENDENCIES OF CHRISTIANITY.

We now proceed to the effects and tendencies of Christianity. If it can be shown that this religion, and this alone, has been the cause of the greatest blessings that mankind have enjoyed, and that, if fully received, it would carry the individual and society to the highest possible state of perfection in this life, and fit man for the highest conceivable state of happiness hereafter,—it must be from God. And this can be shown. Nor, in speaking of this subject, would I conceal any evil that has taken place in connection with the introduction of Christianity, or any iniquity that has been perpetrated by those who have borne its name. I only ask that men will distinguish, as every candid man must, between tendencies and actual results when those tendencies are perversely and wickedly thwarted; and also between names and things.

First distinction.—The persecution by Nero—to illustrate the first distinction—was an evil, and without Christianity it would not have existed. But who or what was the cause of it? Was it the inoffensive

Christians, simply asserting their own inherent right to love the Saviour, and to worship God according to the dictates of their own conscience? or was it the wickedness of Nero and of his creatures? When, at the command of Christ, the devil went out of one who had been possessed, and tore him, and left him as dead, was it Christ who was the cause of this suffering? And thus has it always been with Christianity, whether its object has been to enjoy its own rights or to benefit others. If evil has arisen, it has been because men have persecuted Christians, and have sought to take from them the inalienable rights which God has given; or because, when Christianity has attacked great and deeply-seated evils, as idolatry and slavery, men have clung to these with a wicked pertinacity, and the devil has not been cast out of society without rending it.

Second distinction. — In regard to the second distinction, that between names and things, there is a very general delusion which steals insensibly over the mind from the application of the term 'Christian' to those who are in no sense governed by Christian principle. If men would test the effect of a medicine, they must take that, and not something else which they may choose to call by that name. If they take arsenic, and call it flour, the mere fact that they call it by a wrong name will not prevent its poisonous effects. And so ambition, and pride, and vanity, and malice, and deceit, will produce their own appropriate effects, in whatever form of society they may exist, and by whatever name they may be called. Keeping these two distinctions in view, it may easily be shown that Christianity has really been the cause of no evil, while it has conferred infinite blessings upon mankind, and only waits to be fully received, to introduce a state as perfect as can be conceived of in connection with the present physical constitution of things.

Effects. — Certainly, no revolution that has ever taken place in society can be compared to that which has been produced by the words of Jesus Christ. Those words met a want, a deep want, in the spirit of man. They placed in the clear sunlight of truth a solution of those profound problems and enigmas, in relation to man and his destiny, about which the philosophers only disputed. They more than confirmed every timid hope which the wisest and best of men had cherished.

He pointed men to a Father in heaven, to the mansions of rest which he would prepare. He "brought life and immortality to light."

He erected a perfect standard of morals, and insisted upon love to God and love to man, and he stood before men in the glorious light of his own perfect example.

He spoke, and that spiritual slumber of the race which seemed the image of death was broken up, and a movement commenced in the moral elements that has not ceased from that day to this, and never will cease.

Those who were mourning heard his voice, and were comforted; those who were weary and heavy-laden heard it, and found rest unto their souls.

It stirred up feelings, both of opposition and of love, deeper than those of natural affection. It therefore set the son against the father, and the father against the son, and caused a man's foes to be they of his own household.

Having no affinity with any of the prevalent forms of idolatry and corruption, and making no compromise with them, it turned the world upside down wherever it came. Before it, the heathen oracles were dumb, and the fires upon their altars went out.

It acted as an invisible and secret force on society, communing with men upon their beds by night, dissuading them from wickedness, seconding the voice of conscience, giving both distinctness and energy to its tones, now whispering, and now speaking with a voice that made the stoutest tremble, of righteousness, temperance, and of a judgment to come.

It opened heaven, and spoke to the ear of hope.

It uncovered that world, "where their worm dieth not, and the fire is not quenched."

It was stern in its rebukes of every sin, and encouraged every thing that was "pure, and lovely, and of good report."

Being addressed to man universally, without regard to his condition or his nation, it paid little regard to differences of language, or habits, or the boundaries of states.

Persecution was aroused; it kindled its fires, it brought forth its wild beasts. Blood flowed like water, but the blood of the martyrs was the seed of the church. No external force could avail against a power like this. The word was spoken, and it could not be recalled. The hand of God had made a new adjustment in the movement of the moral world, and the hand of man could not put it back. No other revolution has ever been so extensive or so radical.

Moving on directly to the accomplishment of its own more immediate and higher objects, the voice of Christ has incidentally caused, not only moral, but social and civil revolutions.

It has banished idolatry and polytheism, with their inseparable degradations, and pollutions, and cruelty. Human sacrifices, offered by our own ancestors, by the Greeks, and Romans, and Carthaginians, and the ancient worshipers of Baal and Moloch, — offered now in the islands of the Pacific, and in India, and in Africa, — cease at once where Christianity comes. It was before its light had visited this continent, that seventy thousand human beings were sacrificed at the consecration of a single temple.*

* Prescott's Mexico.

It has banished the ancient games, in which men slew each other, and were exposed to the fury of wild beasts, for the amusement of the people.

It has banished slavery, once so prevalent, from Europe, and from a large portion of this continent.

To a great extent it has put an end to the exposure of infants.

It has elevated woman, and given her the place in society which God designed she should occupy.

By putting an end to polygamy, and to frequent divorces, it has provided for the cultivation of the domestic and natural affections, for the proper training of children, and for all the unspeakable blessings connected with the purity and peace, and mutual love and confidence, of Christian families.

It has so elevated the general standard of morality, that unnatural crimes, and the grosser forms of sensuality, which once appeared openly, and were practiced and defended by philosophers, now shrink away and hide themselves in the darkness.

It has diminished the frequency of wars, and mitigated their horrors.

It has introduced the principle of general benevolence, unknown before, and led men to be willing to labor, and suffer, and give their property, for the good of those whom they have never seen, and never expect to see in this life.

It has led men to labor for the welfare of the soul, and, in connection with such labors, to provide for the sufferings and for the physical wants of the poor; and it is found that these two go hand in hand, and can not be separated.

If there be here and there a mistaken zealot, or a pharisaical professor of Christianity, who would seem to be zealous for the spiritual wants of men, and yet would say to the hungry and the naked, Be ye clothed and be ye fed, — at the same time giving them nothing to supply their wants, — it is also found, not only that the truest regard for the present well-being of man must manifest itself through a regard for his spiritual wants, but also that, when a regard to those wants ceases, the lower charity which cares for the body will decay with it. When the tree begins to die at the top, where the juices are elaborated that nourish it, it will die down. Christianity alone has built hospitals for the sick and for the insane, and almshouses, and houses of refuge, and provided for the instruction and reformation of those confined as criminals. Was there ever any thing in a heathen land like what is to be seen at South Boston? What book is it that the blind are taught to read? If there had been no Bible, and no such estimate of the worth of man as that contains, can any one believe that the great work of printing for the blind would have been performed? or that the deaf and dumb would have been so provided for? When I recently saw those blind children so instructed, and heard them sing, — when I saw thoughts and feelings chasing each other like light and shade over the speaking countenance of Laura Bridgman, deaf, and dumb, and blind, — I could not but feel, though the ordinary fountains of knowledge were still sealed up, yet that in a high sense it might be said to them and to her, as Peter said to Eneas, " Jesus Christ maketh thee whole."

Present effects. — And what Christianity has hitherto done, it is now doing. It is to some extent embodying its force in missionary operations, and it has lost none of its original power. Men are found ready to take their lives in their hands, to forsake their country, and friends, and children, and go among the heathen, for the love of Jesus; and it is found that the same simple preaching of the cross, that was mighty of old to the pulling down of strongholds, is still accompanied with a divine power; and nations of idolaters, savages, cannibals, infanticides, are seen coming up out of the night of paganism, and taking their place among civilized, and literary, and Christian nations.

But indications of something greater. — These, and such as these, are the public, visible, and undeniable effects of Christianity, uniformly produced in any community in proportion as a pure Christianity prevails. To me, however, these are rather indications of a great work, than the work itself. They are but as the coral reef that appears above the surface, which is as nothing to the deep and concealed labors of the little ocean architect. Like that architect in the ocean, Christianity begins at the bottom of society, and works up. It never acts successfully upon the faculties of man as an external force. It must act through these faculties, and hence it can change public institutions and forms of government, and produce those great public effects which are noticed, only as it changes individuals. How immense the work, how mighty the changes, which must have been wrought in individuals, before these embodied and public effects could appear! Such institutions and effects are the results of a life, a vitality, a power; and they stand as the indices and monuments of its action. When I see the earth covered with vegetation, — when I see a vast forest standing and clothed with the green robes of summer, — I know there must have been an amazing amount of elemental action. I think how the atmosphere, and the light, and the moisture, and the earth must have conspired together, and how the principle of vegetable life must have lifted up the mass, particle by particle, till at length it had formed the sturdy trunk, and set his "coronal" of green leaves upon the monarch of the forest. And so, when I see these results, these institutions, standing in their freshness and greenness, — when I see the moral desert budding and blossoming, — I know there must have been the play of moral life, the clear shining of truth, the movement of the Spirit of God, and the deep, though, it may be, silent strugglings of the spirit of man. Then I know that conscience must have been aroused, and that there has been the anxious questioning, and the earnest struggle, and that the tear of penitence has flowed, and that the secret prayer has gone up, and that songs of hope and salvation have taken the place of a sense of guilt and of anxious fear. Then I know that there have been holy lives and happy deaths. Such changes in individuals, and such results, who that lives in these days has not seen? Such changes and results it is the great object of Christianity to produce. When it shall produce these changes fully upon all, fitting them for heaven, then, and not till then, will its tendencies be fully carried out. Then will every thing wrong in the constitution and relations of society be displaced, and without violence, as the organization of the chrysalis is displaced by that of the bright and winged being that is infolded within it, and society shall come forth in its perfect state. Then shall the will of God be done; and this earth, so long tempest-tossed, like a clear and peaceful lake, shall reflect the image of heaven.

Summary and conclusion. — Thus, as well as I was able under the severe pressure of other duties, with a sincere desire to promote the views of the munificent founder of these courses of Lectures, and I trust with some sense of my responsibility to God, have I presented, separately, such arguments as the time would permit for the truth of Christianity; but, if we would see the proof in all its strength, we must look at these arguments in their united force. We know that an argument may be framed from separate circumstances, each of which may have little weight, while the force of the whole combined shall amount to a moral demonstration. It is in this way that some of the separate arguments for Christianity are constructed; but it is not thus that we present these separate arguments as conspiring together. We claim that there are for Christianity many separate infallible proofs, each of which is sufficient of itself; but still, the general impression upon the mind may be increased when they are seen together. We claim that the proofs for the religion of Christ are like those for his resurrection given through the different senses of the disciples. Some believed when they merely saw him; some believed when they saw him and heard his voice. Each of these was a separate and adequate proof; but Thomas thought it necessary, not only that he should see and hear him, but that he should put his finger into the prints of the nails, and thrust his hand into his side. Christ did not ask his disciples to believe without proof then; he does not now. He has provided that which must satisfy, if he be only fair-minded, even an unbelieving Thomas; and this proof, as it comes in from very various and independent sources, is adapted to every mind.

We have seen that there was nothing in the nature of the evidence, or in any conflict of the evidence of testimony and of experience, to prevent our attaining certainty on this subject.

We have seen that there was no previous improbability that a Father should speak to his own child, benighted and lost; or that he should give him the evidence of miracles that he did thus speak.

We have heard the voice of Nature recognizing, by her analogies, the affinities of the Christian religion with her mysterious and complex arrangements and mighty movements.

We have seen the perfect coincidence of the teachings

of natural religion with those of Christianity; and, when Christianity has transcended the limits of natural religion, we have seen that its teachings were still in keeping with hers, as the revelations of the telescope are with those of the naked eye.

We have seen that this religion is adapted to the conscience, as it meets all its wants as a perceiving power, by establishing a perfect standard.

We have seen that, though morality was not the great object of the gospel, yet that there must spring up, in connection with a full reception of its doctrines, a morality that is perfect.

We have seen that it is adapted to the intellect, to the affections, to the imagination, to the conscience as quickening and improving it, and to the will.

That, as a restraining power, it places its checks precisely where it ought, and in the wisest way; so that, as a system of excitement, of guidance, and of restraint, it is all that is needed to carry human nature to its highest point of perfection.

We have seen that it gives to him who practices it a witness within himself.

That it is fitted, and tends, to become universal.

That it may be traced back to the beginning of time.

Such a religion as this, whether we consider its scheme, or the circumstances of its origin, or its records in their simplicity and harmony, we have seen could no more have been originated by man than could the ocean.

We have seen the lowly circumstances, the unprecedented claims, and the wonderful character, of our Saviour.

Around this religion, thus substantiated, we have seen every possible form of external evidence array itself.

We have seen the authenticity of its books substantiated by every species of proof, both external and internal.

We have seen that its facts and miracles were such that men could not be mistaken respecting them, and that the reality of those facts was not only attested, on the part of the original witnesses, by martyrdom, but that it is implied in institutions and observances now existing, and is the only rational account that can be given of the great fact of Christendom.

We have seen, also, that the accounts given by our books are confirmed by the testimony of numerous Jewish and heathen writers.

And not only have we seen that miracles were wrought, and that the great facts of Christianity are fully attested by direct evidence, but we have heard the voice of prophecy heralding the approach of Him who came traveling in the greatness of his strength, and saying, "Prepare ye the way of the Lord."

We have seen this religion, cast like leaven into society, go on working by its mysterious but irresistible agency, transforming the corrupt mass.

We have seen it taking the lead among those influences by which the destiny of the world is controlled, so that the stone which was cut out without hands has become a great mountain.

And finally, we have seen its blessed effects, and its tendency to fill the earth with righteousness and peace.

United testimony. — These things we have seen separately; and now, when we look at them as they stand up together and give in their united testimony, do they not produce, ought they not to produce, a full, a perfect, and abiding conviction of the truth of this religion? If such evidence as this can mislead us, have we not reason to believe that the universe itself is constituted on the principle of deception?

Certainty. — May I not hope, then, that as we have

thus gone together about our Zion, some of you, at least, have felt that her towers are impregnable,—that

"Walls of strength embrace her round"?

May I not hope that you have been led so to see the *certainty* of those things in which you have been instructed, as to gain strength in your own moral conflicts, and to tread with a firmer step, and gird yourselves for higher exertion, in spreading this blessed religion over the world? If so, I have my reward.

www.ingramcontent.com/pod-product-compliance
Lightning Source LLC
Chambersburg PA
CBHW032353230426
43672CB00007B/688